MEDIA MANUALS

Motion Picture Camera and Lighting Equipment

MEDIA MANUALS

Motion Picture Camera & Lighting Equipment

Choice and Technique

Second Edition

David W. Samuelson

Focal Press
London and Boston

Focal Press
is an imprint of Butterworth–Heinemann

 PART OF REED INTERNATIONAL P.L.C.

First published 1977
  Reprinted 1978, 1982
Second edition 1986
  Reprinted 1988, 1990

© **David W. Samuelson, 1986**

British Library Cataloguing in Publication Data

Samuelson, David W.
  Motion picture camera and
  lighting equipment: choice and
  technique.–2nd ed.
  1. Moving-picture cameras
  2. Cinematography – Lighting
  I. Title
  778.5'3   TR880

ISBN 0-240-51261-8

Library of Congress Cataloging-in-Publication Data

Samuelson, David W.
  Motion picture camera and
  lighting equipment.
  1. Moving-picture cameras.
  2. Cinematography – Apparatus
  and supplies.
  3. Cinematography – Lighting.
  I. Title.
  TR880.S313   1986   778.5'3   86-14300

ISBN 0-240-51261-8

Composition by Genesis Typesetting, Laser Quay, Rochester, Kent
Printed and bound by Hartnolls Ltd., Bodmin, Cornwall

Contents

Introduction

The purpose of using motion picture production equipment is to put on to a screen an image which communicates a message or tells a story. The equipment is not an end in itself.

It may well be that the image will be enhanced by the exploitation of the full range of suitable equipment available, but most important, the sensible choice of equipment may do much to make a production economically viable.

This does not necessarily mean either the cheapest or the most expensive.

Equipment is cost effective when it is efficient in its use, time-saving to set up and operate, lightweight to transport and, even in itself, aesthetically pleasing and satisfying to use. Above all, it must put on to a screen a picture of such quality that patrons will choose to see it even if it means paying for the privilege and withstanding the discomfort of leaving their homes to do so. It must be a picture that they will wish to see in preference to seeing or doing something else and be prepared to devote time and attention to.

However, whether the picture is seen in a cinema, on television, or elsewhere, the professional motion picture only achieves success if the client or viewer is prepared to return for more.

The success, quality, and particularly the economics of a production depend as much as anything upon an informed selection and application of hardware used to make it. This book is designed to provide concise and up-to-date access to the essential information for that purpose.

Acknowledgements

When writing a book like this, it is important to have friends from whom you may seek advice or verification of facts or with whom you may simply chat to help sort out your own thoughts on a particular aspect of film making.

Among those upon whom I have imposed while writing this series of books, I would particularly like to thank the following:

My brothers and colleagues at Samuelson Film Service Limited.

Freddie Young, OBE, BSC, three times Oscar-winning Director of Photography.

Jack Hildyard, BSC, Ossie Morris, BSC (and his crew), and Geoff Unsworth, BSC, all Oscar-winning Directors of Photography.

Robert E. Gottschalk, President of Panavision.

Herb Lightman, Editor of American Cinematographer Magazine, who translated my English into American terminology.

Bernard Happé, Technical Consultant to Technicolor Limited.

Tony Lumkin, Technical Advisor to EMI Studios.

Dennis Kimberley and Bertie Davies of Kodak Limited.

Bill Pollard, who designs Depth of Field Calculators.

Geoff Smith and Tom McGuinness, who understand lighting.

Roland Chase of Colour Film Services Limited, who knows 16 mm film.

Bob Pullman, who is an authority on presentation.

Gordon Cooke and Kish Sadhvani of Rank Optics Limited.

Vic Margutti of Rank (Denham) Laboratories Limited.

Dr. Kugler of the metal halide lighting division of Osram Limited.

Tom Ainsworth of the CSI lighting division of Thorn Lighting Limited.

Ed di Gulio and Milt Forman of Cinema Products Inc.

Dick Glickman of Rosco Limited, an eminent lighting consultant.

B. Edwards and D. Boyne of Edwards Brothers Limited, who sorted out the cables.

Stephen Murphy, the former Film Censor, who censored my English.

Harry Waxman and colleagues in the British Society of Cinematographers.

My colleagues in the British Kinematograph, Sound and Television Society and the Association of Cinema and Television Technicians.

And three people who in particular made me want to write this book and made it possible, my late father, G. B. Samuelson, who always told me to be a Technician, never a Producer, my mother, who is a matriarch in the kindest sense of the word, and Elaine.

While much of the artwork in this book has been derived from original photographs taken by the Author or supplied by Samuelson Film Service Limited, some is based on illustrations in catalogues and descriptive literature and the Author wishes to thank the following companies for their cooperation in this respect.

First edition:

Aaton	Kodak
Angenieux	Lowell
Arnold & Richter	LTM
Astro	Marechal
Auricon	Millican
Beaulieu	Minolta
Berkey	Mitchell
BICC	Mole Richardson UK
Cadmium Nickel	Mole Richardson USA
Canon	O'Connor
Chapman	Osram
Cinema Products	PAG
Cine 60	Paillard Bolex
Colortran	Panavision
Dawe	Photosonics
Eclair	Ronford
Elemack	Spectra
Frezzolini	Sylvania
General Camera	Thorn
General Electric	Viten
Ianiro	Yoder

Second edition:

Aaton Cameras	Moviecam International
Alan Gordon Enterprises	Moving Picture Company
American National Standards Institute	Oxford Scientific Films
Arnold and Richter	Panavision
Ballancroft	Photo-Sonics
British Broadcasting Corporation	Rank Strand
Cinema Products	Ronford Baker Engineering
Elemack	Samuelson Group
Fries Engineering	Skycam
IIMC	SMPTE
Imax Systems Corporation	Stabilisation
Insight Vision Systems	Tandy
Midland Pictures Corporation	Thorn EMI
Minolta	Tyler

The Producer's Choice

The choice of the camera crew and their equipment is of major importance in the planning of a motion picture production, bearing in mind the specialised skills of technicians and the variety of equipment available.

Even before the director of photography is chosen, the producer and the director will have made some basic decisions about the way the proposed film is likely to be shot and even more important, where it is intended to be shown.

Formats and cameras

If the film is for cinema release the choice is almost certainly to be one of the 35mm formats, either 'anamorphic' for the most spectacular presentation or 'spherical', with the top and bottom of the picture masked off to make it 'wide screen' (see page 28). Anamorphic lenses compress the picture in the camera by a ratio of 2 : 1. It is subsequently 'unsqueezed' in projection giving a very wide (2·35:1) aspect ratio. Spherical lenses are normal non-anamorphic types.

The residual income from subsequent TV showings is usually an important aspect of most feature film financing and must be taken into consideration although the film may be primarily intended for the cinema.

Film shot 'wide screen' must be adequately composed so that when shown on the TV screen without the top and bottom of the picture cut off, as in the cinema, no microphone boom, lamps, tops of the scenery or tracks etc. on the floor are revealed.

Films shot in the anamorphic format may be printed for TV presentation by the 'pan and scan' method so that only the most important part of the scene is reproduced. This area may be selectively printed and optically panned across the screen as necessary so that close-ups, so vital to good TV presentation, remain large.

If the script calls for the picture to be shot in the 'mobile camera' style, the creative possibilities are increased by the use of modern lightweight equipment which allows sync sound and dialogue shooting with a hand held camera.

If the film is solely for TV presentation, 16mm film and equipment is the probable choice. For TV news, 16mm sound-on-film cameras are the most convenient.

Director of photography's choice

When the director of photography orders equipment for the actual filming, he must know exactly what the script entails

Not unnaturally, budget considerations must also be taken into account and here it must be remembered that to use the most suitable equipment may make it possible to shoot more screen time in a day and thus save money overall.

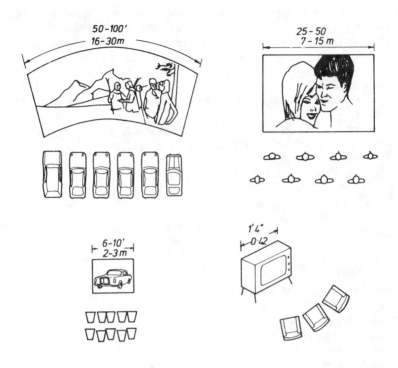

FILM PRESENTATION ENVIRONMENTS

Formats
The drive-in, the showcase movie theatre and the large cinema show: 70mm print-up, 35mm anamorphic and 35mm wide screen.
The intimate cinema, the local movie house show: 35mm anamorphic, 35mm wide screen, 35mm print-up from Techniscope or Super 16.
The industrial and documentary cinema show: 35mm standard, 16mm standard.
Television shows: 35mm anamorphic (pan and scan printed) 35mm spherical and 16mm.

Image area magnification
The quality of the image finally projected on to a screen is the product of many factors, not the least of which is the number of times the picture is enlarged from the original frame size. Magnifications from typical camera *original* and *projected image* sizes are as follows:

Negative Sizes:	Screen Sizes (ft)			Image Magnification
35mm anamorphic	47	×	20	230,600
35mm wide screen 1.85:1	37	×	20	290,000
Super 16 1.85:1	37	×	20	920,000
16mm TV transmitted	1.3	×	1	1,882

Choosing a Camera

The almost endless possibilities of cinematography require a very wide choice of camera and auxiliary equipment. All cameras have certain features in common although no one make incorporates every possible variation. Basic principles, however, are always the same.

Component parts
Light-tight box (camera body) with apertures for lens and film and a lid for access
Movement complete with pull-down mechanism and film registration
Lens complete with mounting and focusing system
Reflex shutter and viewfinder system
Aperture plate and mask
Rear pressure plate
Drive sprocket and guide rollers
Motor and speed control electronics
Ground glass focusing screen
Footage counter
Magazine take-up drive
On-off switch
Battery or other power supply
Tachometer
Trip switches
Viewfinder de-anamorphoser
Viewing glasses
Viewfinder magnifier
Adjustable shutter
Tape hook
Large focusing knob and enlarged focus scale
Built-in exposure meter
Filter holder/sunshade
Video viewfinder system
Computerised motion control

Making the choice
In addition, there is a mass of small design points about each and every camera which makes it different from any other.

In choosing equipment for a particular assignment the cinematographer must know what he has to photograph, how, where, with whom and with how much light.

Whether he is renting or buying the camera may also make a difference. If renting, he can afford to choose a camera which will completely fulfil a specific need but if buying and investing a considerable sum of money he must be sure that what he chooses is sufficiently versatile to fulfil as many of his likely requirements as possible.

THE RIGHT CAMERA FOR THE JOB

Camera types
(Left to right, top to bottom) Beaulieu 4008 (Super 8); Paillard Bolex (16mm wild); Cinema Products CP16RA (16mm sound-on-film); Photosonics (16mm high speed); Eclair NPR (16mm double system sound); Arriflex IιC (35mm wild); Mitchell BNCR (35mm studio); Panavision Panaflex (35mm hand-held silent reflex).

17

The Camera Movement

The basic mechanical principle of a motion picture camera has changed little since before the turn of the century when many inventors, working both independently and in combination, contributed developments which led to cinematography as we know it today.

How the camera works

A strip of transparent material, coated with a light-sensitive emulsion is transported past a lens at its plane of focus and halted briefly while it is exposed to light. Exposure is only made while the film is stationary. To ensure this, an opaque shutter placed between the lens and the film interrupts the light while the film is in motion. The point at which the film is actually exposed frame by frame, is the camera gate. The gate plate incorporates a means of chanelling the film in correct alignment with the lens, holding it flat at the plane of focus and masking off light from all but the actual picture area. Immediately below the gate aperture is the movement which advances the film and holds it securely during the exposure period.

The film has perforations punched at regular intervals along one or both edges to provide a key for the transport mechanism to act upon and to provide a point of reference for each successive picture frame.

During the period when the film must be moved after an exposure and positioned in readiness for the next, claws, which form an essential part of the movement, engage in the perforations and drag the film in a downward direction. The most precise camera movements of all have dual forked pull down claws which engage in four perforations simultaneously. While the exposure is being made the claws are withdrawn from the perforations. They return to the first position in readiness for the next cycle.

A sprocket wheel, located either within the camera body or incorporated in the magazine, draws unused film from the unexposed roll in the appropriate magazine compartment. With its opposite side this sprocket feeds the film (which has now been exposed) continuously onto the take up roll of exposed film. Between the sprocket and the top of the gate, and the bottom of the gate and the take up side of the sprocket the film is threaded in the form of loose loops. These eliminate variations in tension which would otherwise arise between the intermittent movement of the exposing mechanism and the continuous movement of the sprocket and the rolls of film.

The entire operation is carried out within an enclosure which admits light only through the lens and past the shutter.

18

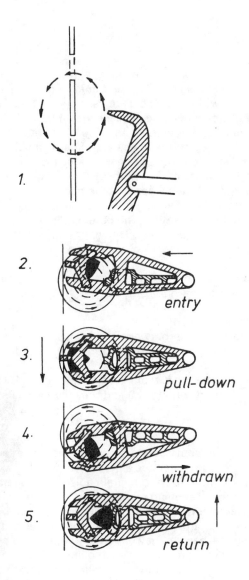

1.

2. *entry*

3. *pull-down*

4. *withdrawn*

5. *return*

CAMERA MOVEMENT

Sinusoidal intermittent movement
1. Pull-down claw enters perforation, pulls film down, withdraws and returns for next cycle.

Arriflex IIC movement
2–5. Arriflex cam and claw intermittent movement, stages of operation.

Registration

Certain high precision cameras incorporate locating, or registration pins which hold the film in exact registration, one frame with the next, relative to the perforations while the exposure is being made. This ensures particularly steady pictures and is essential if any double printing is to be done subsequently without the two or more images appearing to 'float' relative to each other. Absolute image steadiness also enhances the general definition and 'sharpness' of the picture.

To allow for very slight variations in width of film stock due to shrinkage and variations in the distance apart of the perforations, only one of the two registration pins (the one on the side of the film opposite to the soundtrack), fully fits the perforation. The other is slightly narrow and fits closely only in the vertical direction. The machining tolerances of registration pins is to within one tenth of a thousandth of an inch (0·00254mm).

For precise registration the same perforation relative to the frame which is located by the fully fitting pin in the camera, is also used in optical printers, process projectors and all other equipment where optimum image steadiness is required.

Other cameras rely upon pressure between the front and rear surfaces of the gate and on the edges of the film to maintain steadiness during exposure.

In the Arriflex IIC camera the claw remains motionless for 1/150 second after pull down and before withdrawal and thus partially acts as a registration pin.

Camera noise

A most important aspect of modern camera design is the noise level while running. It is preferable to manufacture a movement which makes little noise in the first place than to have to contain noise subsequently with heavy blimping and sound deadening materials.

Cameras with close tolerance registration pin movements often incorporate a means of fine adjustment of the pitch and stroke of the claw so that the pull-down mechanism may be tuned to the actual perforation pitch of the film until the camera runs most quietly. This adjustment may have to be made every time the camera is reloaded to take up the small difference between one roll of film and another.

FILM REGISTRATION

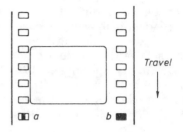

Pin positions
The position of 35mm registration
pins relative to the aperture.
A. Vertical fitting.   B. Full fitting.

Travel

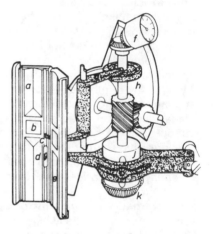

Arriflex 16BL movement
a. Aperture plate;   b. Aperture;
c. Registration pin;   d. Pull-down
claw;   e. Rear pressure plate;
f. Tachometer;   g. Registration pin
cam;   h. Mirror shutter;   i. Shutter
drive shafts;   j. Film transport
claw;   k. Bevel gear to transfer
drive from motor.

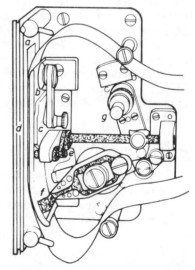

Original Mitchell movement
(Later models incorporate variable
pitch adjustment.)
a. Aperture plate;   b. Register
plate;   c. Pressure plate;   d. Matte
slot;   e. Registration pins;   f. Dual
forked pull-down claws;
g. Registration pin throwout (used
when threading the camera.)

21

The Shutter

The period of time that the film emulsion is exposed to light is dependent both upon the speed (frames per second), of the camera and the angular opening (cut out) of the shutter. The faster the camera or the smaller the shutter opening, the less the exposure. Most cameras have shutter openings of 170, 175 or 180° which, at camera speeds of 24 or 25 fps may, for all practical purposes, be taken as 1/50 second exposure. The reciprocal of the exposure, i.e. 1/second=fps×360÷shutter (angle) degrees.

Light efficient shutters
One or two makes of camera have a maximum shutter opening of 200° or more. A 200° shutter, for instance, gives an exposure of 1/43 sec. at 24 fps. Such shutters afford an increase in exposure equivalent to 1/6 stop in comparison with the normal 175° shutter opening, enough to be noticeable when shooting by available light and significantly cost saving in the number of lights, and even electricians, required to light a large night exterior scene. The wider the shutter opening the greater the image blur of a moving subject, making it possible to do faster pans without fear of strobing or skipping. Conversely, narrower shutter openings give sharper individual pictures but increase the possibility of pan shots showing railing fences which appear to vibrate, or wheels appearing to be motionless or even rotating backwards.

Smaller-than-average shutter openings
Some cameras, especially high speed models, have shutter openings of 120° or less and allowance for this fact should be made when determining correct exposure. Other makes of camera which incorporate a beam splitting reflex viewfinder system or a variable shutter which may be adjusted while the camera is stationary (and the lens removed) create the possibility that the effective exposure is less than normal. Before shooting with such a camera the cameraman should always check what the difference is and, in the case of the variable shutters, that it is set as required, and make an exposure allowance accordingly.

Shooting a TV screen
Certain cameras have shutters of a very precise opening which automatically permit direct filming off a domestic TV set without showing a shadow (hum) bar. This opening must be exactly 144° on a 24 fps camera where the mains power frequency is 60Hz and 180° on a 25 fps camera where the mains frequency is 50Hz.

Exposure times at various shutter angles (24fps)

Shutter angle (degrees)	Exposure at 24 fps (nearest whole number)	Effect on exposure		Shutter angle (degrees)	Exposure at 24 fps (nearest whole number)	Effect on exposure	
220	1/39	Increase 1/3 stop		120	1/72	Decrease 2/3 stop	
210	1/41	,, 1/3 ,,		110	1/79	,, 2/3 ,,	
200	1/43	,, 1/6 ,,		100	1/86	,, 2/3 ,,	
190	1/45	,, 1/6 ,,		90	1/96	,, 1 ,,	
180	1/48 (1/50 at 25 fps)	Normal		80	1/108	,, 1 ,,	
175	1/49	,,		70	1/123	,, 1 1/3 ,,	
172·8	1/50	,,		60	1/144	,, 1 2/3 ,,	
170	1/51	,,		50	1/173	,, 2 ,,	
160	1/54	Decrease 1/3 stop		40	1/216	,, 2 1/3 ,,	
150	1/58	,, 1/3 ,,		30	1/288	,, 2 2/3 ,,	
144	1/60	,, 1/3 ,,		20	1/432	,, 3 ,,	
140	1/62	,, 1/3		10	1/844	,, 4 ,,	
130	1/66	,, 1/3 ,,		5	1/1728	,, 5 ,,	

The $1/x$ of a sec. exposure at 24 fps may easily be found (using an electronic calculator) by dividing 8640 by the shutter angle (9000 for 25 fps).

Adjustable shutters

Many cameras incorporate a 'variable shutter', the angular opening (cut-out) of which is adjustable. The most sophisticated cameras permit this operation to be carried out while the camera is actually running.

Under normal circumstances the speed of a motion picture camera must remain at a constant 24 or 25 fps and therefore any modification to the period of exposure may only be made by varying the shutter opening. As a fully open shutter giving the maximum possible exposure is also the norm (exposure being controlled by altering the lens aperture) it follows that exposure may only be shortened and not increased by manipulation of the shutter opening.

Maximum shutter openings vary slightly between makes of cameras but are most usually between 170° and 180° and are considered, for all practical purposes, to give an exposure of 1/50 second at 24/25 fps.

Halving the shutter opening reduces the exposure by the equivalent of one full stop of lens aperture. Thus, if the shutter opening is reduced from 180° to 90° and it is desired to maintain the same exposure and camera speed, the lens aperture must be opened by one full stop to compensate. Reducing the shutter opening to 45° halves the exposure again, and so on. Variations of shutter opening do not affect depth of field.

Exposure control
Shutter openings are sometimes reduced to permit wider lens apertures to be used when reduced depth of field effects or optimum optical definition is required. (Most lenses produce their best definition at an aperture two or three stops down from maximum and performance falls off markedly at the very small apertures of *f* 16 or *f* 22.)

Variable shutters which may be adjusted while the camera is running are preferred when an 'in shot' exposure change is required – when panning from a dark scene to a lighter one or vice-versa. The alternative method, changing the exposure by adjusting the lens aperture, alters the optical characteristics of the lens and is usually noticeable in the screen image.

Additional refinements to 'in shot' adjustable shutter controls are: adjustable limit stops at either end of the movement to permit the cameraman to make an adjustment to a predetermined position while watching the action, a remote control to enable a director of photography to make an adjustment without interfering with the operators freedom of movement, an indicator disc which gives a visual check on the exact shutter position.

Effect of shutter opening (cut out) on exposure

180° = normal exposure;
90° = half normal exposure
(add 1 stop);
45° = quarter normal exposure
(add 2 stops);
$22\frac{1}{2}$° = eighth normal exposure (add three stops).

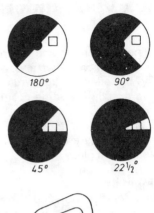

180°   90°

45° $22\frac{1}{2}$°

Arriflex IICV adjustable shutter camera

Typical of many camera types where the shutter may be adjusted only while the camera is stationary.
a. Shutter adjusting knob;   b. Mirror reflex shutter;   c. Adjustable shutter segment;   d. Film gate. In the example shown the shutter is set at an angle of 120°.

Panavision R-200° camera shutter control

This may be adjusted between 200 and 50° while the camera is running. Limit stops permit adjustment to a pre-determined position while watching the action rather than the camera. An indicator disc below shows actual position and setting of the shutter.

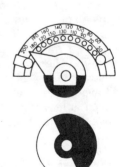

25

Reflex Viewfinder Systems

For aiming the camera and composing the picture, reflex cameras have a viewfinder which allows a view through the actual taking lens. This is achieved by reflecting light from that lens on to a ground glass screen placed in exactly the same position relative to the lens as is the film in the camera gate.

The ground glass may be of exactly the same proportions as the aperture in the gate or larger; the limits of the useful picture area are engraved on the glass.

Rotating mirrors

The light for the viewfinder may be reflected intermittently from a mirror incorporated in the shutter itself, or rotating synchronously with it. Mirrored shuttered systems (rotating, oscillating or reciprocating) give bright pictures despite the fact that the operator does not see the picture during the actual periods of exposure. This intermittent period of blindness is only a problem when filming a practical TV set, where a black or white band may appear on the TV screen and not be seen by the camera operator, or when filming by strobe lighting where the period of illumination for exposure purposes is in the order of 1/10,000th of a second and occurs only during the shutter's 'open' period.

Partial reflectors

Alternatively, light for viewfinding may be diverted to the ground glass by a partial mirror in the light path – a glass membrane (pellicle) or a solid glass prism block. Pellicles are liable to shatter if roughly handled; thick prism blocks may distort the image. especially with wide angle and zoom lenses, unless the lenses are specially computed and manufactured to take into account the extra thickness of glass. Special zoom lenses incorporating partially reflecting prism blocks allow reflex viewing on non-reflex cameras.

As all partial mirror systems divert a portion of the light from the film, exposure must be increased to compensate. In the case of cameras retro-modified with pellicles, the cameraman must increase the exposure by $\frac{1}{2}$–$\frac{2}{3}$ of a stop. Cameras incorporating prism blocks make allowances by quoting in the instruction manual an exposure 'time' which is less than the period when the shutter is open. Reflex lenses have the differences incorporated in the 'T' stop calibration.

The image

Viewfinder systems incorporate an optical arrangement which magnifies the image for the benefit of the operator. Some systems also show the image to be magnified in excess of the limits of the frame.

Lenses which incorporate a partial mirror reflex system often use an

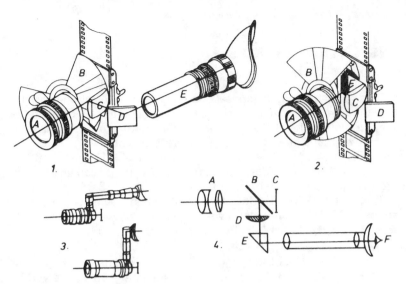

VIEWFINDING SYSTEMS

1, 2. Arriflex IIC mirror reflex viewfinding system

When the shutter is closed and the film transported, all light from the lens is reflected on to a ground glass screen viewed by the operator.   2. While the film is stationary the shutter is open and all the light falls on the film.   A. Lens; B. Mirror Shutter;   C. Ground glass;   D. Right angle mirror;   E. Viewfinder; F. Film plane.

3. Reflex zoom lenses

Non-reflex cameras may be given 'through the lens' viewfinding capability by the use of a reflex zoom lens. The rear section incorporates a partial reflecting prism which diverts a portion of the light from the film to the viewfinder. The light loss is accounted for in the 'T stop' calibration. For instance, an *f*2.2 lens may be rated at T2.5. A long eyepiece is advantageous when using the camera on a tripod, the short when shoulder supported.

4. Partial reflection

A partial mirror is set permanently between the lens and the film plane, reflecting a portion of the light in to the viewfinder. Exposure must be increased by 1/2–2/3 stop.   A. Lens   B. Partial reflector (pellicle or prism);   C. Film plane;   D. Ground glass;   E. Right angle prism;   F. Viewfinder optical system.

aerial image for most of the picture area with only a small central area of ground glass for focusing purposes. This gives a much brighter picture overall, diverts less light from its primary function of exposing the film but makes focusing by eye more difficult, particularly in brightly lit conditions when both the camera lens and the operator's eye are well stopped down. Mirror shutters and pellicles should never be touched with bare fingers and should only be cleaned, on location, with an airspray.

The Ground Glass

Most cameras have interchangeable ground glasses to suit the aperture plate or gate mask fitted to the camera and/or to the presentation format for which the film is intended. Within a frame area the following alternative ground glass markings are usually available:

Academy (1·37 : 1) within the full frame (1·33 : 1) area; 1·66 : 1, 1·75 : 1 or 1·85 : 1 'widescreen' projection within Academy; 70mm (2·2 : 1) projection within the anamorphic (2·35 : 1) frame; 'Techniscope' (2·35 : 1) for two perforation pulldown modified cameras; ISO, US or European TV safe areas within Academy or 16mm; 16mm (1·34 : 1); 'Super 16' (1·66 : 1).

Projector aperture dimensions

Ground glasses are marked according to projector dimensions. With the exception of full frame, Techniscope and standard 16mm, the vertical centre line of the picture frame is offset to the right of the centre line of the film to accommodate the sound track. This is expressed as a distance from the guided edge of the film and in the case of 35mm is 0·738in. (18·75mm), of Super 16, 0·352in. (8·94mm) and Super 8, 0·170in. (4·32mm).

Dimensions (mm)	Area (sq. mm)		Dimensions (in.)	Area (sq. in.)
35mm				
23.66 x 17.78	421	Full frame	0.931 x 0.700	0.652
21.29 x 17.78	378	Anamorphic	0.828 x 0.700	0.587
19.13 x 16.97	325	70mm print from 35mm anamorphic	0.753 x 0.668	0.503
20.96 x 15.29	320	Academy	0.825 x 0.602	0.497
20.96 x 12.62	265	1·66 : 1	0.825 x 0.497	0.410
20.96 x 11.96	251	1·75 : 1	0.825 x 0.471	0.389
20.96 x 11.33	237	1·85 : 1	0.825 x 0.446	0.368
20.12 x 15.09	304	TV transmitted area	0.792 x 0.594	0.470
18.11 x 13.58	246	TV safe action (1)	0.713 x 0.535	0.381
16.10 x 13.08	211	TV safe title (2)	0.630 x 0.475	0.299
22.05 x 8.89	196	Techniscope	0.868 x 0.350	0.304
16mm				
11·63 x 7·26	86	Super 16 (1·66 : 1)	0·458 x 0·286	0·133
11·63 x 6·27	73	Super 16 (1·85 : 1)	0·458 x 0·247	0·113
9·65 x 7·26	70	Standard	0·380 x 0·286	0·109
9·65 x 5·21	50	1·85 : 1	0·380 x 0·205	0·078
9·35 x 7·01	66	TV transmitted	0·368 x 0·276	0·102
8·40 x 6·31	53	TV safe action (3)	0·331 x 0·248	0·082
7·48 x 6·07	45	TV safe title (4)	0·293 x 0·221	0·065
8mm				
5·31 x 4·01	21	Super 8	0·209 x 0·158	0·033

Corner radii

TV safe action and safe title areas have rounded corners as follows: (1) 0·14in. (3·6mm), (2) 0·13in. (3·2mm), (3) 0·07in. (1·7mm), (4) 0·06in. (1·5mm).

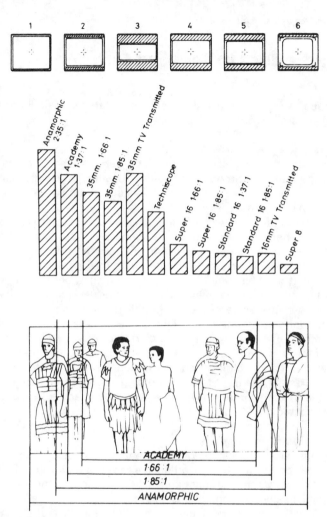

IN THE VIEWFINDER

Ground glass markings
Typical ground glass markings on 35mm cameras: 1. Anamorphic film format for optical sound;   2. Standard film format   3. Techniscope;   4. Wide screen (1.85:1);   5. Wide screen (1.66:1);   6. 1SO-TV (with safe action area).

Negative areas
Comparison of total negative areas on main formats.

Screen ratios
Comparative screen ratios of main formats.

Super 16
A Super 16 ground glass might also have two vertical lines engraved 0·331 in. (8·41mm) apart to indicate 'television safe action' area coincident with the height dimension.

29

Viewfinder Optical System

To produce a bright, large and correctly orientated viewfinder image an optical system is required.

The eyepiece position
In times past, the eyepiece was invariably set in the same plane as the rear of the camera, the most convenient position when the camera is mounted on a tripod etc. and especially convenient when used with a geared pan and tilt head.

For hand holding, however, the eyepiece cup is better situated on a plane with the film gate so that the camera sits balanced about the operator's shoulder. Steadiness is derived from the side of the face and hands, arms and elbows being well dug-in to the operators waist.

The worst possible situation for hand holding is one where the only point of contact with the operator is the rubber eyepiece cup (with the front of the lens as far away from the point of human contact as possible) and with the entire weight of the camera supported by arms outstretched. This form of hand holding is even worse if the operator must, at the same time, do his own focus and zoom adjustments.

Ideally, a hand holding camera should have alternative eyepiece positions, one at the front for hand holding and an extension module to bring it level with the rear for use when the camera is tripod, dolly or crane mounted.

The eyepiece functions
The magnifying optical viewfinder may be quickly adjusted to (calibrated) points to accommodate the individual eyesight defects of different cameramen. The most convenient eyepiece is the 'multi angle' type which in any position, retains an erect image.

In very cold working conditions the rear glass surface of the eyepiece can be treated with an anti-mist coating or heated to prevent it from clouding over with condensation.

Eyecup
It is a basic principle of hygiene that where a camera is constantly used by many people, the part which is pressed against the operator's eyes, the eyecup, should have some form of clean covering. A disposable antiseptic eyepiece serves the purpose except for operators who are allergic to rubber. They can use a chamois leather cover. A deep eyecup should have a small hole to avoid a suction effect on the operator's eyeball.

Panavision Panaflex
The camera in the hand holding mode.

Panavision Panaflex
Camera with viewfinder extension fitted for use when the camera is tripod- dolly-
or crane-mounted.

Eclair NPR
Camera fitted with an orientatable viewfinder, here used for low angle shooting.

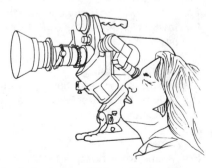

Eclair NPR
Camera fitted with an Angineux swivelling viewfinder, here used for overhead
shooting.

Viewfinder: Additional Facilities

The viewfinder systems on studio cameras incorporate a number of additional facilities which aid in composing and assessing a scene.

Magnification
Most studio-type cameras incorporate a supplementary magnifier in the viewfinder system which enables the operator or focus assistant to greatly enlarge the centre of the picture as an aid to critical focusing by eye. This facility may also be used by the director of photography when using a contrast-viewing filter, to study in detail the lighting effect of a particular part of the picture area.

Some cameras incorporate a zoom magnification system which remains in focus through the range. This may serve not only as a focusing and lighting aid but also, because it remains in focus at all times, for partial magnification during the actual shooting. On older cameras the magnifier may only be set in one of two positions of magnification and, unless *fully* set, a false degraded focus effect is seen.

Illuminated ground glass markings
Some cameras incorporate a facility to make the ground glass frame line markings glow a dull red or yellow colour. This is particularly useful when shooting in low-key lighting conditions when otherwise the limitations of the frame area cannot be seen against a dark background.

Viewing filters
The most sophisticated cameras have facilities for introducing special contrast-viewing filters into the viewfinder system. These are used by directors of photography during the lighting operation as an aid to assessing the overall contrast and lighting balance of the scene. By reducing the adaptability of the human eye with a viewing filter the ratio of key to fill lighting and the general contrast level may easily be seen. The cameraman should not look through the contrast-viewing filter for too long at one time lest his eye accommodates to the effect. For colour photography suitable filters are Kodak 500/20 or 2×ND 0·9 for daylight and a Kodak 548/1 or Wratten 78B (pale blue) + ND 0·5 for tungsten light.

De-anamorphosing
Many 35mm cameras have a de-anamorphosing optic incorporated in the viewfinder system to 'un-squeeze' the image when using anamorphic lenses.

Newsreel cameras
Some one-man operated 16mm cameras have viewfinder indicators showing lens aperture, sound recording level and/or camera 'off-speed' where a crystal controlled motor is fitted.

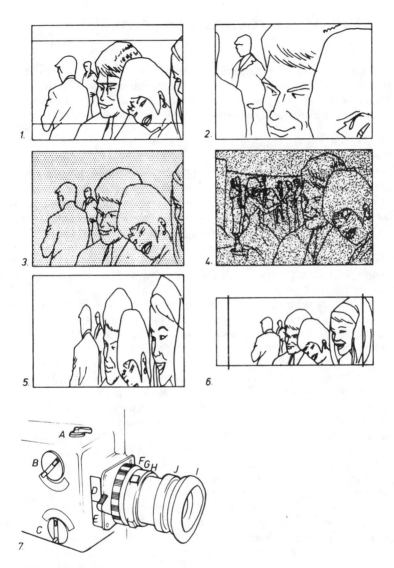

THE VIEWFINDER

Additional markings
1.Normal spherical image with centre cross and 1:1.85 markings;
2. Magnified image;   3.Daylight viewing filter;   4. Artificial light
viewing filter in position;   5. Uncorrected anamorphic image;   6. De-squeezed
anamorphic image with 70mm print-up markings.

Panavision PSR eyepiece and controls
A. Viewfinder 'open-close' control;   B. Spherical 'de-anamorphose'
control;   C. Viewing filters selection and control;   D. Image magnification
control;   E. Image magnification control & marking panel;   F. Ring to adjust
eyepiece to individual sight;   G. White bezel for marking eyepiece settings;
H. Locking ring;   I. Chamois cover;   J. Operator's eyepiece.

Video Viewfinder systems

The addition of a video camera to share the light available to the camera operator's viewfinder permits the director, and anyone else, to see the scene exactly as it is seen by the operator as the scene progresses. The image may be recorded and replayed after the rehearsal/take is complete.

Choice of video cameras

The image focused on a ground glass screen, which is what is seen by the video viewfinder camera, is inevitably deficient in many ways, not least of which is definition, making it very difficult to get a satisfactory video image for reproduction on a large video monitor. The image is grainy, lacks fine detail, usually has bad flicker (unless the image is reflected by a pellicle mirror, rather than a spinning mirror), lacks luminous intensity if a fast film stock is being used or the exposure is low key, and the ground glass illumination may be uneven from side to side, top to bottom or centre to corners. There are also problems with video cameras which do not accurately scan the frame.

In early days, industrial closed-circuit television cameras, primarily designed for surveillance work, were fitted to film cameras, but now special-purpose video cameras are available. These sharpen the image by enhancing the edges of objects, and have an automatic black-level facility to set the black level to the darkest part of the picture, automatic gain control to optimise the video camera exposure level, circuitry to increase and modify the contrast range to bring out fine detail, a frame store to eliminate flicker by storing a good image and playing it back during the blank period, sensitivity into the infra-red range to extract maximum illumination (useful with tungsten lighting but not with MH light which has no IR component), and facilities for evening-out the exposure and aligning the image in any direction.

Video assist cameras are smaller and lighter than heretofore; additional facilities available are automatic lens iris control (may be used to compensate for the light loss when the film camera is running), superimposed ground glass frame lines in black or white (depending if the image is light or dark), superimposed images from previous takes used as a guide for subsequent image combining on an optical printer, superimposed time code and take identification (usually SMPTE code), reverse and inverse scan switching, switchable 625/525 line standards, genlock synchronisation to an external source, facilities to run the video recorder automatically when the film camera is switched-on, on-board power supply, on-board low-power video transmitter for cableless operation, and colour.

Especially bright monitors and anti-reflection filters are available for use in bright ambient light conditions.

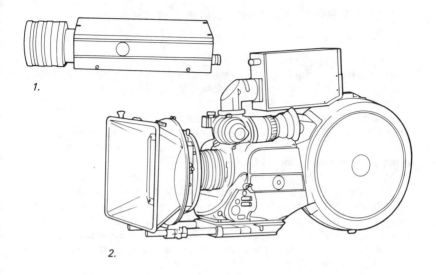

1.

2.

3.

Video viewfinders
1. Insight purpose-built video camera for video viewfinding; 2. Arriflex VAFE
(Video Assisted Film Editing) colour video camera mounted on a 35BL III; 3. The
Director and other members of the crew can see the same image as the camera
operator while the film is being shot.

Sports and Monocular Finders

When shooting sporting events or wildlife involving fast-moving relatively small subjects (golf balls, skiers on a mountainside, birds and small animals) with long focus lenses, an auxiliary viewfinder may be helpful.

The most satisfactory system of sports finder is a six times magnification monocular with a simple cross line sight in its centre set along the reflex viewfinder eyepiece so that it exactly coincides with the position of the operator's left eye.

Monocular finders are made to be clamped on to the sides of most types of camera used for long-lens sports filming. The finder has lateral adjustment to allow for the separation of the cameraman's eyes, forward and backward adjustment so that it may be set to coincide with the plane of the camera eyepiece and rotational movement to adjust to the centre of the picture (or with the centre cross, usually engraved on the camera viewfinder).

In practice, the cameraman finds the subject using the monocular with his left eye, brings it in to the centre of the engraved cross, after which he uses the normal camera viewfinder, with his right eye, for accurate framing and focus.

Simple sports finders
A simple means of improvising a sports finder is for the cameraman to tape a piece of soft wire to the front end of a long telephoto or zoom lens with a small 'knob' on the end of it. This knob should be so positioned so that the cameraman looks through the viewfinder with his right eye the knob lines up with the centre of the picture.

When making such an improvised finder it may be necessary to set-up the camera, complete with magazine, in the position in which it is to be used so that the optical centres between the cameraman's eye and the knob are aligned as they will be when shooting.

White line sports finders
Some sports finders show a white centre cross and/or a number of white concentric circles superimposed on a magnified image. Such systems are useful when the subject is predominately dark but are of little use when trying to find and follow an object set against the sky or snow.

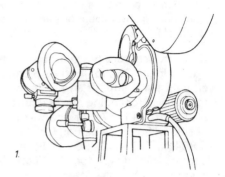

Sports finder attachment
1. Arriflex 16ST camera with auxiliary Samcine monocular sports finder clamped on the side.

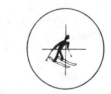

1.

2. Subject
Naked eye view of skier on a mountain.

2.

3. Monocular view
The monocular finder has a centre cross to assist in keeping even a rapidly moving distant subject correctly located in the field of view.

3.

4. Viewfinder
The image is correctly positioned in the picture area as seen in the ordinary viewfinder.

4.

Aperture Plate

The aperture plate is that part of the camera against which the film is held during the exposure period and which forms the 'window' at the point of focus.

Camera aperture plate dimensions

Professional 35mm motion picture cameras may be supplied with either a full (silent) or an Academy aperture plate with the possibility of masking or changing the aperture to other formats as required. The Academy (1·37 : 1) camera aperture is 0·864×0·630in. (21·95×16mm). Anamorphic filming is done with an aperture of 0·864×0·732in. (21·95×18·59mm), 12% larger in area than Academy. Cameras modified for the Techniscope two perforation pulldown system must be fitted with a half frame aperture which is 0·868×0·373in. (22·05×9·47mm), 49% smaller than anamorphic. Process plates i.e. films for back or front projection, are often with full aperture, 0·980×0·735in. (24·89×18·67mm), 32% larger in area than Academy.

Widescreen films 1·66 : 1, 1·75 : 1 or 1·85 : 1, should be shot with an appropriate mask to limit the picture area to that intended for projection in the cinema. This removes responsibility for the composition of the picture from the local projectionist and returns it to the camera operator who has rather more artistic training. Also, extraneous objects, such as lights, microphones and inadmissible areas of the naked human body may be definitely excluded from the screen.

Checking the gate

Professional motion picture cameras allow easy access to check that no loose hair or piece of dirt has lodged along any edge, which would be seen as an ugly ragged silhouette on the screen. On Mitchell, Panavision, XR35 and Arriflex 35BL cameras this is done by removing the front aperture plate bodily and holding it up to the light. On Arriflex IIC cameras the rear pressure plate may be opened up and the film slipped to one side. The aperture can then be viewed *in situ* with the aid of a pen light. On Eclair cameras the clip-on magazine may be removed to inspect the aperture plate (care being taken not to dislodge any dirt).

Any dust or hairs in the aperture plate may be removed with an air bulb or aerosol spray. Emulsion which has built up must be removed with an orange stick, taking very great care not to scratch the metal.

Marker light

Aperture plates often incorporate a small cut out or a hole for a sync marker system. A tiny lamp placed immediately in front of the cut or hole, may be illuminated in synchronism with a tone on the sound track to make a mark at the beginning of each take.

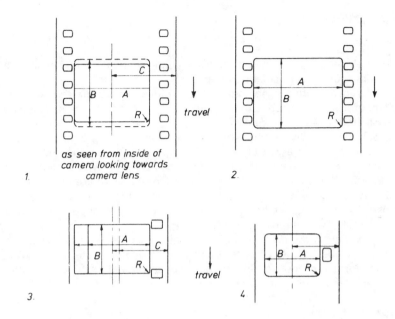

1. *as seen from inside of camera looking towards camera lens*

2.

3.

4.

travel

CAMERA APERTURES

Camera apertures are made slightly larger than printer and projector apertures so that any minor edge imperfection may be hidden in printing and projection.
Ground glasses are marked according to projector apertures.
The aperture plates of most professional cameras may be removed for inspection and cleaning and on 35mm cameras the mask may be interchanged to suit different formats.

35mm camera aperture sizes
1. Academy & Anamorphic;   2. Full frame as seen from inside of camera looking towards camera lens.

Dimensions					
Academy		Anamorphic		Full frame	
A 0.864in	21.95mm	0.864in	21.95mm	0.980in	24.89mm
B 0.630in	16.00mm	0.732in	18.59mm	0.735in	18.67mm
C 0.738in	18.75mm	0.738in	18.75mm		
R 0.030in	0.80mm	0.030in	0.80mm	0.030in	0.76mm

Dimensions					
Standard 16		Super 16		Super 8	
A 0.404in	10.26 mm	0.488in	12.4 mm	0.245in	6.22mm
B 0.295in	7.49 mm	0.295in	7.49mm	0.166in	4.22mm
C 0.314in	7.998mm	0.352in	8.94mm	0.170in	4.32mm
R 0.015in	0.38 mm	0.015in	0.38mm	0.005in	0.13mm

Lenses

No single lens yet designed can possibly fulfill all the demands of any but the most complacent cinematographer.

Fixed focal length lenses may be subdivided into normal, wide angle, telephoto, wide aperture (super-speed or ultra-speed) and close focusing (pack-shot or table-top) categories.

Zoom lenses may be subdivided into several distinct groups. There are those which have a 3, 5, 6 or 10 : 1 range of focal lengths and are of particularly high quality, in some cases equalling or even bettering the optical performance of fixed focal length lenses. There are the standard 10 : 1 types, those which start with a wider angle than normal, those with close focusing capabilities, those with a 20 : 1 range and those incorporating a reflex viewfinding facility.

In addition, there are a number of highly specialised lenses available. These include flat field lenses for use on animation rostrums, copying lenses for use on optical printers, and periscope and pitching lenses for ultra-low-angle and miniature cinematography.

Optical design

Claims and statements made in respect of the design aspects of lenses can be misleading. What really matters is what the image looks like on the screen and the usefulness of any additional features.

Cameramen are well advised to make their own comparison tests to assess the optical quality, freedom from distortion, colour quality, focal length and aperture etc. and disregard all claims relating to glass types and grinding techniques. It may happen that a type of glass recommended by one manufacturer may have been tested and rejected by another, grinding techniques claimed to be advanced by one may have been used long ago by another and even discarded in favour of some newer technology and additional facilities incorporated may have little practical application.

In considering lenses take care to ensure that they are suitable for the camera with which they are intended to be used. If any modifications are required they should not involve the additional expense of remounting all the owner's existing lenses which he still chooses to use.

Choosing suitable lenses

Many aspects affect the choice of lenses. Some the user may wish to buy, if he owns his own camera. Others, required only occasionally may be more economic to hire, as needed. Some of the most desirable are not even available for outright sale but only for hire.

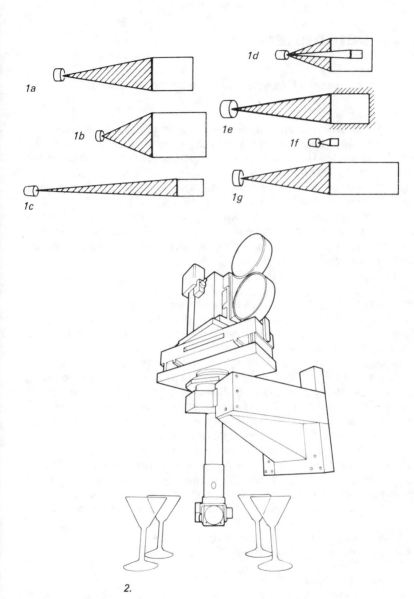

Lenses and their jobs
1a. Normal lens, b. Wide angle, c. Telephoto, d. Zoom, e. Wide aperture, f. Close focusing, g. Anamorphic; 2. Snorkel lens on a motion controlled camera, used for filming from inaccessible viewpoints.

Lens Parameters

In choosing lenses the following aspects must be considered.

Focal length
The angle of view depends upon the focal length of the lens and the format size. The greater the focal length or the smaller the format, the smaller the angle. The smaller the angle the smaller the portion of the subject, and the less background, is included in the shot.

For similar angles of view, lenses used on 16mm cameras are approximately half the focal length of those used on 35mm.

Zoom lenses may be set to any number of different focal lengths within the range of that particular lens, or adjusted (zoomed) in shot to give the effect of magnifying or reducing the image size within the frame as filming proceeds.

Aperture
The amount of light which is allowed to pass through a lens, for exposure purposes, is controlled by an 'iris diaphragm'. This is an expandable and reducible annular ring set within the lens which restricts the flow of light, as a tap controls water.

The degree of opening is quoted in terms of *f* stops and T stops.

The *f* stops are arithmetically derived factors calculated by dividing the focal length by the effective diameter of the lens in use at that particular stop. Hence a 50mm focal length lens which has an effective diameter of 25mm at maximum aperture is said to be an *f2* lens. When that diameter is restricted (stopped down) the exposure is reduced.

T stops are photometric measurements of the light actually transmitted by a lens system. On the very latest lenses employing sophisticated multi-layer coatings, *f* stops and T stops are almost identical. On older lenses the exposure difference may be about 1/3rd stop, or on lenses incorporating a reflex viewfinder system, one whole stop.

Lenses need to be calibrated with both apertures: T stops for exposure control, *f* stops for calculating depth of field.

Back focal distance
This is the distance from the rear element of the lens to the film plane. It must be sufficiently great to avoid interfering with the mechanical parts of the camera.

Lens barrel diameter
This is the diameter of the lens in its mounting and the lens opening in the camera. If that is restricted it will not be possible to use the widest aperture lenses with that particular camera.

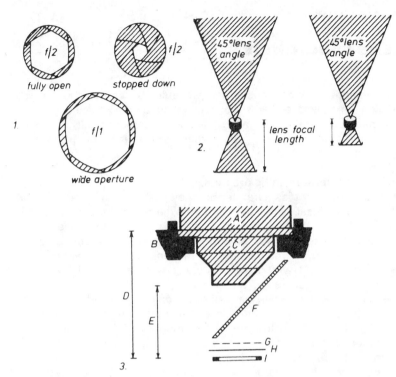

LENS SPECIFICATIONS

Lens apertures
1. An f-stop is an arithmetical factor calculated by dividing the focal length of a lens at infinity by the effective diameter of the stop in use.

Lens angles
2. To cover the same angle, 16mm lenses must be approximately half the focal length required to cover a 35mm frame.

Lens mounting restrictions
3. A. Lens;   B. Camera;   C. Lens barrel diameter;   D. Flange focal distance;   E. Back focal distance (allowing for corner to be cut off lens);   F. Reflex mirror;   G. Focal plane adjustable shutter;   H. Gelatin filter holder;   I. Film plane.

Entrance pupil
A lens may be considered to be a collector of rays of light which converge from many angles to form a single point. The point at which they apparently cross is called the entrance pupil. A knowledge of where this lies may be important when front projection, model and glass process shots are being set up.

The entrance pupil should not be confused with the front nodal point, which is where the rays of light actually cross after having been refracted by the front elements of the lens.

Lens Mountings

A knowledge of what lenses are available for, or may be fitted to, individual makes of cameras may well influence the choice of a camera for a particular filming assignment. Not all lenses, especially of the wide angle, wide aperture and anamorphic types, may be fitted to all cameras.

Choosing a camera to fit the lens
Several aspects of camera design may restrict the choice of lens: available back focal distance; the internal diameter of the lens mounting aperture; strength and size of the lens mount; positive angular positioning, necessary for anamorphic lenses. These must be considered in relation to the diameter of the lens at the point where it is to be accommodated within the camera lens aperture and the type of focusing system necessary.

Because space must be allowed between the lens and the film plane to accommodate the aperture plate, the shutter and the reflex system, there is a limit to how close the rear element of a lens may be mounted in relation to the film. This is known as the minimum back focal distance.

Lenses which are larger in diameter cannot be mounted within narrow lens mounts. Fixed focal length lenses must be able to move forwards from the film plane, to focus to close range. This means a sleeve within a sleeve, which also takes up space.

It is not practical to mount a long and heavy lens on a small lens mount without additional support, especially if that mount itself is only set within an insubstantial lens turret. 'Hard front' modifications to existing turret cameras make it possible to mount heavy lenses without a support bracket.

Anamorphic lenses must be mounted in a very exact azimuth (angular positioning) and cannot be used in the mountings of the bayonet or screw-in type where the lens is rotated to an indefinite position to be secured.

Wide angle, wide aperture, zoom and anamorphic lenses, in particular require that the flange focal depth (the distance from the front of the lens mount to the film plane) must be held to within very close tolerances or else considerable loss of definition will result.

Choosing a lens to fit the film format
Although lenses designed for 35mm formats may be used on 16mm cameras, it is not considered good practice to do so. Such lenses are designed to give optimum performance over a greater diagonal and must inevitably suffer some central fall-off compared with those specifically designed for 16mm usage. Because the image they produce is of limited size, 16mm type lenses cannot be used on 35mm cameras.

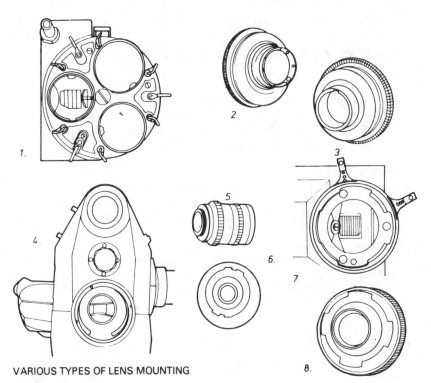

VARIOUS TYPES OF LENS MOUNTING

Arriflex mounts

1. The port on the left is a steel bayonet type and those on the right the original standard Arri mount. Lenses with a standard type mount may be used in a steel bayonet type port but not vice-versa.   2. Steel bayonet.   3. Standard.

Eclair 16 NPR camera

4. Usually fitted with a 'C' mount port (above) and an Eclair mount port (below).   5. 'C' mounted lens.   6. Eclair mounted lens.

Panavision and BNCR

7 & 8. Port and lens mount

All types of Panavision cameras have the same mounts so that all Panavision lenses are interchangeable between all cameras. The BNCR and Panavision mounts are similar, the Panavision one being slightly smaller.

C mount

The C mount, with 1in. (25·4mm) diameter, 32 threads per in., 0·690 (17·53mm) flange focal distance, is fitted to many 16mm cameras. Certain wide aperture wide angle lenses are only available in this mount. The C mount is not as strong as clamp ring or bayonet mounts and in consequence any heavy lenses (zooms etc.) so mounted must be given additional support. The threaded portion of 'C' mounted lenses can usually be rotated independently of the lens, so that when screwed into the camera the focus and aperture index marks (and focal length in the case of a zoom lens) may be conveniently positioned. It is possible to use adapters for Arri or Eclair-mount lenses on a C mount camera but not vice-versa.

45

Lens Focal Lengths and Angles

A choice of lens focal lengths is essential.

Short focal lengths give wide angle pictures with broad horizons. Long focal length (including telephoto) lenses restrict the breadth of the background in relation to the foreground.

'Normal' lenses

Such lenses are the standard set of fixed focal length lenses normally available for a camera. The focal length ranges from about 25 to 100mm for the 35mm formats, 12·5 to 50mm for 16mm. The wider lenses in the range may be of the inverted telephoto type (see below). Maximum apertures are usually T2 or T2·5.

'Macro' or close-up lenses have special optics and extended focusing for shooting at closer range than normal, say 1:1 object to image ratio. They may be any focal length from wide angle to telephoto, but 40, 55, 90 and 100mm lenses are most often preferred.

Telephoto lenses

Telephoto lenses are long focus lenses, whose special optics reduce the back focal distance so that they may be shorter overall than their focal length.

These lenses range from about 150mm focal length for 35mm usage, and 75mm for 16mm work to 1000mm. The longest lenses are normally available for either gauge. Maximum apertures depend upon focal length – T4 or wider for the shorter focal lengths, T8 for the 1000mm.

Catadioptric or mirror telephoto lenses are even more compact, employing a double reflecting mirror principle to reduce their overall length. Because the design cannot use a diaphragm, exposure must be controlled either by neutral density filters or adjusting the camera shutter.

Wide angle or inverted telephoto lenses

Wide angle lenses range between 10–20mm in focal length on 35mm film. Some use inverted telephoto or retrofocus construction, an optical principle which increases the back focal distance. Such lenses are particularly suitable for reflex motion picture cameras where the mirror shutter, or other image reflecting system, requires space, inhibiting the rear lens element from being set close to the film plane.

'Fish-eye' or 'bug-eye' lenses (either special inverted telephoto lenses or optical attachments for normal length focal lenses) give an extreme wide angle of view regardless of image distortion. Some such lenses cover a complete 180° hemisphere, or more.

To minimise distortion, ultra wide angle lenses should be used with the camera absolutely level on both axes.

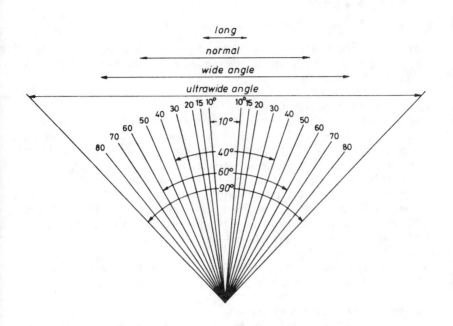

long

normal

wide angle

ultrawide angle

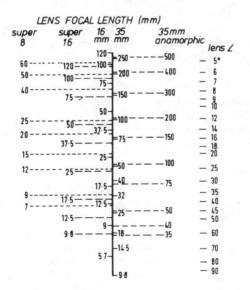

LENS FOCAL LENGTH (mm)

super 8	super 16	16 mm	35 mm	35mm anamorphic	lens ∠
		120	250	500	5°
60	120	100	200	400	6
50	100				7
40		75	150	300	8
	75				9
					10
		50	100	200	12
25	50	37·5			14
20	37·5		75	150	16
					18
15		25			20
12	25		50	100	25
		17·5	40	75	30
9	17·5	12·5	32		35
7					40
	12·5	9	25	50	45
				40	50
9·8			18	35	60
		14·5			70
5·7					80
		9·8			90

LENS ANGLES AND FOCAL LENGTH

Main categories of lens shown in relation to their angles of view. The table shows the equivalent focal length in each format for these angles of view.

47

Lens Types

Additional scope may be added to the possibilities of cinematography by the use of lenses which incorporate special optical features in addition to that of focal length.

Wide aperture (super or ultra speed)

Wide aperture lenses are principally used to obtain sufficient exposure in conditions of low level available light, especially where it would be impractical or expensive to use extra illumination to light the scene. Most advantageous are the 'wide angle wide aperture' lenses which cover the type of scene which would be most expensive to light.

Typically, 35mm wide aperture lenses have apertures of T1·3 and T1·4. Some 16mm cameras may be fitted with such lenses as 15mm f1·3 and 25mm f0·95. Due to the restrictions of back focal distance and the internal diameter of the lens mount, not all wide aperture lenses may be accommodated on all cameras.

Long focus wide aperture lenses are often used by creative cinematographers to acquire a minimum depth of field effect.

Zoom or varifocal length lenses

The focal length of zoom lenses may be altered over a range of 3 : 1, 5 : 1, 6 : 1, 10 : 1 or even 20 : 1. Typical examples are lenses which may be used at any focal length between 20 and 100mm (5 × 20mm), 25 and 250mm (10 × 25mm) and 25 and 500mm (20 × 25mm) on 35mm cameras, and 10 to 100mm (10 × 10mm) and 12·5 to 250mm (20 × 12·5) on 16mm cameras.

The latest 3 : 1, 5 : 1, 6 : 1 and even 10 : 1 zoom lenses available for 16 and 35mm cameras produce images which, in quality, are as good as some of the best fixed focal length lenses available.

Range extenders increasing the focal length by 1·5 or 2 times may be used with zoom lenses, with some loss of effective aperture and often with a great loss of definition.

Anamorphic

'Scope' lenses, such as the Panavision Anamorphic, horizontally compress the picture in the camera by a ratio of 2 : 1, to be expanded subsequently by a similar lens in the projector. In effect, anamorphic lenses take in an angle twice as wide as normal (or spherical) lenses but of unaltered height. The anamorphic format has a 2·35 : 1 ratio. Anamorphic lenses are available in all special types necessary for creative cinematography (i.e. normal, telephoto, wide angle, macro, wide aperture and zoom).

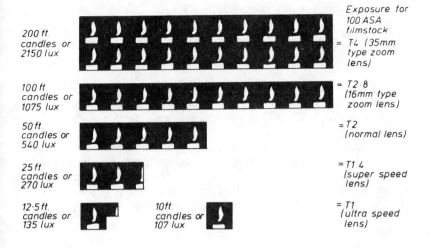

	Exposure for 100 ASA filmstock
200 ft. candles or 2150 lux	= T4 (35mm type zoom lens)
100 ft. candles or 1075 lux	= T2.8 (16mm type zoom lens)
50 ft. candles or 540 lux	= T2 (normal lens)
25 ft. candles or 270 lux	= T1.4 (super speed lens)
12.5 ft. candles or 135 lux	10 ft. candles or 107 lux = T1 (ultra speed lens)

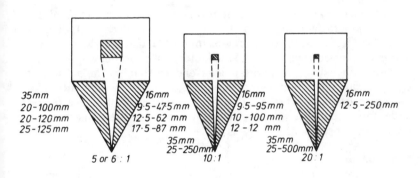

35mm	16mm	16mm	16mm
20-100mm	9.5-47.5 mm	9.5-95mm	12.5-250mm
20-120mm	12.5-62 mm	10-100mm	
25-125mm	17.5-87 mm	12-12 mm	
	35mm	35mm	35mm
	25-250mm	25-250mm	25-500mm
5 or 6 : 1		10 : 1	20 : 1

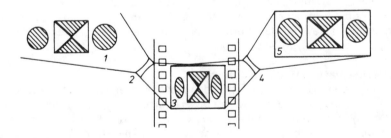

LENS TYPES AND WHAT THEY DO

Wide aperture lenses
Wide aperture lenses which pass more light than normal lenses, make some scenes more economical to light.

The flexibility of zoom lenses
Technical zoom focal length ranges from 35mm and equivalent 16mm lenses.

Anamorphosis
1. Original scene;   2. Anamorphic camera lens;   3. Anamorphic image with 2:1 horizontal squeeze;   4. Anamorphic projection lens;   5. Projected image.

49

Lens/Camera Compatibility

Having taken delivery of a camera and lens which are not his everyday equipment, a cameraman should carry out a series of tests to assess the optical/electrical and mechanical potential of all the equipment in combination.

Failure to do so prior to an expensive or unrepeatable sequence or shot may be construed as negligence. Unless proper mechanical and optical tests are carried out beforehand by the user, the suppliers of the equipment will undoubtedly disclaim responsibility in the event of a fault showing up after the equipment has been removed from their premises.

Tests should be both visual and photographic.

Lens support

Heavy lenses may require additional support in addition to that afforded by the camera lens mount particularly with turret cameras lacking a solid 'hard front'. Some types of lens mounting, particularly those with a clamp ring locking system, can satisfactorily support heavier lenses.

When checking a supported lens ensure that the lens fits in the camera squarely and is neither drooping down, forced upwards or displaced to one side. This is particularly important in the case of zoom, wide angle and wide aperture lenses where accurate registration is of the utmost importance.

Collimation

A collimator is used to check that a lens will focus on infinity, and in the case of zoom lenses, hold this point of focus throughout the zoom range. Quite small and inexpensive portable collimators are available and should form an essential part of a cameraman's tool kit when he is travelling away on location to places where camera engineering support is unlikely to be available.

Intermediate distance calibration

Scale markings on a lens should be checked against measured distances and those obtained by eye focusing on the ground glass. Although it is probably unnecessary to check every distance every day, a regular check, even daily, of one distance, say 6ft. or 2m is a wise precaution which may show up any fault as it begins to develop.

Many zoom lenses are not calibrated accurately enough to be focused against taped distances and if this form of operation is contemplated and the lens has not already been individually checked and engraved then the focus assistant must make his own markings, perhaps on a piece of camera tape.

CAMERA AND LENS

Collimator
1. To check that the lens will focus on infinity a collimator is used.

What is seen
2. The graticule seen through the collimator should appear sharp and clear.

Heavy lenses
3. A heavy lens should be adequately supported, positively secured and in correct alignment to the camera.

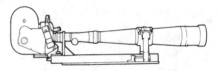

Calibrations
4. Lens calibrations should agree with eye focusing and taped distances.

No lens is perfect but some are more acceptable than others.

Lens Assessment

The equipment suppliers may have checked a lens in terms of its MTF (technically sophisticated method), by collimation and/or by projection on an optical bench. But to the layman such means will not demonstrate exactly how the resultant pictures are likely to look on the screen, the criterion by which user tests should be judged.

Photographic testing

To be meaningful, a test subject must be chosen which contains detail of equal size in all areas, is of high contrast, contains straight horizontal and vertical lines, is sufficiently large to be photographed by the widest angle lens and is repeatedly available so that tests, which may have to be shot over a period of days, may be compared with one another.

A properly designed focus chart of sufficient size, is the ideal but failing this sheets of printed matter will suffice. The detail should not be so fine that a normal lens is unable to resolve it. The target should be mounted absolutely square-on to the camera and evenly lit from opposite sides. No bright light or reflection should shine onto the lens.

What to check for

Definition: The ability to separate detail both in the centre of the picture area and in the corners. There will inevitably be some fall-off in performance off-axis. Most lenses produce optimum results two stops down from full aperture (i.e. two stops smaller than maximum) down to about f11, after which the quality deteriorates rapidly. The effect of aperture on performance should be checked. Zoom lenses should be checked at various focal lengths, moving the camera in relation to the test target to keep the image size constant.

Geometry: Parallel lines on the test target should photograph as parallel.

Colour Fringing: The interface between blacks and whites should not be discoloured.

Contrast: Whites should be clear and blacks dense. A good lens should produce a picture of acceptable definition, with good contrast.

Vignetting: A frame should be equally exposed overall and not darker in the corners.

Zooming: While zooming, a mark in the centre of the test target should not wander excessively, focus should be maintained within tolerances and the mechanical operation of the lens should be smooth. Focal length should not change when the lens is focused (most do!).

Infinity: This point of focus is best checked with a collimator with film actually running through the camera. Additionally, a distant object should also be photographed.

Aperture: Lenses set at similar T stops should produce negatives of equal density.

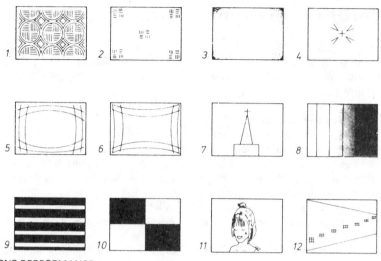

LENS PERFORMANCE

Qualities by which lenses are assessed:
1. Good resolution; 2. Good off-axis and central performance; 3. No vignetting; 4. Minimal axial drift while zooming; 5. Minimal barrel or, 6. pincushion distortion; 7. Proper infinity focus; 8. Aperture (exposure) consistent with different lenses; 9. Minimal colour fringing; 10. Contrast: dense blacks, clear whites; 11. Good flesh tone colour; 12. Acceptable figures for extremes of field depth.

Colour Fidelity: A set of lenses should produce pictures of similar colour balance. The most important colour to be photographed is that of the human face. A pretty girl of average flesh tone, seated in front of large areas of even tone, is the ideal test subject.

Depth of field: The distance in front of and behind the point of focus which is acceptably in focus may be influenced by a number of factors. Only a film test, with objects placed at different distances, will show exactly the depth of field of any particular lens or focal length.

Intermediate distances: Scale markings should be compared with measured distances and those obtained by eye focusing on the ground glass.

Projector line-up leader

At the same time as shooting lens tests prior to shooting a feature film it is common practice to also shoot a 'Projector Line-up Leader' which may be attached to the beginning of each days rushes (dailies). This should display the title of the film, a focus chart (for the projectionist to focus up on in advance) and pointers which show the screen limits (1·66 : 1, 1·85 : 1, 2·35 : 1 etc.) to ensure correct projector racking and screen masking.

Finding the Point of Focus

For the purpose of focusing, distance may be measured either by a tape measure or by visual observation of the image on the ground glass focusing screen.

Measuring the distance

If focusing is to be done with the aid of a tape measure, it is advisable when using a strange camera, to make tests beforehand to check that the distances marked on the lens are accurate. This is particularly important with zoom lenses, the engraved distances of which may sometimes be described as only 'approximate'.

When using a tape measure the loose end should be attached to the camera (by a special hook provided on most cameras) on a plane with the film.

In those parts of the world where some metric and some feet-and-inches scaled lenses are to be found, it is useful to have a tape measure scaled in metric units on one side and feet and inches on the reverse.

When focus must be split between a near and distant object, measurements must be taken to both points and the optimum setting calculated by reference to a depth of field calculator or table.

Focusing by eye

Focusing by eye depends for accuracy upon the setting of the ground glass in relation to the film plane and the personal judgement of the individual. It may be very difficult or even impossible to tell what is 'in focus' and what is 'out', particularly when usir.g a well stopped down and/or wide angle lens, in conditions of bright ambient light, and when shooting in a smoky or haze-laden atmosphere, against the sun, or through fog or filter diffusers. Even in more favourable conditions it may be difficult to judge the acceptibility of depth of field by eye when working close to the limits. Consequently, feature film focus assistants always use a tape measure in preference to eye focus unless it is impossible to do so. In such circumstances a focusing system which incorporates an image magnification facility is a great advantage. On some cameras the only magnification is incorporated in the viewfinder extension unit.

Before focusing a lens visually, the person doing so should first ensure that the eyepiece is set to suit his eyesight. This is done by adjustment until the engraved markings of the grain of the ground glass itself are most sharply defined.

When focusing by eye, the lens should be focused from the close point towards infinity over the area of minimum depth of field.

Focusing zoom lenses

It is usual to set zoom lenses to maximum focal length when eye-focusing. This enlarges the image detail and reduces the depth of field.

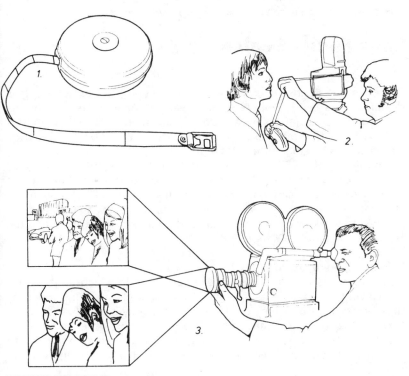

DETERMINING FOCUS

1. Tape measure with ft and in on one side and metric markings on the reverse. 2. Focusing by tape measure. 3. When focusing a zoom lens it is possible to zoom in to enlarge the image as an aid to critical focusing.

Care should be taken when using this method while shooting at full aperture, as some lenses of older design may change focus as the lens is zoomed.

Similarly, a focus shift will be generated in zoom lenses by the use of a rear gelatine filter. This also will only be noticeable at or near full aperture.

Focusing on the move

When artists and the camera are likely to move about in relation to one another during a complicated take, a focus assistant will often put small pieces of tape or chalk marks on the floor as reference points. Alternatively he may make a little map noting the distances according to features in the set. If an artist has to walk at a constant distance from a camera which is itself being moved, as a guide a piece of wood can be fixed to the dolly to touch the artist just out of shot.

It must be possible to set the lens focus accurately to the point of focus.

Lens Focus Scales

There is no consensus of opinion among camera and lens manufacturers as to where it is most convenient to display the engraved focus distances in relation to the camera. The most common, and perhaps the most ergonomically acceptable position is at '3 o'clock' when looking at the front of the lens.

On the Mitchell S35R camera however, the lenses are usually scaled at 9 o'clock, which means that the focus assistant must stand on the motor side of the camera. On the Arriflex IIC and 16ST and many 16mm-type lenses the markings are at 12 o'clock, making it almost impossible to work as a two man team if the operator is very tall and the assistant comparatively short.

Focus display systems

Studio cameras usually have large focus controls which engage in a geared ring around the lens. These focus controls are surrounded by large white discs on which the focus scalings may be boldly displayed, enabling the focus assistant to see at a glance where the lens focus is set. These white discs are interchangeable and must be matched to each lens. If they are magnetised it makes changing a more rapid process.

Arriflex blimps have focus strips which must be changed when the lens is changed. A special strip must be made for every lens on every camera in every blimp. They are rarely, if ever, interchangeable.

A follow focus matte box with a white disc focus display (and provision for two rotating and sliding filters) is available as a non-proprietary accessory for the Arriflex IIC camera.

Focus and zoom focal length display discs are similarly available for 16mm Angenieux zoom lenses. These enable the cameraman operating on his own to see at a glance (using his left eye) where his lens focus and zoom is set without taking his eye away from the viewfinder eyepiece.

Where no adequate focus scale is displayed a piece of white camera tape may be attached to the lens barrel on which to make marks.

Remote focus

There are times when there is no space available for the assistant to stand on either side of the camera to adjust the focus during the course of a shot. On these occasions, a remote focusing system may be attached.

With Panavision cameras, a flexible drive shaft may be attached to the focus control on either side or at the rear of the camera. The latter facility is particularly useful when working in a narrow corridor where, if necessary, the focus assistant may stand behind the operator.

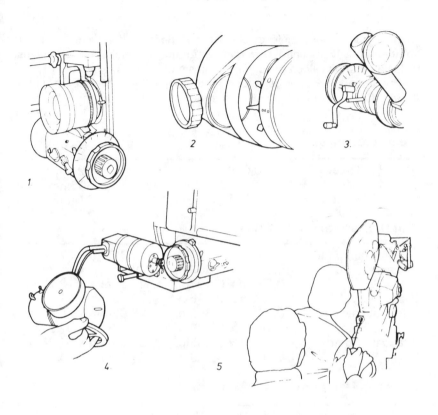

FOCUS CONTROL

1. Panavision PSR follow focus system.   2. Samcine follow focus matte-box for Arriflex IIC.   3. Focus ring attached to an Angenieux reflex zoom lens.
4. Remote focusing by Selsyn drive.   5. Remote focusing by flexible cable.

Image Size Calculation

With a pocket electronic calculator it is possible for even the least mathematically inclined cameraman to quickly make his own lens calculations. All calculations must be in similar units, i.e. mm or in.

If you work in inches, lens focal lengths must be converted from mm to in.; if done in metric measurements, the feet and in. must be converted.

Some basic figures

1 millimeter =	0·0394in.	1 inch =	25·4mm
1 meter =	39·37in.	1 foot =	305mm
100 meters =	3937in.	1 yard =	914mm

Aperture widths and heights

35mm anamorphic	0.838in.x 0.700in.	21.29mm x 17.78mm
Academy	0.825in.x 0.602in.	20.96mm x 15.29mm
1·66 : 1	0.825in.x 0.497in.	20.96mm x 12.62mm
1·85 : 1	0.825in.x 0.446in.	20.96mm x 11.33mm
Techniscope	0.868in.x 0.350in.	22.05mm x 8.89mm
Super 16mm	0.464in.x 0.286in.	11.79mm x 07.26mm
Standard 16mm	0.380in.x 0.286in.	09.65mm x 07.26mm
Super 8	0.209in.x 0.158in.	05.31mm x 04.01mm

Lens focal lengths expressed in inches

mm		in.	mm		in.	mm		in.	mm		in.	mm		in.
5·7	=	0·22	20	=	0·80	50	=	2·00	150	=	6	400	=	16
10	=	0·40	25	=	1·00	75	=	3·00	180	=	7	500	=	20
12·5	=	0·50	32	=	1·25	90	=	3·50	200	=	8	600	=	24
15	=	0·60	35	=	1·40	100	=	4·00	250	=	10	1000	=	40
17·5	=	0·70	40	=	1·60	125	=	5·00	300	=	12	1200	=	48

The formula

Four components produce the object/distance/focal length/image equation:

Object size (O)   — Object to lens distance (D)
Lens focal length (F)   — Image size (I)

Put algebraically the basic formula is:

$$\frac{\text{Object size (O)}}{\text{Image (I)}} = \frac{\text{Distance (D)}}{\text{Focal length (F)}}$$

For example if an object is 1000mm wide and 10,000mm away the lens focal length is 100mm and the aperture width to be filled is 10mm:

$$\frac{1000}{10} = \frac{10,000}{100}$$

It should be noted that this simple formula is only acceptably accurate where the distance is many times greater than the focal length of the lens.

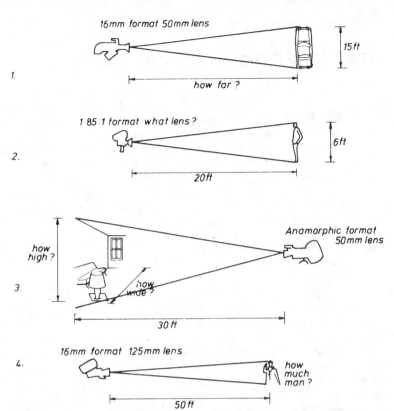

1. *16mm format 50mm lens*

how far?

15 ft

2. *1·85:1 format what lens?*

20 ft

6 ft

3. *how high?* *how wide?* *Anamorphic format 50mm lens*

30 ft

4. *16mm format 125mm lens*

how much man?

50 ft

LENS IMAGE SIZE FORMULAE

The four basic formulae (terms defined on page 58) are: $D=O \times F \div I$; $F=D \times I \div O$; $O=D \times I \div F$; $I=F \times O \div D$. Here are four practical situations to which they are applied to solve a problem.

1. An object 15ft long must be included in a shot. The format is 16mm (standard), the lens 50mm. How far away must the camera be?

Distance
$D=O \times F \div I$; $D=15ft \times 50mm \div 0.380in$;
$D=180in \times 2in \div 0.380in$; $D=947in=79ft$.

2. A man six feet high must fill a 1.85:1 frame from 20ft away, what lens should be used?

Focal length
$F=D \times I \div O$; $F=20ft \times 0.446in \div 6ft$;
$F=240 \times 0.446in \div 72in$;
$F=1.48in=35mm$.

3. How high and wide must a set be built to fill an anamorphic frame with a 50mm lens, 30ft away?

Height
$O=D \times I \div F$; $O=30ft \times 0.7in \div 50mm$;
$O=360 \times 0.7in \div 2in$; $O=126in=10ft 6in$.

Width
$O=D \times I \div F \times 2$;
$O=30ft \times 0.838in \div 50mm \times 2$;
$O=360in \times 0.838in \div 2in \times 2$;
$O=302in=25ft 2in$.

4. A man 6ft high is filmed from 50ft away with a 125mm lens, how large will the image be on film in relation to a 16mm format?

$I=F \times O \div D$; $I=125mm \times 6ft \times 50ft$;
$I=5 \times 72 \div 600in$; $I=0.6in$.

A 16mm frame is 0.286in high, therefore from this distance the man will be half length in the frame, approximately.

In the case of anamorphic cinematography, this formula applies only to the vertical dimensions of the picture. To calculate measurements relating to the horizontal plane the lens focal length (F) should be halved or the image width (I) doubled.

Close Focusing by Extension

When shooting closer to the subject than the focusing mount of the normal lens allows, it may be exchanged for a lens with a special double or triple extension mount. These macro lenses most often come in focal lengths of 40, 55, 90 and 100mm. Their close focusing possibilities may be further increased by the use of extension tubes which place the lens at an even greater distance from the film plane. Extension tubes may also be placed between a normal lens and the film plane, for close focusing. To obtain the best optical performance by this means the lens should be reversed so that the front element faces the film.

Extension tubes can not be used with anamorphic, wide-angle or zoom lenses and with these it is necessary to use diopters (supplementary close-up lenses) for very close range work.

Image:object ratios

When referring to the magnification (or reproduction) ratio of a picture, the first number always refers to the size of the image on the film and the second to the size of the object photographed. The cameraman must visualise the ratio as seen from the motor side of the camera looking towards the subject. Thus, a 1 : 2 magnification ratio means that the image on the film, regardless of the size of the film, is half the size that the object photographed is in reality. Because the magnification ratio takes no account of film size the ratio must be twice as great with 35mm film compared with 16mm in order to fill the screen to the same proportion.

A 1 : 1 ratio means that the image and the object are the same size, although if it fills a 16mm frame it will only half fill a 35mm format. The amount of extension required for a 1 : 1 ratio is twice the focal length of the lens.

The depth of field for a given magnification ratio is the same whether a 40mm lens is used 80mm away or a 90mm lens is used 180mm away. The only difference is that more background is included with the 40mm lens and there would be more space for lighting using the longer focal length.

Exposure

Whenever an object is less than 10 focal lengths away from the camera the exposure must be increased beyond that calibrated on the lens to compensate for the extra extent by which the light is being dispersed.

The simplest way to calculate the increased exposure factor is to add one to the magnification number and multiply the result by itself. Thus, for a two times magnification $2+1=3$, $3\times3=9$. A factor of 9 means an exposure increase of a little over 3 stops.

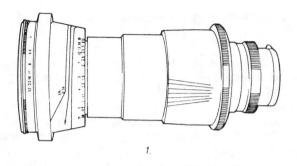

1.

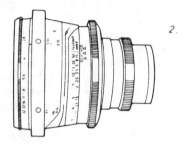

2.

EXTENSION FOCUSING

Typical macro lens in triple extension mount. 1. Focused down to 1:1 magnification ratio. 2. Focused on infinity.
Where an exposure factor is calculated the following table gives the equivalent exposure increase in stops.

Exposure factor table

Factor	1.5	2	3	4	6	8	12	16	24	32	64	128	256
Exposure increase (stops)	$\frac{1}{2}$	1	$1\frac{1}{2}$	2	$2\frac{1}{2}$	3	$3\frac{1}{2}$	4	$4\frac{1}{2}$	5	6	7	8

Lens extension tables

Object to image ratio	Width of object to fill frame		Extension forward of infinity		Exposure increase
	35mm	16mm	40mm lens	90mm lens	stops
1:2.5 (0.4:1)	2in 50mm	0.9in 23mm	0.7in 17mm	1.5in 37mm	1
1:2 (0.5:1)	1.6in 41mm	0.8in 20mm	0.8in 20mm	1.8in 45mm	$1\frac{1}{4}$
1:1	0.8in 20mm	0.4in 10mm	1.6in 40mm	3.5in 90mm	2
2:1	0.4in 10mm	0.2in 5mm	3.2in 80mm	7in 180mm	$3\frac{1}{8}$
4:1	0.2in 5mm	0.1in 2.5mm	6.3in 160mm	14in 360mm	$4\frac{1}{2}$
8:1	0.1in 2.5mm	0.05in 1.25mm	12.6in 320mm	28in 720mm	$6\frac{1}{4}$

Close Focusing by Diopters

If a positive supplementary lens is placed in front of any camera lens, the range over which the camera may be focused is reduced.

Optical considerations

A simple meniscus lens of one meter focal length is said to have a focal length of one 'diopter'. If placed in front of another lens focused on infinity it will shift the point of sharp focus from infinity to one meter. A '+2 diopter' is a supplementary lens of half a meter focal length, and if placed in front of a normal lens set at infinity causes that lens to be focused sharply at $\frac{1}{2}$ meter (19·70in.) distance. A '+4 diopter' is $\frac{1}{4}$ meter focal length, and so on. The plus sign indicates that it is a positive lens. More than one diopter lens may be used at a time, in which case the effectiveness is almost the sum of their dioptric powers. Thus when a +1 and a +2 diopter are combined they become almost a +3 diopter.

Diopters should be placed in front of the prime lens with their uncurved side towards the subject. When two diopters are used together the most powerful should be placed closest to the front element of the prime lens.

Diopters make the focal length of the prime lens slightly shorter, thus reducing by a small amount, the close-up capability. A 100mm lens becomes 90·91mm with a +1 diopter, 83·33mm with a +2 and 71·43mm with a +4. Diopters require no exposure compensation. For optimum results lenses should be stopped down to at least f 8 when a diopter is used. Combinations of diopter lenses must be eye focused through a reflex viewfinder system and the lens scalings ignored.

Full cover diopters

Many zoom lenses, which cannot be focused closer than about 4ft 6in. are supplied with two diopters. The No. 1 permits focusing between 5ft 8in. and 3ft 3in. and the No. 2 between 3ft 6in. and 2ft 8in. Used together the range is 2ft 8in. to 2ft 3in.

Split diopters

When two parts of a scene, set at widely different distances from the camera which cannot be spanned by depth of field, need to be held in sharp focus, it is possible to place a 'split diopter' (a full diopter cut in half) over just a portion of the prime lens, the other part of the picture being focused in the normal manner. Thus it is possible to set up a shot with one person placed just a few inches away from the camera and another set 20 feet away and hold both in focus. When setting up split diopter shots care must be taken to blend the join between two parts of the shot against a line or natural break in the background. The part of the lens covered by the split diopter has in effect, a wider angle of view than the remainder.

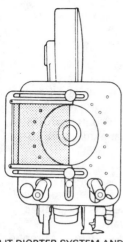 

A SPLIT DIOPTER SYSTEM AND ITS EFFECT

Split diopter lens

A split diopter mounted in front of an Arriflex 35 IIC camera. The half lens can be positioned anywhere in relation to the picture frame. Here it is seen set up exactly in the middle of a scene covering only the right hand side of the scene.

Diopters with 35mm type zoom lens table

Diopter power	Focus distance marked on lens ft	Focus distance with diopter Ft in		Modified focal length Focal length (mm) marked on lens					
				25	32	50	75	100	250
				Focal length lens with diopter					
$+\frac{1}{4}$D	Inf	14	2	25.5	33	52	79	106	260
	25	9	7						
	15	7	10						
	10	6	5						
	6	4	8						
	5	4	1						
$+\frac{1}{2}$D	Inf	7	8	26	34	54	83	112	270
	25	6	3						
	15	5	7						
	10	4	10						
	6	3	11						
	5	3	6						
+1D	Inf	4	4	27	37	58	92	126	284
	25	4	0						
	15	3	9						
	10	3	6						
	6	3	1						
	5	2	10						
+1.5D	Inf	3	3	28	40	63	104	146	305
	25	3	1						
	15	3	0						
	10	2	10						
	6	2	7						
	5	2	6						
+2D	Inf	2	9	29	43	69	119	172	329
	25	2	7						
	15	2	7						
	10	2	6						
	6	2	4						
	5	2	3						

Depth of Field

If a lens is focused at a certain distance there will be an area in front and behind which also appears to the viewer to be acceptably in focus. This is called 'depth of field' and should not be confused with 'depth of focus' which refers to the distance the film plane may vary in relation to the lens.

Theoretical considerations
The longer the focal length of the lens the less the depth of field.
The closer the point of focus to the camera the less the depth of field.
The wider the aperture the less the depth of field.
The depth of field may be estimated if the following assumptions are made:
1. The out-of-focus image of an imaginary point source of light (having luminance but no magnitude) is a perfect circle – the 'circle of confusion'.
2. Images made up of circles of confusion below a certain critical diameter are considered to be 'in-focus', while those above this diameter are considered to be 'out-of-focus'.

Although the truth of both these assumptions is debatable, tables based on them have proved to be a useful guide in practice.

Early tables and calculations were based on a circle of confusion 1/500in. (0·05mm) for 35mm work and 1/1000in. (0·025mm) for 16mm. Rank Optics Limited, however, publish tables for Cooke Varotal zoom lenses based on the more exacting standard of 0·027mm (1/950in.) for 35mm, recommending 0·013mm (1/2000in.) for 16mm. Angenieux use 0·030mm (1/850in.) for both 35 and 16mm.

Practical considerations
1. The public accepts some out-of-focus effect beyond the plane of focus as a natural part of the photographic process.
2. If out-of-focus objects are dark or under-lit, they may still appear acceptable on the screen; other objects, out-of-focus by the same amount, but brightly or over-lit, may be quite unacceptable.
3. High definition lenses have less acceptable depth of field than those which are inherently 'soft'. The use of a diffuser on a lens will increase the apparent depth of field.
4. Zoom lenses have less depth of field at close range than fixed focus lenses of the same focal length and aperture. This fact is taken into account in the latest depth of field tables and calculators.
5. The resolving power of the film stock will also affect depth of field. There appears to be less with ultra fine grain emulsions where what is sharp looks sharper, and therefore what is unsharp is less acceptable.
6. The assumption that the circle of confusion for 16mm work must be

CONDITIONS AFFECTING DEPTH OF FIELD

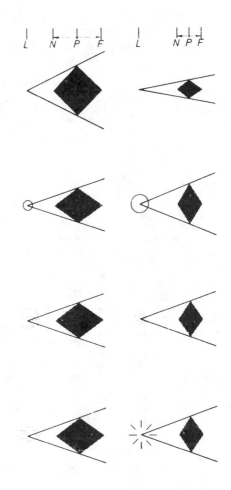

Focal length
Short focal length lenses give most depth of field.
Long focal length lenses give little depth of field.
L = Lens; N = Near point of acceptable focus; P = Point of focus; F = Far point of acceptable focus.

Aperture
Small aperture gives great depth of field.
Wide aperture gives shallow depth of field.

Circle of confusion
Large circle of confusion gives, in effect, more depth of field.
Small circle of confusion gives, in effect, less depth of field.

Lighting
Soft lighting; Poor lens quality; Fog and diffusion filters; Coarse grain filmstock; Fixed focal length lenses give more apparent depth of field.
Hard lighting; High definition lenses; Clear ambience; Fine grain filmstock; High quality zoom lenses, make the depth of field more critical.

about half that for 35mm may not be justified in practice because the conditions for viewing are usually quite different.
7. Depth of field calculations are based on *f* stops. Tables (as those on the next pages) showing depth of field in relation to T stops have been calculated to allow 1/3rd stop difference between *f* and T calibrations.

Depth of Field Tables—Metric

Nearest and Furthest Point of Acceptable Focus

LENS APERTURE	LENS FOCAL LENGTHS IN RELATION TO LENS APERTURE										

For 0·05mm circle of confusion use tables as printed.
For 0·025mm circle of confusion transpose focal lengths two columns to right.
(Note: ⅓rd stop has been allowed for the difference between f and T stops).

Aperture											
T2				21	25	30	35	42	50	60	70
2·8			21	25	30	35	42	50	60	70	84
4		21	25	30	35	42	50	60	70	84	100
5·6	21	25	30	35	42	50	60	70	84	100	120
8	25	30	35	42	50	60	70	84	100	120	140
11	30	35	42	50	60	70	84	100	120	140	170
16	35	42	50	60	70	84	100	120	140	170	200
22	42	50	60	70	84	100	120	140	170	200	241

POINT OF FOCUS MEASURED FROM FOCAL PLANE — Meters

FIXED FOCAL LENGTH LENSES and most 16mm TYPE ZOOM LENSES

Meters	N/F											
1·0	N	0·6	0·72	0·78	0·84	0·88	0·91	0·93	0·95	0·96	0·97	0·98
	F	2·5	1·65	1·40	1·25	1·17	1·11	1·08	1·05	1·04	1·03	1·02
1·2	N	0·72	0·82	0·89	0·97	1·02	1·07	1·10	1·13	1·15	1·17	1·18
	F	4·41	2·30	1·84	1·58	1·45	1·37	1·31	1·28	1·26	1·24	1·23
1·3	N	0·75	0·86	0·95	1·03	1·09	1·15	1·19	1·22	1·25	1·26	1·27
	F	5·37	2·72	2·1	1·76	1·61	1·5	1·44	1·39	1·36	1·34	1·33
1·5	N	0·82	0·94	1·05	1·15	1·23	1·3	1·35	1·39	1·42	1·44	1·46
	F	18·7	3·82	2·69	2·16	1·93	1·78	1·69	1·63	1·59	1·56	1·54
1·7	N	0·87	1·02	1·14	1·27	1·36	1·45	1·51	1·56	1·59	1·63	1·65
	F	Inf	5·54	3·43	2·60	2·27	2·07	1·95	1·86	1·83	1·77	1·75
2·0	N	0·94	1·11	1·26	1·42	1·54	1·66	1·74	1·81	1·8	1·91	1·93
	F	Inf	11·2	4·98	3·4	2·86	2·53	2·35	2·23	2·15	2·10	2·07
2·5	N	1·03	1·25	1·44	1·66	1·82	1·98	2·11	2·21	2·29	2·35	2·39
	F	Inf	Inf	10·2	5·20	4·02	3·40	3·08	2·88	2·75	2·67	2·62
3·0	N	1·07	1·36	1·59	1·86	2·07	2·28	2·24	2·59	2·71	2·79	2·85
	F	Inf	Inf	33·4	8·03	5·51	4·41	3·89	3·57	3·37	3·25	3·17
5·0	N	1·24	1·65	2·0	2·45	2·84	3·26	3·62	3·94	4·22	4·43	4·58
	F	Inf	Inf	Inf	Inf	21·6	10·8	8·12	6·85	6·15	5·75	5·51
8·0	N	1·36	1·87	2·35	3·0	3·6	4·3	4·95	5·59	6·15	6·61	6·95
	F	Inf	Inf	Inf	Inf	Inf	60·0	21·0	14·1	11·5	10·1	9·42
17·0	N	1·47	2·1	2·71	3·62	4·54	5·73	6·95	8·28	9·56	10·7	11·7
	F	Inf	Inf	Inf	Inf	Inf	Inf	Inf	82·0	35·1	25·0	21·0
Inf	N	1·62	2·42	3·29	4·74	6·48	9·22	12·9	18·4	26·0	37·1	52·0

35mm ZOOM LENSES (T stops)

Meters	N/F											
1·5	N	0·97	1·08	1·16	1·24	1·3	1·35	1·39	1·42	1·44	1·46	1·47
	F	5·55	2·86	2·27	1·95	1·8	1·69	1·63	1·59	1·56	1·54	1·53
1·7	N	1·03	1·16	1·26	1·36	1·44	1·51	1·55	1·6	1·62	1·64	1·66
	F	13·0	3·94	2·86	2·35	2·11	1·96	1·88	1·82	1·79	1·76	1·74
2·0	N	1·1	1·27	1·39	1·53	1·63	1·73	1·79	1·85	1·89	1·92	1·94
	F	Inf	6·87	4·05	3·04	2·64	2·4	2·27	2·18	2·13	2·09	2·06
3·0	N	1·28	1·53	1·74	1·98	2·18	2·38	2·52	2·64	2·73	2·81	2·86
	F	Inf	Inf	18·9	6·97	5·03	4·12	3·75	3·48	3·33	3·22	3·16
5·0	N	1·47	1·84	2·18	2·61	2·99	3·41	3·72	4·03	4·26	4·46	4·59
	F	Inf	Inf	Inf	Inf	18·3	9·79	7·78	6·64	6·07	5·69	5·49
10·0	N	1·66	2·17	2·68	3·4	4·14	5·05	5·79	6·64	7·32	7·99	8·44
	F	Inf	Inf	Inf	Inf	Inf	Inf	40·4	20·8	15·9	13·4	12·29
20·0	N	1·77	2·38	3·03	4·02	5·12	6·64	8·03	9·8	11·4	13·2	14·51
	F	Inf	Inf	Inf	Inf	Inf	Inf	Inf	Inf	85·2	41·64	32·33
Inf	N	1·89	2·63	3·49	4·99	6·7	9·69	13·1	18·8	26·0	38·0	52·0

Depth of Field Tables: Ft & In.
Nearest and Furthest Point of Acceptable Focus

LENS APERTURE — LENS FOCAL LENGTHS IN RELATION TO LENS APERTURE

For 1/500in. circle of confusion use tables as printed.
For 1/1000in. circle of confusion transpose focal lengths two columns to right.
(Note: ⅓rd stop has been allowed for the difference between *f* and T stops).

LENS APERTURE											
T2				21	25	30	35	42	50	60	70
2·8			21	25	30	35	42	50	60	70	84
4		21	25	30	35	42	50	60	70	84	100
5·6	21	25	30	35	42	50	60	70	84	100	120
8	25	30	35	42	50	60	70	84	100	120	140
11	30	35	42	50	60	70	84	100	120	140	170
16	35	42	50	60	70	84	100	120	140	170	200
22	42	50	60	70	84	100	120	140	170	200	240

POINT OF FOCUS MEASURED FROM FOCAL PLANE — FIXED FOCAL LENGTH LENSES and most 16mm TYPE ZOOM LENSES

POINT OF FOCUS MEASURED FROM FOCAL PLANE												
3-0	N	1-11½	2-2½	2-4¾	2-6½	2-8	2-9	2-9¾	2-10½	2-11	2-11¼	2-11¾
	F	6-7¼	4-8½	3-11¾	3-7¾	3-5½	3-3½	3-2½	3-1¾	3-1¼	3-0¾	3-0½
3-6	N	2-2½	2-5½	2-8¼	2-10¾	3-0½	3-2	3-3	3-3¾	3-4½	3-5	3-5¼
	F	9-3¼	6-0¾	5-0¾	4-5¼	4-1¾	3-11	3-9½	3-8½	3-7½	3-7	3-6¾
4-0	N	2-4	2-8½	2-11¾	3-2¾	3-4¾	3-6¾	3-8	3-9¼	3-10	3-10¾	3-11
	F	15-5	7-9¾	6-2½	5-3½	4-10½	4-6¾	4-4¾	4-3¼	4-2¼	4-1¼	4-1
4-6	N	2-6	2-11¼	3-2¾	3-6½	3-9	3-11¼	4-1	4-2½	4-3½	4-4¼	4-4¾
	F	25-2	10-1	7-6¼	6-2¾	5-7¾	5-2¾	5-0	4-10	4-8¾	4-7¾	4-7¼
5-0	N	2-7½	3-1½	3-5¾	3-10	4-1	4-4	4-6	4-7¾	4-8¾	4-10	4-10¾
	F	75-0	13-1	9-1	7-3	6-5½	5-11¼	5-7½	5-5¼	5-3½	5-2¼	5-1½
6-0	N	2-10½	3-5¾	3-11	4-4½	4-8¾	5-0½	5-3½	5-5¾	5-7½	5-9	5-9¾
	F	Inf	23-10	13-2	9-7¼	8-3	7-5	6-11½	6-7½	6-5¼	6-3½	6-2½
8-0	N	3-3	4-0½	4-8	5-4	5-10½	6-4½	6-9¼	7-1	7-4	7-6½	7-8
	F	Inf	Inf	30-2	16-2	12-8	10-9	9-10	9-2¼	8-9	8-6¼	8-4½
10-0	N	3-6¼	4-5¾	5-3	6-1¾	6-10¼	7-6¾	8-1½	8-7¼	9-0	9-3½	9-5¾
	F	Inf	Inf	Inf	27-6	18-7	14-9	13-0	11-11	11-4	10-10	10-7
15-0	N	3-11¾	5-3	6-4	7-8½	8-10¼	10-1	11-1½	12-0	12-11	13-5	13-10
	F	Inf	Inf	Inf	Inf	50-0	29-6	23-1	19-11	18-2	17-0	16-5
25-0	N	4-5	6-0¾	7-7	9-7¾	11-7	13-9	15-9	17-9	19-3	20-10	21-11
	F	Inf	Inf	Inf	Inf	Inf	Inf	61-0	42-7	36-9	31-4	29-3
50-0	N	4-10	6-10	8-11	11-11	15-0	19-0	23-0	27-4	32-0	35-7	38-9
	F	Inf	Inf	Inf	Inf	Inf	Inf	Inf	Inf	200-0	100-0	70-0
Inf	N	5-4	7-11	10-9	15-7	21-3	30-3	42-3	60-3	80-0	120-0	170-0
						35mm ZOOM LENSES (T stops)						
5-0	N	3-2	3-7	3-10	4-1½	4-3¾	4-6	4-7½	4-8¾	4-9½	4-10¼	4-10¾
	F	19-9	9-9	7-8	6-6¼	6-0¼	5-7¾	5-5½	5-3¾	5-2¾	5-1¾	5-1¼
6-0	N	3-6	4-0	4-4	4-9	5-0	5-3	5-5¼	5-7	5-8¼	5-9½	5-10
	F	177-0	16-2	10-11	8-7	7-8	7-0½	6-8¾	6-5¾	6-4	6-2¾	6-2
8-0	N	3-11	4-7	5-2	5-9	6-2	6-8	7-0	7-3	7-5¼	7-7¼	7-8½
	F	Inf	94-0	23-0	14-1	11-8	10-2	9-10	8-11½	8-8	8-5½	8-4
10-0	N	4-3	5-1	5-9	6-7	7-3	7-11	8-4	8-10	9-1¼	9-4¼	9-6¼
	F	Inf	Inf	70-0	23-1	16-11	13-10	12-7	11-8	11-1	10-9	10-6
15-0	N	4-9	5-11	6-11	8-3	9-4	10-7	11-5	12-4	13-0	13-6	13-11
	F	Inf	Inf	Inf	154-0	43-3	26-11	22-2	19-4	17-10	16-10	16-4
20-0	N	5-1	6-5	7-8	9-5	10-11	12-8	14-0	15-5	16-5	17-5	18-0
	F	Inf	Inf	Inf	Inf	195-0	51-0	35-11	28-10	25-8	23-6	22-6
50-0	N	5-8	7-7	9-7	12-6	15-8	19-10	23-6	28-3	31-2	36-0	38-10
	F	Inf	Inf	Inf	Inf	Inf	Inf	Inf	260-0	120-0	82-6	70-3
Inf	N	6-2	8-8	11-5	16-4	22-0	31-9	43-0	61-7	85-6	125-0	170-0

Hyperfocal Distances

When filming under newsreel and documentary conditions it is sometimes necessary to set the focus of a lens so that the greatest possible depth of a scene, from infinity forwards, is acceptably in focus.

This distance depends upon the focal length of the lens and the aperture to which it is set.

The precise point at which the focus should be set under these circumstances is called 'hyperfocal distance'. The nearest point of acceptable focus is half the hyperfocal distance.

Practical considerations

Opening the aperture by two stops makes the hyperfocal distance twice as far away from the lens; stopping down by two stops makes it half the distance away.

By remembering the *f* 1 hyperfocal distance for a given focal length, it is possible to calculate mentally the hyperfocal distance for any aperture, simply by dividing the *f* 1 distance by the aperture to be used.

Thus if a cameraman remembers the figure 320 in relation to a 50mm lens he simply divides that by 4 to find the hyperfocal distance for that lens at *f* 4 (80ft), by 8 to find the hyperfocal distance at *f* 8, and so on. If he then sets his 50mm lens at *f* 4 to 80ft, he will know that everything between 40ft and infinity will be acceptably sharp.

Lens	Circle of confusion	Hyperfocal distance (*f* 1)	Working aperture	Hyperfocal distance	Nearest point of acceptable focus
50mm	1/1000	320ft (96m)	*f* 2	160ft (48m)	80ft (2 4m)
50mm	1/1000	320ft (96m)	*f* 4	80ft (2 4m)	40ft (12m)
50mm	1/1000	320ft (96m)	*f* 8	40ft (12m)	20ft (6m)
50mm	1/1000	320ft (96m)	*f* 16	20ft (6m)	10ft (3m)

f 1 Hyperfocal distances

1/1000in. circle of confusion at *f* 1

12·5mm lens =	20ft	(6m)
17·5mm lens =	40ft	(12m)
25 mm lens =	80ft	(24m)
35 mm lens =	160ft	(48m)
50 mm lens =	320ft	(96m)
100 mm lens =	1280ft	(192m)

Depth of field is very often a matter of personal judgement and these figures should be taken only as a guide in the first place. For more accurate calculations depth of field tables or a calculator should be consulted.

Zoom lenses have less depth of field at short focusing ranges than fixed focal length lenses, particularly in the direction of the camera.

HYPERFOCAL DISTANCE

Wide angle lens; Long focus lens;
Lens well stopped down; Wide
aperture.
NF = Point of near focus;
F = Point of focus.

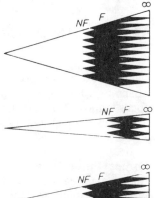

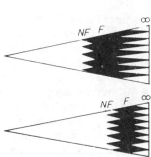

HYPERFOCAL DISTANCE CALCULATIONS SIMPLIFIED

f/no	Lens focal lengths						
1					9	11	12.5
1.4				9	11	12.5	15
2			9	11	12.5	15	17.5
2.8		9	11	12.5	15	17.5	21
4	9	11	12.5	15	17.5	21	25
5.6	11	12.5	15	17.5	21	25	30
8	12.5	15	17.5	21	25	30	35
11	15	17.5	21	25	30	35	42
16	17.5	21	25	30	35	42	50
22	21	25	30	35	42	50	60

Circles of confusion	Hyperfocal distances						
0.001in	2ft 6½in	3ft 7in	5ft 3in	7ft 3in	10ft 6in	14ft 9in	20ft 6in
0.002in	1ft 3in	1ft 9½in	2ft 7in	3ft 7½in	5ft 3in	7ft 4in	10ft 6in
0.025mm	0.8m	1.1m	1.6m	2.2m	3.2m	4.5m	6.3m
0.05mm	0.4m	0.56m	0.8m	1.1m	1.6m	2.2m	3.2m

f/no	Lens focal lengths						
1	15	17.5	21	25	30	35	42
1.4	17.5	21	25	30	35	42	50
2	21	25	30	35	42	50	60
2.8	25	30	35	42	50	60	70
4	30	35	42	50	60	70	84
5.6	35	42	50	60	70	84	100
8	42	50	60	70	84	100	120
11	50	60	70	84	100	120	140
16	60	70	84	100	120	140	170
22	70	84	100	120	140	170	200

Circles of confusion	Hyperfocal distances						
0.001in	29ft 6in	41ft	59ft	82ft	118ft	164ft	236ft
0.002in	14ft 9in	20ft 6in	29ft 6in	41ft	59ft	82ft	118ft
0.025mm	9m	12.5m	18m	25m	36m	50m	72m
0.05mm	4.5m	6.3m	9m	12.5m	18m	25m	36m

69

Range Extenders

When a camera crew must travel lightly or compactly, weight and space may be saved by using a range extender to increase the effective focal length of a lens instead of carrying separate long focus lenses. This is a supplementary optical element mounted between lens and camera.

Optical limitations

Range extenders are available for certain telephoto and zoom lenses, which will increase their focal lengths by factors 1·5, 2 and even 3 times. They reduce the effective aperture of a lens by a factor equal to the square of their magnification. Thus, a 2 X range extender used with a 400mm *f* 4 telephoto lens converts it into 800mm working at *f* 8.

Unless range extenders are designed specifically for particular lenses they may impair the optical quality of the image. The degradation in quality sometimes looks worse through the viewfinder when seen on a ground glass screen, than it appears on the film. They are not satisfactory for lenses of normal or short focal length and are best used with any lens stopped down at least two stops.

Combination lens outfits

A further means of economising in weight and space when transporting very long telephoto lenses and to give a choice of focal lengths available is to combine a single central portion of a lens with two alternative front elements of different focal lengths. A range extender may also be added.

Typical of such outfits is the Kilfit Combi lens. Here 400 and 600mm optical units may be fitted on to a common lens barrel which incorporates the focusing system, the exposure control (iris), the support system and the means of attaching the lens to the camera mounting. A 2 X range extender may be fitted between the rear of the lens barrel and the mount giving the possibility of a 400, 600, 800 or 1200mm lens as required. As the same iris is used to control the exposure of all focal lengths alternative sets of calibrations must be used commencing with T4, 5·6, 8 and 11 respectively.

Another type of combination lens, the Astro Telestigma uses alternative rear elements to give focal lengths of 175, 225, 250 and 315mm at maximum apertures of *f* 3·5 to *f* 6·3. This lens is exceptionally light in weight and compact, and is ideal when the ultimate in portability is required. For 16mm usage, it is a useful additional lens to complement a 12–120mm zoom.

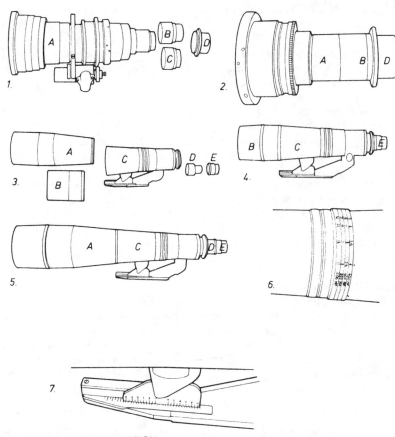

RANGE EXTENDER APPLICATION

Typical 10 × 25mm zoom lens with range extenders
1 & 2. With the camera mount screwed directly onto the rear of the lens the
focal length range is 25–250mm.
With a 2 × range extender placed between the lens and the lens mount the range
becomes 50–500mm.
With a 1.6 range extender the range becomes 40–400mm. There is always
some loss in optical quality when a range extender is used.
A. Zoom lens;   B. 2 × Range extender;   C. 1.6 × range extender;   D. Lens
mount.

Telephoto combination lens with range extenders
3. The central section of a combination lens incorporates the iris ring, the focusing
system and the lens support.
A. 600mm element;   B. 400mm element;   C. Central section;   D. 2 × Range
extender;   E. Lens mount.
4. 400mm T4 mode;   5. 1200mm TII mode;   6. Alternative aperture
markings. Here seen set for: T4 as a 400mm lens, T5.6 as a 600mm, T8 as an
800mm, and TII as a 1200mm;   7. Vernier focusing scale.
When focusing very long lenses the amount of lens extension is so little that the
only practicable means of marking is by a Vernier 400–600–800–1200mm
combination lens.

Optical Accessories

Multi facet prisms or lenses may be placed in front of a suitable prime lens to produce special optical effects in the camera, which would otherwise have to be made by optical printing.

Multi image prisms

Multi facet prisms, which form a multiplicity of similar images offer one of the most popular trick effects. There are two types, those which form images in a radial pattern and those which form images side-by-side and parallel.

The radial type may have a plain central segment so that an unaffected image remains in the centre of the picture.

Multi image prisms must be used with lenses of about 50mm focal length for the 35mm formats and 25mm for 16mm usage. They may be rotated 'in-shot' to produce an effect of a number of images rotating about the centre of the screen.

Multi image lenses

These optical units take the form of a large number of negative lenses used in conjunction with a single complementary positive lens. The negative lenses are usually set in such a manner as to give a multi image effect but with the boundaries of each image more clearly defined than with multi image prisms. The images are usually formed either in a grid pattern or radially like a telephone dial. They must be used with 100mm lens for 35mm work and with a 50mm lens for 16mm.

Prismatic attachments

A turn-over, or dove prism can turn an image upside down or reverse it laterally. When the prism is rotated 'in shot' the picture turns over in the reverse direction. When the image is the right way up it is reversed left to right.

This unit can not be used with wide angle prime lenses.

A 45° prism may be used to shoot scenes with the camera set at 90° to the action. The image is reversed left to right.

The Samcine inclining prism is used for low or high angle cinematography; the image is correctly orientated top to bottom and left to right. It may be used with prime lenses of 25mm focal length for the 35mm formats or 12·5 for 16mm cameras and with no appreciable loss of exposure, definition or any image distortion.

Fish eye lens

This is a supplementary lens which is placed in front of a 50mm (or 25mm for 16mm usage) prime lens to give an ultra wide angle (or bug eye) coverage, albeit distorted.

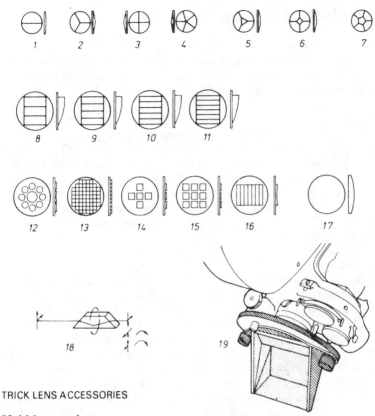

TRICK LENS ACCESSORIES

Multi-image prisms

Radial type prisms giving: 1. two; 2. three; 3. four and 4. five images.
5, 6 and 7. Radial type multi-image prisms with clear central segments.
Parallel type multi-image prisms giving 8. three; 9. four; 10. five and 11. six side-by-side images.
12–16. Multi-image lenses used in combination with the positive lens 17.
Dove turn over prism 18. The image may be rotated but is always upside down or reversed.
19. Samcine prism, is used in front of normal prime lens and gives an extremely low angle view. The image remains correctly orientated with no distortion and with little light loss.

Effects iris

A large iris which may be placed in front of any lens to give an 'iris-in' or 'iris-out' effect. One must be able to mount the iris with its centre anywhere relative to the picture area.

Mattebox Sunshade

The mattebox sunshade serves the dual purpose of shading the front element of the lens and any filter from stray light and of providing a mounting for 'in front of the lens' filters.

Filter holding
For creative cinematography, accommodation must be provided for at least two or three filters. Polarisers, stars, nets and graduated filters may need to be rotated about the optical axis. A sliding facility may also be desirable to position graduated filters precisely where they are wanted relative to the picture in any lateral direction. Simple filming operations require only a single filter holder (for a colour correcting filter) usually circular and retained by a filter ring screwed directly to the front of the lens.

Sunshading
If a lens hood is attached directly on to the front of the lens it is often circular in shape, especially if the front element of the lens must be rotated for focusing. Such sunshades are comparatively inefficient in comparison with a rectangular type which follows closely the straight line edge of the picture frame. When lenses of longer focal length are used with a rectangular sunshade the efficiency may be increased further by adding a hinged top flap or slide-in masks, each one made to clear only the angle of view of a particular focal length lens.

Another efficient form of sunshade is the bellows type, which may be racked out to the limits of the picture, depending upon the lens in use. But it must be racked back sufficiently when a lens is replaced by another of slightly wider angle.

Extra shading may also be provided by the use of a 'french flag', a small opaque sheet of aluminium, normally 12 × 6in., anodised matte black and attached to an articulated arm that may be positioned exactly as required.

If the cut-out at the rear of the filter holder is larger than the diameter of the lens, no stray light from behind must shine on the rear surface of the filter and so reflect back into the lens. Protection may be provided by a flap of opaque black cloth attached to the rear edge of the matte box or by placing a wide annular ring, called a donut, around the lens to the outside limit of the filter.

Checking for cut-off
No sunshade 'cut-off' must appear around the edge of the picture. This should be checked by looking through the reflex viewing system and holding a pointed object, such as a pen or pencil, to each edge of the picture. If the point can be seen, the sunshade must be obtruding into the picture area.

74

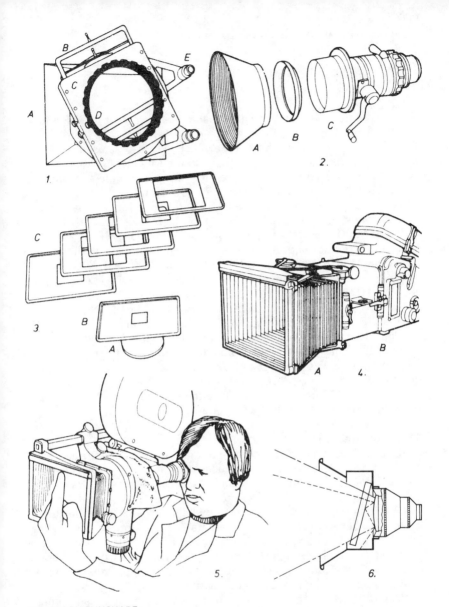

MATTEBOX SUNSHADE

1. Filter holding mattebox   A. Mattebox/sunshade; B. 2 × Sliding filter tray; C. Rotating filter tray holder; D. Bezel to take a circular polar screen; E. Camera attachment point.

2. Sunshade/filter for simple filming   A. Circular sunshade; B. Filter retaining ring; C. Angenieux 10 × 12·5 zoom lens.

3. Panavision sunshade and masks   A. Panavision sunshade; B. Sunshade mask; C. Masks for various lenses.

4. Bellows method   A. Extendible bellows sunshade; B. Arriflex 120S blimp.

5. Cut-off   Checking for cut-off by placing a finger to the inside edge of a bellows sunshade while looking through the reflex viewfinder.

6. Panavision filter tilting mattebox   Used to eliminate secondary reflected ghost images; a. light ray, b. filter (may be tilted 15% up or down), c. lens element, d. housing with anti-reflection coating.

Film Magazines

Unless it is purely a daylight spool loading camera each model has its own type of magazine. The only exceptions are the Mitchell 400 and 1000ft (120 and 300m) 35mm type which may also be used on the CP XR35 and Panavision PSR cameras, and the Mitchell 400 and 1200ft (120 and 360m) 16mm types which may be used on the Auricons and Auricon conversions, the CP16s, the TGX16 and certain high speed cameras, as well, of course, as on all 35 and 16mm Mitchell cameras.

Magazines may be available in various sizes for various cameras, 400 and 1000ft for the Arriflex 35BL, the Panavision PSR (which has a special low profile magazine housing to take advantage of the smaller magazine) and the Mitchell S35R. Normally, 200 and 400 (60 and 120m) magazines are used with the Arriflex IIC but with special modification a 1000ft type may be used. For the Eclair CM3, Camematic and GV35 100, 200 and 400ft magazines are available and 250, 500 and 1000ft (75, 150 and 300m) for the Panavision Panaflex.

Most 16mm cameras intended for sync sound shooting normally accept 400ft magazines but may be adapted to 1200ft if a take of up to 33 min running time is envisaged. Exceptions are the Beaulieu News 16 and the Canon Scoopic 200 which accept only 200ft spools. The Eclair ACL will take 200 or 400ft magazines, the Paillard Bolex R16 and Rex a 400ft and the Beaulieu R16 a 200ft magazine.

Magazine design

Film magazines may accommodate the film in two separate compartments in tandem (like Mickey Mouse ears), in a single displacement compartment where the space vacated by the unexposed film is taken up by the exposed, or side by side coaxially.

Magazine take-ups may be driven by belts or gears from the camera motor or a separate motor in the camera body. Or they may have their own individual motors, which in the case of the Arriflex 16St must be changed from one magazine to another whenever the camera is reloaded. The motors incorporated in the Panavision Panaflex have a heater system for low temperature operation.

Where 400ft belt driven magazines are fitted to cameras primarily used with 1000ft loadings, extra idler pulley wheels on the side of the magazine obviate the need to change to a shorter belt when the smaller magazine is used. When the magazines have their own motors, ensure that the electric contacts are always clean.

Film windings

All modern cameras use film wound 'emulsion in' but some take up in a clockwise direction 'emulsion out' and others anti-clockwise. Some coaxial magazines take up on the viewfinder side of the camera, some on the reverse.

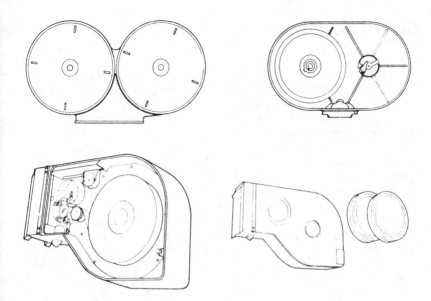

FILM MAGAZINE TYPES

Separate compartments placed side by side; Single compartment displacement method where space vacated by one roll is taken up by the other; Cheek to cheek compartments; comparison in size between 400ft 16mm magazine and 2 × 200ft film cans.

With one minor exception all 35mm cameras take only roll wound film but most 16mm cameras can take film on rolls or spools. This means that they must have adapter centres which convert from the square spindles required for spools to the round centres required for cores. Special care should be taken when unloading 16mm magazines not to send the core adaptors to the laboratory with a roll of film. Replacements are expensive. Also, the magazine will be useless for roll film until a replacement is obtained. The interior of a magazine should be kept clean, loading should only be done in a dust- and hair-free atmosphere and the cameraman should ensure that he has spare take-up cores to hand.

Spool Loading

The 35mm Bell and Howell Eymo camera (with rare exceptions) takes 100ft spools of film only, runs at 90ft per min, and has a maximum run on one winding of about 22 sec. It is a difficult camera to reload in the rain or under shell fire and yet very much of the best real action footage shot during World War II was obtained with just such cameras. The modern generation of cameramen should remember this when considering whether to take a 16mm camera which takes a $5\frac{1}{2}$ min. 200ft (60m) roll of film or an 11 min 400ft magazine.

The great advantage of spool loading film is the scope for operating at some range from base, car or camera cases and yet carry a plentiful supply of spare film in the pockets without the need for a spare magazine. Naturally, any newsreel cameraman who is prepared for all eventualities should always have spare film immediately to hand in case of a camera jam or the unforseen event-of-a-lifetime. The same case applies to shooting say, on a mountain or anywhere involving great distances; more film can be carried for the same weight on spools than in magazines.

Loading with spool-wound film

The reloading of spool wound film should be done in as shaded a place as can be found and as rapidly as possible to avoid unnecessary edge fogging. A routine must be thought out and followed. A good system is to go in to the shade, lay the camera or magazine exposed film side upwards, open the can of fresh film and, without removing the protective binding, put this roll of film into a pocket or other dark place. Open the camera or magazine. Remove the roll of exposed film, put it in a can and replace the lid as quickly as possible. Take care not to prise apart the flanges of the daylight spool when removing it from the camera. If necessary, turn the camera or magazine upside down to remove the used film spool. Take the empty spool from the top compartment and place it somewhere handy. Take the unexposed film from its dark place, remove the protection paper and put the spool in position. Thread the film through the gate and attach it to the take-up spool. Now run a little to make sure all is well and taking up satisfactorily (beware of take-up spools with bent flanges). Close the door and run on about 6ft (2m). The camera is now ready for use. When taping up the exposed roll either write the roll number or make an appropriate number of thumb tears in the edge of the label so that later the rolls can be properly marked for the laboratory to process in the correct order.

To preserve the last few frames of an exposed roll unloading should be done in the dark. If this facility is not available the camera or magazine may be wrapped in a coat or anorak and the cameraman's arms put through the sleeves backwards. The can should be well marked for the laboratory 'Open in a dark room only'.

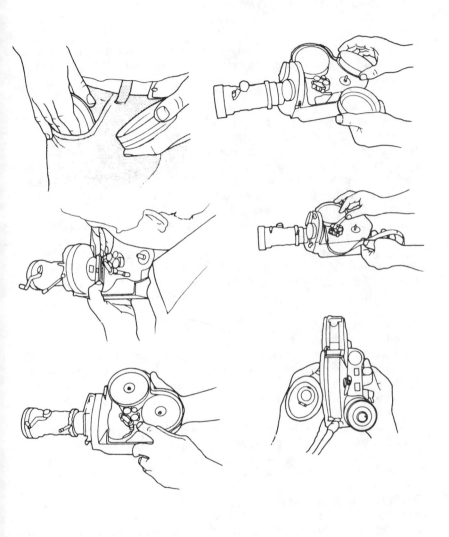

SPOOL LOADING

Put the unexposed roll of film in your pocket. Remove the exposed roll from the camera. Check the gate for hairs or dirt. Reload the camera. Test that it is running satisfactorily. Check the camera speed on the tachometer.

Sync Camera Speeds

Before a motor is selected to drive a camera it is necessary to know a little about camera speeds and the degree of accuracy of the speed required.

Sound speeds

The standard speed for motion picture cameras and projectors is 24 frames per sec (fps), which must be accurately maintained if there is to be no variation in the speed of the action or the pitch of the sound.

An exception is in those countries where the AC frequency of the electricity supply is 50Hz and where film is scanned for TV transmission at a rate of 25 fps. In consequence, films made especially for TV presentation in those countries are shot at 25 fps.

The running time for film shot at 24 fps and presented at 25 fps is reduced by approximately 4% and suffers from the sound being pitched slightly higher. At 24 fps, 35mm film runs at 90ft (27·4m) per minute and 16mm at 36ft (11m) per min. At 25 fps the speeds are 93·75 and 37·5ft (28·6 and 11·4m) respectively. To convert 24 to 25 fps multiply by 1·0416 and to convert 25 to 24 fps multiply by 0·96.

Synchronisation

Sound, when it is recorded on a separate $\frac{1}{4}$in magnetic tape, must have a recording of the camera speed alongside the audio track. This recording, known as pilotone or sync pulse, is used as a reference when the sound is transferred to sprocketed tape prior to the editing stage and ensures that the track maintains exactly the same physical length as the picture.

A pilotone or pulse signal may be generated either from a crystal oscillator (where such a means is used to control the camera motor) from an AC supply (when an AC motor is used) or from a small alternator attached to the camera, in which case any form of motor may be used.

Checking camera speeds

Almost all cameras incorporate an fps indicator.

Where a crystal motor is used, camera speed must be maintained more accurately than can be read off the usual camera speed tachometer. So an electronically operated method of warning the cameraman that the camera is running 'off speed' is provided. This may take the form of either a warning light or a buzzer.

Crystal controlled motors must be checked frequently to ensure the absolute accuracy of speed and, more important, that the speed of the camera is identical to that of the generated crystal pilotone pulse of the recorder with which it is used. This may be done by checking against a master crystal or by using the recorder crystal to control a strobe light for that purpose.

TIME AND FOOTAGE

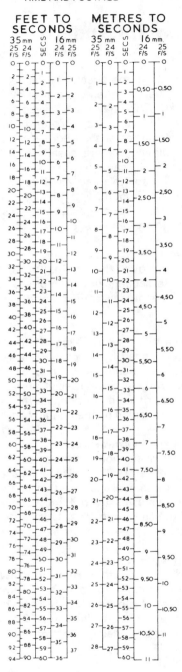

FEET TO SECONDS | METRES TO SECONDS

Variable Camera Speeds

There are occasions when the director or the cameraman may wish to adjust the apparent speed of the action or to make a scene last longer or pass more quickly. This may be achieved by running the camera faster or slower than the eventual projection speed.

A camera may be run faster than normal to slow down action. For example, in sports filming camera speeds of 70–120fps are usually considered to be fast enough for 'slow-motion' presentation, 250–500fps for action analysis and 28–40fps for cameras positioned close to the action and shooting with long lenses, to make the movements match wide angle coverage by more distant cameras. Slow-motion is often used to give an artistic 'lyrical' effect to a scene.

Speeded-up motion
A camera may be run slower than normal to speed up the tempo of a scene, to make chase sequences look more exciting, to make movements of larger-than-life models appear realistic, and for comedy effect.

Off-speed sync sound
It is possible to shoot sync sound off-speed if the sound is subsequently transferred to normal speed by a special process which stretches or reduces the length of the sound track without affecting the tone or pitch of the sound. This is done on a special play-off head which either deletes minute periods of sound or adds momentary blank spaces at a rate which cannot be detected by the human ear.

Model and miniature cinematography
When filming reduced-scale models the camera must be speeded-up to make movements appear realistic. The increase depends upon the speed and scale of the model, its direction and movement relative to the camera, and its supposed speed. Similar allowances must be made when filming miniaturised explosions, fires, water movement (waves, rain, dam bursts etc.) and free-falling objects.

Exposure compensation
When the speed of the camera is changed allowance must be made when setting the exposure. Many makes of 16mm camera especially designed for speeds of up to 250–500fps have interchangeable shutters, the widest of which is often only 120°. In this case an extra half stop should always be added to the exposure.

Calculating exposure
The reciprocal of the exposure, i.e. $1/x$ sec.$=$fps.$\times360\div$shutter degrees. With a 170–180° shutter $1/x$ sec.$=$fps.$\times2$. For a 120° shutter $1/x$ sec.$=$fps.$\times3$.

VARIABLE CAMERA SPEED TABLES

Camera speed (fps)	6	8	12	16	24	25	32	48	64	96	128	250
Feet per minute												
35mm film	22·5	30	45	60	90	93·75	120	80	240	360	480	937
16mm film	9	12	18	24	36	37·5	48	72	96	144	192	375
Meters per minute												
35mm film	6·86	9·14	13·7	18·3	27·4	18·6	6·6	54·9	73·2	10	146	286
16mm film	2·74	3·66	5·49	7·32	11	11·4	14·6	22	29·3	44	59	114
Exposure – sec.												
170–180° shutter	1/12	1/16	1/24	1/32	1/50	1/50	1/60	1/100	1/125	1/200	1/250	1/500
Exposure – adjustment												
Stops	−2	−1½	−1	−½	normal	−½	+1	+1½	+2	+3	+4	

Time taken for a roll of film to pass through the camera. 35mm – min‑sec.

Camera speed		6	8	12	16	24	25	32	48	64	96	128	250
Ft.	Mtrs												
50	15	2-13	1-40	1-7	0-50	0-33	0-32	0-25	0-17	0-13	0-8	0-6	0-3
100	30	4-26	3-20	2-13	1-40	1-6	1-4	0-50	0-34	0-26	0-16	0-12	0-6
200	61	8-54	6-40	4-26	3-20	2-13	2-8	1-40	1-7	0-50	0-33	0-25	0-13
300	91	13-20	10	6-40	5	3-20	3-12	2-30	1-40	1-15	0-50	0-38	0-19
400	122	17-47	13-20	8-53	6-40	4-26	4-16	3-20	2-13	1-40	1-7	0-50	0-26
500	152	22-13	16-40	11-7	8-20	5-33	5-20	4-10	2-47	2-5	1-24	1-3	0-33
1000	305	44-26	33-20	22-13	16-40	11-7	10-40	8-20	5-33	4-10	2-47	2-6	1-6

Time taken for a roll of film to pass through the camera. 16mm – min‑sec.

Ft	Mtrs	6	8	12	16	24	25	32	48	64	96	128	250
50	15	5-34	4-10	2-47	2-5	1-23	1-20	1-2	0-41	0-31	0-21	0-16	0-8
100	30	11-7	8-20	5-33	4-10	2-47	2-40	2-5	1-23	1-2	1-41	0-31	0-16
200	61	22-13	16-40	11-7	8-20	5-20	5-10	2-10	2-47	2-5	1-23	1-2	0-32
300	91	33-20	25	16-40	12-30	8-20	8	6-15	4-10	3-7	2-5	1-34	0-48
400	122	44-27	3-20	22-13	16-40	11-7	10-40	8-20	5-33	4-10	2-47	2-5	1-4
500	152	55-33	41-40	27-47	20-50	13-53	13-20	10-25	6-56	5-13	3-28	2-36	1-20
1000	305	111	83-20	55-33	41-40	26-40	26-40	20-50	13-53	10-26	6-56	5-12	2-40
1200	366	133	100	66-40	50	33-20	32	25	16-40	12-30	8-20	6-15	3-12

The effect of Camera Speed on Object Speed when projected at 24 fps

Actual Object Speed	6	8	12	16	24	25	32	48	64	96	128	250
10	40	30	20	15	10	9·6	7·5	5	3·75	2·5	1·88	0·98
20	80	60	40	30	20	19·2	15	10	7·5	5	3·75	1·92
30	120	90	60	45	30	28·8	22·5	·5	11·25	7·5	5·63	2·88
40	160	120	80	60	40	38·4	30	20	15	10	7·5	3·84
50	200	150	100	75	50	46	37·5	25	18·75	12·5	9·38	4·8
60	240	180	120	90	60	57·6	45	30	22·5	15	11·25	5·76
70	280	210	140	105	70	67·2	52·5	35	26·25	17·5	13·13	6·72
80	320	240	160	120	80	76·8	60	40	30	20	15	7·68
90	360	270	180	135	90	86	67·5	45	3·75	22·5	16·88	8·84
100	400	300	200	150	100	96	75	50	37·5	25	18·75	9·6

The effect of camera speed on time when projected at 24 fps
Time taken to project sec.

Action Time	6	8	12	16	24	25	32	48	64	96	128	250
10	2·5	3·33	5	6·66	10	10·42	13·3	20	26·6	40	53·3	104
20	5	6·66	10	13·33	20	20·83	26·6	40	53·3	80	106·6	208
30	7·5	10	15	20	30	31·25	39·9	60	80	120	160	313
40	10	13·3	20	26·66	40	41·67	53·2	80	106·6	160	213	417
50	12·5	16·6	25	33·33	50	52·08	66·5	100	133	200	266	521
60	15	20	30	40	60	62·5	79·8	120	160	240	320	625
100	25	33·3	50	66·6	100	104·12	133	200	267	400	533	1042

Camera Motors

The camera motor may be a battery powered unit with the speed controlled by highly sophisticated electronics. Many forms are used.

Crystal motors

Crystal oscillator controlled DC servo motors, better known as 'crystal motors' are the preferred means of driving a motion picture camera. Their speed is accurate to within 0·001% (10 parts in a million). If used in conjunction with a similarly controlled sync pulse generator attached to the sound recorder, one or many cameras may be used simultaneously without any cable connection between camera and recorder. Such accuracy ensures that even the longest possible take, 1200ft. of 16mm (33 min.) will not be out of sync by more than ± half a frame by the end of the roll.

Crystal motors are usually switchable 24/25 or 24/30 fps. When using an unfamiliar camera check that the right speed is selected and that the sound recorder is similarly set. Many crystal motors also incorporate a variable speed (usually 8–40 fps) facility.

Accessory control units are available to slave crystal control motors to external sources such as a mains frequency to eliminate HMI flicker, or to a process projector for front projection work.

Other motors for sync and sound shooting

Battery powered governed motors operate at speeds accurate to within 1·5%. When fitted to lightweight hand held cameras and used for shooting sep-mag sync sound a pulse generator on the camera supplies a speed reference signal recorded simultaneously with the sound.

Non-sync motors

DC (wild) motors usually have a speed range of 4–40 fps, are often reversible and are not suitable for use when shooting sync sound.

High speed motors are available for certain cameras when filming 'slow-motion'. The Arriflex 11CHS is capable of speeds of up to 60–70 fps and the Mitchell S35R, 128 fps. Cameras which operate at speeds in excess of 128 fps usually have integral motors.

Single-shot motors are used for animation or time-lapse work.

Stepper motors are used when a camera is controlled by computer or other electronic device. Stepper motors advance by exact, countable and repeatable increments and are thus particularly suitable for motion control cameras.

Non-electric camera drives

A clockwork driven camera may have to be used in exceptionally cold conditions and must be used when shooting in an explosive atmosphere – a coal mine or a tank formerly filled with petroleum spirits.

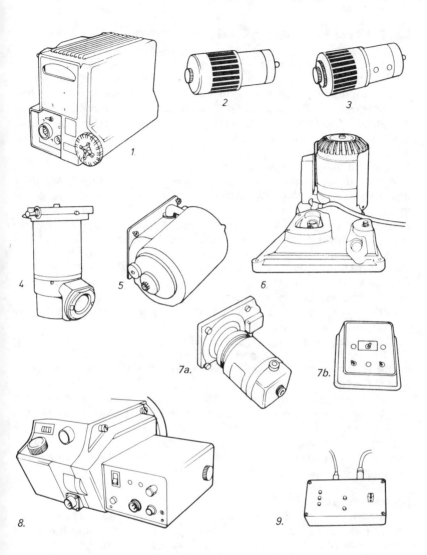

TYPES OF CAMERA MOTOR

1. Crystal controlled. The typical speed accuracy 0.001% or better.
2. Governor controlled. This has a typical accuracy of 1.5%.
3. Wild. Speeds adjustable over a wide range and reversible.
4. High speed. This motor is designed for faster than normal operation.
5. Multi duty. This may be run off either alternating or direct current supplies.
6. Synchronous. Speed locked to an alternating current supply.
7a. Single shot and 7b. Control box. For frame by frame operation.
8. Fries all-in-one motor for Mitchell S35R. Operates at 4–128 fps, 24, 25 & 30 fps crystal control, single frame and interval, forward and reverse, slave mode and auto mirror positioning.
9. Control unit to slave a Panaflex camera to a process projector; a. Sync signal from projector, b. control signal to camera.

85

Camera Battery Connection

The camera to battery cable is one of the simplest pieces of 'cinematographic' equipment, and the most unreliable. It tends to fray and break internally and because it is impractical to check the internal condition (there may be just one strand remaining intact) a spare should always be readily to hand.

Camera to power supply cables

Camera cables, connecting plugs and the polarity of pin connections, though universally used are totally unstandardised. If in doubt, a test meter should always be used to check that the voltage and polarity of a power supply is as required for a particular camera. Cables which carry DC need only be 2-core but AC mains should always use a 3-core cable to ensure that all equipment is correctly earthed (grounded). Three phase supplies require a 4-core cable. With a simple wild DC motor, the polarity of the connections is unimportant but any motor containing electronic speed control, especially crystal control, must be connected with the correct polarity or substantial damage may be caused and the camera rendered inoperative.

Certain cameras using a 12 volt DC supply, most notably the Eclair 16NPR and ACL and some Arriflex 16 and 35 BL cameras use a Canon XLR 4-pin plug with connections as follows: Pin 1=12 volts Negative, Pins 2 and 3=Pulse, Pin 4=12 volts Positive. There should be a 64 ohms resistor wired between pins 1 and 2. Batteries equipped with this plug often also incorporate a Canon XLR 3-pin socket outlet for the camera to recorder pulse lead. This is usually connected to pins 1 and 2 and pin 3 is vacant. (Cables of any length inevitably introduce voltage drop and cables of abnormal length should either be of heavier gauge or the supply voltage increased).

Remote switching

It is sometimes desirable, particularly when shooting sporting events, to have a remote camera on-off switch which may be taped to the tripod head pan handle. With a simple motor this may take the form of an off-on switch in the battery-to-camera lead. With motors incorporating sophisticated electronic speed control circuitry such a switch may cause damage, as may remote control by simply plugging-in and un-plugging the camera lead from the battery.

Spare batteries

Like the cable which connects it to the camera, the camera battery is an item of equipment curiously prone to unpredictable failure and in consequence a spare should always be to hand. Indeed, when filming an unrepeatable event it is wise to have a spare battery standing by with a cable already plugged in to allow a quick change.

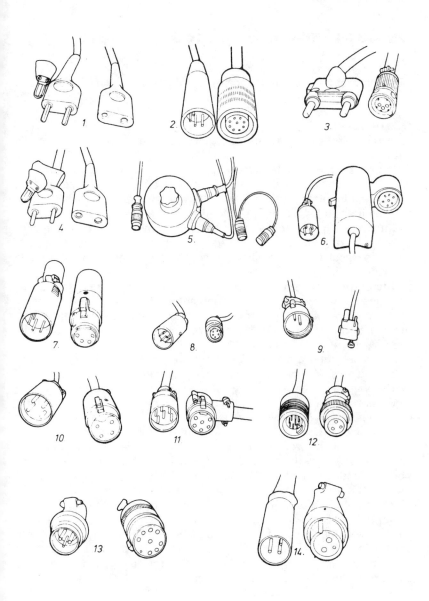

BATTERY TO CAMERA CONNECTORS

1. Arriflex 16ST;   2. Arriflex 16 & 35BL;   3. CPD crystal motor for Arriflex II;
4. Arriflex IIC;   5. Arriflex IIC high-speed;   6. Arriflex IIC sync motor with phase
splitter;   7. Eclair NPR;   8. Eclair ACL;   9. Eclair CM3;   10. 4-pin large Canon
used for 3 phase main;   11. Mitchell BNC sync motor;   12. Mitchell S35R wild
motor;   13. Panavision silent reflex;   14. Panavision Panaflex.

Camera Power Supplies

With the exception of the few cameras which are driven by clockwork, all cameras require an electric power supply, either DC or AC.

DC supplies

Transportable cameras are normally operated off rechargeable batteries.

In choosing a suitable battery for a camera, consideration must be given to the voltage requirements of the camera motor, the capacity of the battery in relation to the power drawn by the camera, the length of film required to be run by a single charge, the ease of recharging and maintenance, the suitability of the battery if it must be operated in conditions of extreme cold and its weight in relation to voltage and capacity, particularly if it must be carried by the camera operator while shooting.

The power requirements of different models of camera differ widely. Voltages vary between 6 and 36v and current between 1 and 15 amps, with an initial switch-on surge which may be two or three times the running current. Certain AC/DC motors may be operated from 96, 110 or 240 volts AC or DC supplies.

When selecting a fuse or circuit breaker for a camera battery, consideration must also be given to the surge current.

The voltage of a DC battery may be increased by adding cells in series or reduced by removing cells, and the capacity of a battery may be increased by wiring two batteries in parallel.

A popular form of battery for powering a portable camera is a battery belt which may be worn by the camera operator. Many 16mm cameras, and all 8mm, have the batteries mounted actually on or in the camera body or handle. Battery cells used in battery belts or built into cameras are invariably of smaller capacity than other camera batteries and extra care must be exercised to ensure that they are not over-discharged.

Some battery belts incorporate a small charging system of the capacitor type. While safe for 120 v supplies they may be dangerous if used with 240 v. Transformer type chargers are safe, more reliable and more economical. If the charger is suitable for dual voltage operation, care should be taken to ensure that it is correctly set.

AC supplies

Synchronous motors, other than electronically controlled DC motors, require a single or three phase mains supply, either 50 or 60 Hz. If an AC motor is operated on a frequency for which it is not designed, it will result in an incorrect camera speed. A three phase synchronous motor may be operated off a single phase supply by the use of a phase splitter wired in to the connecting cable or supplied as a separate unit.

AC may be generated from a DC supply either by means of a rotary

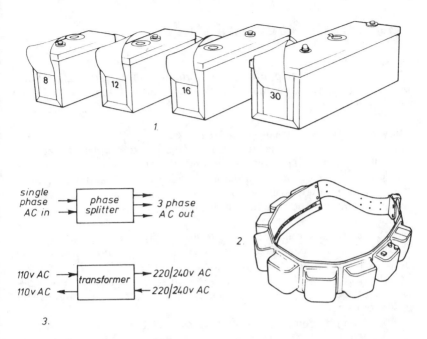

1.

single
phase → ┌─────────┐
phase → │ phase   │ → 3 phase
AC in → │ splitter│ → A C out
       └─────────┘

2.

110v AC → ┌───────────┐ → 220/240v AC
110v AC ← │transformer│ ← 220/240v AC
          └───────────┘

3.

SOURCES OF POWER

Batteries etc.
1. Batteries of similar capacity but of different voltages.
2. Batteries may be held on a belt worn by the cameraman. This is a 8/16 volt battery belt.
3. A phase splitter may be used to convert single phase AC to three phase AC. A transformer may be used to increase or reduce AC voltage.

converter or by an inverter. Some inverters produce an AC current which has a 'square wave' rather than a 'sine' wave and will not run a camera motor smoothly.

The voltage of an AC supply may be reduced by means of either a diode or a transformer. Diode devices are compact, lightweight and inexpensive. The power which emanates from them, however, is not AC but pulsed DC which is unsuitable for AC motors, chargers and other electronic devices which may be destroyed if run from such current. Transformers are heavy and bulky by comparison. They may only be used with an AC supply. The power out-put has the same frequency characteristic as that put in, and they may be used either to step down or step up a voltage, but check that the transformer is capable of handling the current required.

Lead Acid Accumulators

The traditional lead sulphuric acid accumulator in its various forms has been used to power cameras ever since Edison's electrically driven camera of 1887.

Fully sealed and maintenance-free type

For transportable use the most practicable are the types of lead acid accumulator which are fully sealed and in which the electrolyte takes the form of a jelly or an absorbent felt requiring no maintenance other than recharging. By comparison with car batteries they are light in weight, compact and function in any position other than permanently upside down.

Lead acid accumulators or batteries produce an on-load nominal voltage of 2 v per cell which reduces continuously until it drops to the fully discharged voltage of 1·65 v per cell. The capacity of the battery to produce power is affected by the rate of discharge. The lower the discharge rate compared to the capacity of the battery, the greater the power output.

For strength, compactness, efficiency, reliability and convenience, fully sealed lead acid accumulators are supplied made up in to blocks of 3 or 6 individual cells, with voltages of 6 and 12 v respectively. Capacities available range from 2 to 30 Ah at a 20 Ah rate. Fully sealed lead acid accumulators should be charged at temperatures above freezing point but may be discharged at temperatures as low as 0°F (−20°C) and retain their charge at temperatures as low as −20°F (−30°C). The upper temperature limit for these accumulators is 110°F, (45°C).

The rate of self discharge of these batteries is very low, amounting to 3% under normal conditions, or somewhat higher when it is exceptionally warm and humid.

Car batteries

In their more domestic form, car batteries are heavy, liable to leak acid if tipped even slightly from an upright position and require a great deal of maintenance which includes replenishing the electrolyte with chemically pure water. Although comparatively inexpensive initially, it is debatable whether, considering how much maintenance they require, their shorter life and the damage they do when spilled, make them cheap in the long run. When a very great deal of power is required however, open lead acid accumulators may have to be used.

Car batteries are available in various capacities that range up to 100 Ah or more. Traction type cells, of 500 Ah rating, may be used to power brute arc lamps in travelling and inaccessible situations. Car batteries, supplied in wooden boxes, are still sometimes used to power studio cameras with AC motors, from inverters or rotary converters.

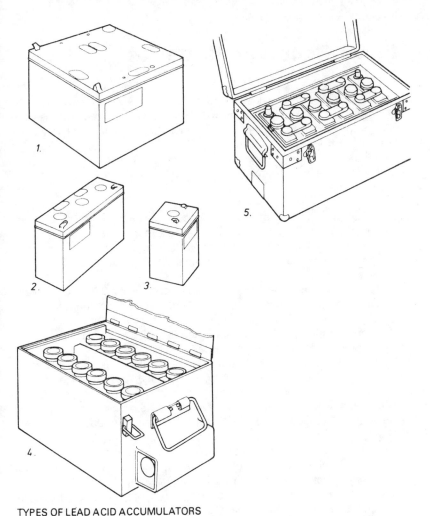

TYPES OF LEAD ACID ACCUMULATORS

Fully sealed lead acid accumulators.   1. 12v 20Ah;   2. 6v 7.5Ah;   3. 2v
7.5Ah;   4. 'Unspillable' type lead acid accumulator, 12v 36Ah;   5. 'Heavy
duty' car battery type lead acid accumulator, 12v 72Ah.

    Great care must be taken not to tip over this type of accumulator or
battery as spilled sulphuric acid will cause untold damage. Should acid
be spilled it must not be touched and everything that has been con-
taminated should be immediately swabbed down with copious
amounts of clean water. The state of charge of an open type lead acid
accumulator may be ascertained by checking the specific gravity of the
electrolyte with a hygrometer. Open cell lead acid batteries should be
topped-up with distilled water whenever the level of the electrolyte falls
below the top of the plates.

Nickel Cadmium Batteries

Sintered plate sealed nickel-cadmium cells have, to a large extent, replaced lead/sulphuric acid accumulators as the preferred batteries for powering portable motion picture cameras. They are comparatively light in weight, compact, may be used in any position, travel well, require little maintenance other than recharging and, amortized over a life expectancy of five years, are comparatively inexpensive.

Capacity

A fully charged nicad cell of the type used to power cameras produces an on-load voltage of 1·2 per cell which remains almost constant until 80% of the capacity is consumed, when it drops rapidly.

To ensure maximum life and reliability, the following should be observed:

Battery voltage must never be allowed to drop below 1·1 volts per cell.

Recharging rate should not exceed 1/10 the capacity unless a very sophisticated system is used.

Discharge amperage should not exceed 20 times the capacity.

Battery temperature should not exceed +110°F, (+45°C).

Exactly how much current a battery produces depends upon: its rating (cameras are usually run off 10 hour rated cells); the rate of discharge drawn by the cameras; the ambient temperature; how fully the battery was charged; what discharge it stands before one or more cells goes into reverse polarity; how long the battery has been stored and at what temperature since charging; and its age.

If nicad batteries are constantly subjected only to shallow discharging before being recharged as though they were fully discharged they develop a 'memory effect' and, with time, will only be capable of delivering a limited amount of current when required. To avoid this, care should be taken not to recharge fully charged batteries and all batteries should occasionally be discharged very deeply before re-charging.

If a nicad battery is over-discharged, individual cells will go into a state of reverse polarity. Usually this is not serious and such cells will normally right themselves when recharged.

Temperature

Sintered plate nickel cadmium cells should be charged at temperatures between 50° and 95°F (+10 to +35°C) and may be discharged between −40 and +130°F (−40 to +55°C). Their capacity is, however, reduced by about 20% between 32 and 0°F (0 to −20°).

Below freezing point, nickel cadmium batteries store their power very well but are inefficient in delivering it. This problem may be alleviated by battery belts, kept warm by being worn by the crew beneath their anoraks.

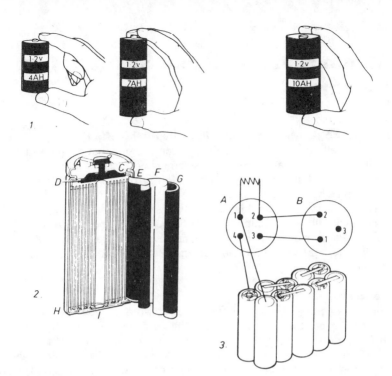

NICKEL CADMIUM CELLS

1. 1.2v Nickel Cadmium cells of different capacities.
2. Construction of a typical Nickel Cadmium battery cell.
A. Cover;   B. Central button (Positive pole);   C. Safety vent;   D. Positive connections;   E. Positive plate;   F. Separator;   G. Negative plate;   H. Nickel-plated steel case;   I. Negative connections.
3. Arrangement of cells for a 12v battery and pin connection for XLR Canon plugs.

Charging

Nickel cadmium batteries must be charged by a constant current charger at a rate not exceeding one tenth of the capacity. Hence the charging rate for 5Ah cells should not exceed $\frac{1}{2}$ amp. Overcharging reduces the life of a battery and if done to excess causes gasses to build up internally. Battery portable lights should never be used immediately after a battery is taken off charge as there is a high chance of blowing the bulb by applying too high an initial voltage. Several minutes should be allowed to elapse for the voltage to stabilise. Cells become quite warm as they reach their fully charged condition.

A nickel cadmium battery self-discharges all the time. At 60°F (20°C) it loses only 20% of its charge in a year but at 115°F (45°C) it should be recharged at least weekly, whether used or not.

35mm Hand-holdable Silent Reflex Cameras

Arriflex 35BL, Moviecam and Panavision Panaflex

The ideal all-purpose motion picture camera is one that combines all the attributes of the traditional studio camera, especially those of image steadiness and silence of operation (24db or better), with that of being suitable for hand-held shooting.

The latest and most sophisticated cameras for 35mm feature, TV and TV commercial film production, the Arriflex 35 BL III, the Moviecam Super and the Panavision Golden Panaflex, achieve these standards and yet are acceptably light in weight, well balanced and tailored to fit the human shoulder.

General specifications

These cameras all incorporate a register-pin movement for image steadiness, but they usually achieve their quietness, in part, by isolating the lens mount, and therefore the lens also, by a sandwich of hard rubber bonded between the camera movement and the lens mount and isolating both from the camera body and sometimes, even, the camera body from the tripod mounting. For this reason they may not be suitable for critical special-effects shooting where optimum image steadiness is imperative.

They all incorporate an adjustable shutter to make it possible to shoot by metal halide lighting at 24 fps with 50 or 60Hz power supplies; the Panaflex has a shutter that opens to 200° and can be adjusted in shot.

They all have orientatable eyepieces and viewfinder de-anamorphosing facilities. Some, but not all, incorporate an illuminatable ground glass reticule, an eyepiece optic heater to prevent misting-up, viewfinder contrast filters and image magnification, and behind-the-lens filtering.

They may all be run under crystal speed control at 24/25 or 24/30 fps and at variable speeds of about 12–30 fps. All can generate a pilotone signal. All have available electronic accessories for remote switching and speed control and to synchronise the camera with any external source including a TV screen, HMI lighting or a process projector. Moviecam offer an electronic malfunction diagnoser and an electronic clapperboard.

All may be used with small or large film magazines on the rear to give a low profile and good balance or alternatively, in the case of the Moviecam or Panaflex, on top to give a shorter overall length. All have facilities for video viewfinding. The Panaflex may be fitted with a pellicle reflex system in place of the rotating mirror, to eliminate video viewfinder flicker.

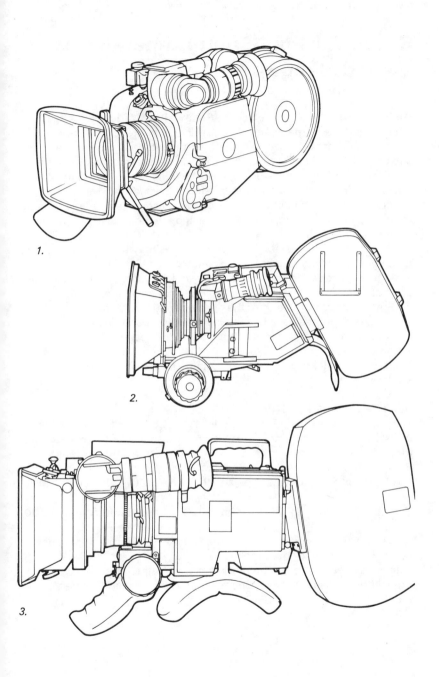

35mm SILENT REFLEX CAMERAS IN HANDHOLD CONFIGURATION

1. Arriflex 35 BL III; 2. Moviecam Super; 3. Panavision Golden Panaflex.

Silent Reflex 35mm Cameras for Tripod Usage

Arriflex 35BL, Moviecam Super, Panavision Golden Panaflex

These versatile cameras in their basic configuration, with a short eyepiece and small capacity magazines mounted on the rear, may be used either hand held or on a tripod head (see previous page), but with the addition of an extension to the viewfinder tube, a 1000ft (300m) magazine on the top, a large follow-focus control and, very often, an auxiliary video viewfinder (video assist) they become particularly suitable for mounting on a tripod, dolly or crane and for shooting in any studio or location environment.

The extended eyepieces of all these cameras may be tilted up or down to position the eyepiece optic in a position convenient for the operator to look through regardless of camera tilt, and may be held in a constant position in space as the camera is tilted up and down by the use of a link arm fitted between the end of the eyepiece and the tripod head.

The extension eyepiece usually includes an image-magnifying objective and sometimes viewing contrast filters (see page 32).

Cameras in this mode are always fitted onto sliding baseplates to enable the cameras to be set in balance regardless of what lens or magazine is fitted.

Panavision Panaflex X

This incorporates most of the features of the Golden Panaflex, and takes the same lenses, magazines and other accessories, but has a straight-through viewfinder which is very bright and less expensive to manufacture, and rent, than an orientatable type.

A Panaflex X is often taken as a second camera to a Golden Panaflex.

Cinema Products XR35, Mitchell BNCR, Panavision Super R-200, et al.

These are reflex studio cameras manufactured using a film transport mechanism taken from a non-reflex Mitchell NC or BNC. Although somewhat heavy and out-moded compared to the latest cameras, they are still much used where economy is more important than transportability.

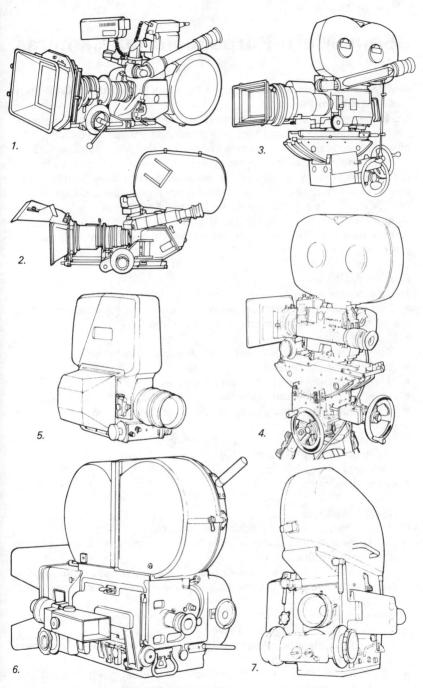

SILENT REFLEX CAMERAS FOR TRIPOD USAGE

1. Arriflex 35BL III; 2. Moviecam Super; 3. Panavision Golden Panaflex;
4. Panavision Panaflex X; 5. Cinema Products XR35; 6. Mitchell BNCR;
7. Panavision Super R-200.

35mm Multi-Purpose Reflex Cameras

Arriflex 35 III, Cinema Products FX35, Fries 35, Mitchell S35R MkII and Panavision Panastar

These cameras are the workhorses of second-unit and special-effects shooting where optimum image steadiness, camera speed versatility and other special features are of more importance than camera quietness.

While many older non-reflex 35mm cameras are still used for special-effects work, all the above cameras have rotating-mirror reflex shutters and both the Fries and the Panastar may be supplied with a pellicle mirror as an alternative. All but the Arri 35 III have focal-plane shutters which may be adjusted in-shot. The Arri 35 III has an adjustable shutter blade behind the reflex mirror which may be adjusted to set positions.

Special facilities

These cameras incorporate the following facilities:

- Close-tolerance registration pin movements and solid movement to lens mounting for maximum image steadiness.
- High-speed running capability up to 128 fps.
- Slow running, single shot and interval shooting capability.
- Reverse running capability.
- May be synchronised to an outside source.
- Facilities to view through the film gate to check synchronisation.
- Facilities to view through a cut frame accurately aligned in front of the ground glass.
- Interchangeable aperture plates, including full frame.
- Facilities for split frame masking.
- Comprehensive multi-stage matte boxes.
- Video viewfinding.

Optional facilities

Certain cameras have unique facilities available:

- Exposure control device (2 × polar filters) electronically coupled to the camera speed (Panastar).
- Lens mounting fixed to camera base, and camera body which moves backwards and forwards to focus to maintain constant lens nodal positioning (Fries).
- Soundproof blimp (S35 MkII).
- Under-slung magazines (S35 MkII).
- Interchangeable motors permitting stepper and other special motors to be fitted (Fries and S35 MkII).
- Nodal mounting adaptor to position lens nodal point in rotational centre of a Panahead camera mounting (Panastar).
- Turnover mount (Panastar).
- Car mount to brace camera in hazardous conditions (Panastar).

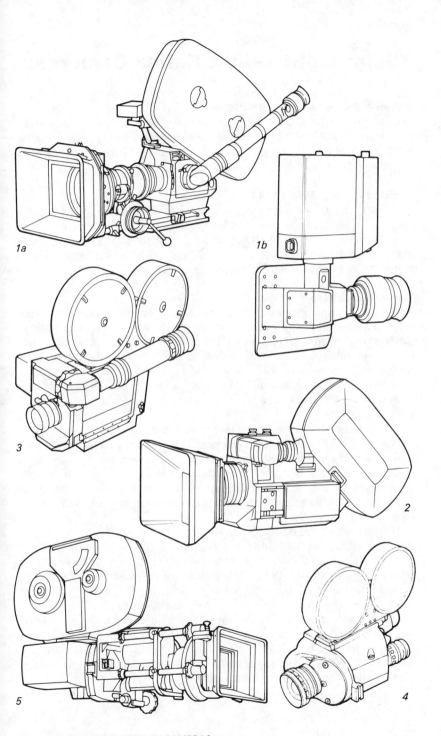

35mm MULTI-PURPOSE REFLEX CAMERAS
1a. Arriflex 35 III in full studio mode; 1b. Alternative video viewfinder door; 2.
Cinema Products CP35; 3. Fries 35R3; 4. Mitchell S35 Mk II; 5. Panaflex Panastar.

35mm Lightweight Reflex Cameras

Aaton 8-35 and Arriflex 35 IIIC

The Aaton 8-35 is a completely new design of 35mm camera broadly based on the Aaton 7 16mm camera, while the Arriflex IIIC can trace its lineage directly back to the first-ever spinning-mirror reflex camera introduced by Arnold & Richter in 1938.

Arriflex IIC and Eclair CM3

These are somewhat older cameras, first produced before the age of the zoom lens, which had three-lens lens turrets to offer documentary and news cameramen a rapid choice of lens focal lengths. In recent times many of these cameras have been converted to single-port hard-fronts to support a heavy zoom lens in accurate register.

Camera facilities

All these cameras are designed for maximum versatility in the portable camera mode, at minimum cost, commensurate with the requirements of professional usage. Quietness of operation and a standard of image steadiness suitable for multiple-pass special-effects work are not primary design considerations. All are eminently suitable for hand-holding, incorporate a rotating-mirror reflex viewfinding system, can be run at a wide variety of camera speeds, and take any suitably mounted lens from 9·8mm upwards.

The Aaton 8-35 is lightweight, low profile and has a single lens port.

The Arriflex IIIC has a single lens port, a 12v motor which doubles as a handgrip and which may be run forwards or backwards at 5–50 fps or at 24/25 fps under crystal control, a shutter with a maximum opening of 165° which may be adjusted while the camera is stationary, and interchangeable doors with a choice of cranked (for hand-holding), orientatable and fixed viewfinder optics.

The Arriflex IIC has a triple lens turret with the lenses closely set (heavy lenses must always have additional support), a 16v variable-speed motor which may be exchanged for a governed or a crystal-controlled motor, a mains motor or, on the HS model, a motor which can run as fast as 80 fps. The shutter normally has 165° fixed opening, but the shutter of the VS model may be adjusted while the camera is stationary.

The Eclair CM3 has a divergent three-lens turret which allows wide-angle and long lenses to be used simultaneously on the same turret without cutting in on one another, a variable shutter (while the camera is stationary) with a maximum opening of 200°, and clip-on magazines. It is particularly good for steady hand-holding.

100

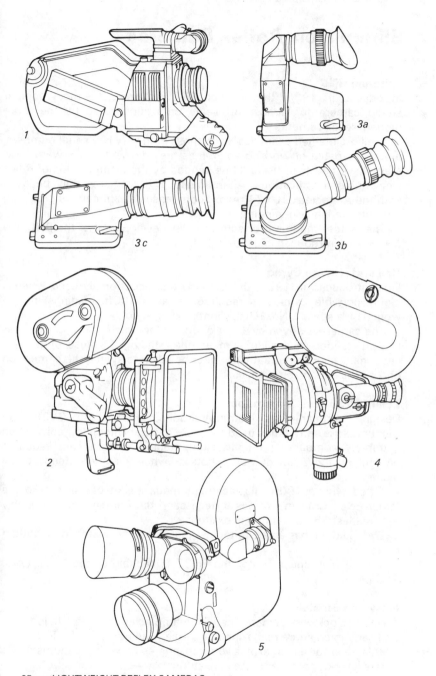

35mm LIGHTWEIGHT REFLEX CAMERAS

1. Aaton 8-35; 2. Arriflex III C; 3. Optional Arriflex III C doors, a. with cranked eyepiece for hand-holding, b. with orientatable eyepiece, c. with fixed eyepiece; 4. Arriflex IIC; 5. Eclair CM3.

35mm Non-Reflex Cameras

Mitchell BNC
Introduced in 1938, the Mitchell BNC remained the most popular studio camera for almost 30 years until superseded by the more modern reflex cameras.

Well maintained examples, even those with very low serial numbers, are still capable of working as well as they did when they were new. Many have had their useful life extended by the incorporation of reflex viewfinding modifications. Alternatively, BNC cameras may be used with the Angenieux 10×24 reflex zoom lenses as a means of providing through-the-lens viewfinding.

The factory-made mirror shutter reflex development of the BNC, the BNCR, was introduced in January 1968.

Bell and Howell Eymo
First introduced in 1925, the Eymo is still occasionally used when a highly portable camera is required. It takes 100ft. loadings of film wound on a special 'No. 10' daylight loading spool.

The camera is driven by a clockwork motor which runs approximately 22ft. (under 15 sec.) of film at one winding. Because of the exceptionally short run great care must be taken to switch the camera on only as the action commences.

Eclair GV35 and Camematic
Designed primarily as instrumentation cameras, the GV35 and Camematic is sometimes used for more general cinematography when extremely compact and lightweight electric cameras are required, particularly for 'point of view' shots or when a camera needs to be hidden.

Fitted with a 100ft. displacement magazine (it can also take the larger Eclair CM3 magazines if necessary) the Camematic is probably the smallest 35mm camera in existence.

Electric drive has an advantage in that it may be switched on and off remotely.

With a high speed motor the GV35 is capable of speeds of up to 150fps.

Newman Sinclair
A classic clockwork camera, the Newman Sinclair takes 200ft. loadings and can run an entire magazine at a single winding.

It is ideal for use in explosive atmospheres and other circumstances where it is not possible to use an electric motor.

Arritechno 35
Especially intended for X-ray and instrumentation work.

102

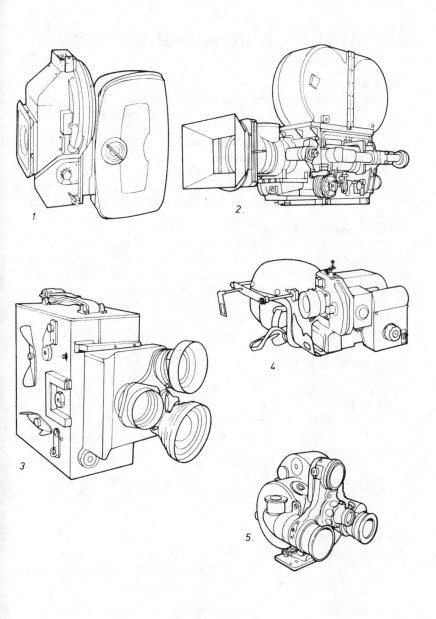

NON-REFLEX CAMERAS

1. Arritechno 35;   2. Mitchell BNC with Angenieux 10 × 24 reflex zoom
lens;   3. Newman Sinclair model N (reflex model);   4. Eclair Camematic fitted
onto a crash helmet;   5. Bell and Howell Eymo.

35mm Ultra-high-speed Cameras

Image 300

Like all other high-speed cameras, the Image 300 was originally designed and built for scientific research and analysis purposes, being subsequently modified and rebuilt for theatrical and similar types of film production.

The Image 300 can be run at 10 pre-set camera speeds, from 24 to 300 fps, has six pull-down claws and two register pins, a rotating-mirror reflex viewfinder system, an integral video viewfinder, a 120° shutter opening, a BNCR lens mount, interchangeable ground glasses and side-by-side 1000ft. film magazines. It has a single-phase 115v, 50/60Hz, AC motor.

Photosonics 35mm–4ML

The Photosonics 4ML is a medium-high-speed camera with an intermittent pin-registered film movement capable of variable speeds up to 200 fps. Its principal features include interchangeable 200, 400 and 1000ft. magazines, interchangeable 28v DC or 115v AC motors, and provision for remote control. While not having a reflex shutter which may be used while the camera is running, it has a boresight viewing system which may be attached in place of the film magazine for accurate frame alignment.

Photosonics 35mm–4E

The Photosonics 4E is an intermittent, pin-registered high-speed camera capable of speeds up to 360 fps. The film movement has 12 pull-down claws, all hollowed out for lightness, 4 register pins and a vacuum gate system which sucks the film into register during the exposure period and blows it off the register pins before pull-down. It has an integral through-the-lens viewing system which may only be used while the camera is stationary, a 120° shutter and 400 or 1000ft. magazines. For theatrical use it has a BNCR lens mount and interchangeable ground glasses. Various motors are available, some of which require a three-phase AC supply.

Photosonics 35mm–4B

The Photosonics 35mm–4B is an ultra-high-speed rotary-prism camera capable of speeds up to 3250 fps. The 4B utilises a rotary prism, which operates in synchronisation with a disk shutter placed between the prism and the film, to compensate for the continuous movement of the film. At top speed, 1000ft. of film passes through the camera in less than 5 seconds, making the synchronisation of switching on the camera and of triggering the event to be filmed a very important factor in using a camera such as this. The images are reasonably steady, and although the image covers a full silent frame the top and bottom tend to be a bit blurred. The shutter opening is 72°. Various motors are available, some of which are three-phase and have an initial power surge of 60 amps.

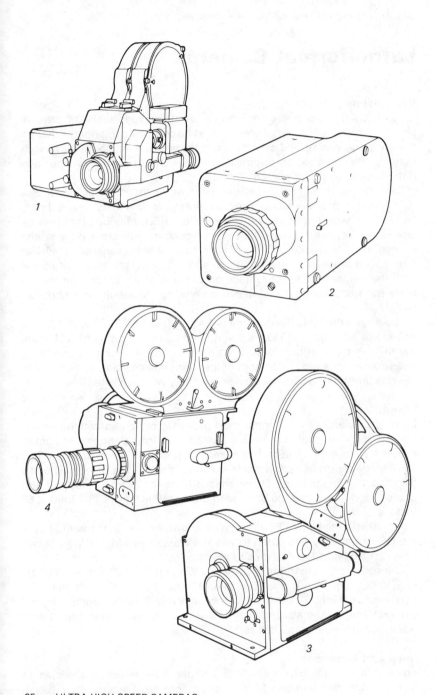

35mm ULTRA-HIGH-SPEED CAMERAS

1. 300 fps Image 300; 2. 200 fps Photosonics 35-4ML; 3. 360 fps Photosonics 35-4E;
4. 3250 fps Photosonics 35-4B.

Large-format Cameras

Vistavision

Large-format cameras are extensively used for special-effects process shooting where a number of scenes must be combined together, either on the optical printer or by front projection, to produce a piece of film which may be intercut with an original, first-generation negative without any noticeable image degradation.

Cameras built for the Vistavision process in the mid 1950s are at a premium for process work. Their advantage is that they use ordinary 35mm film, with the image set lengthways, which may be processed by any laboratory. The camera types often encountered are a large studio model, based on the original Technicolor 3-strip camera, a similar high-speed model, capable of 60 fps, and a lightweight 'butterfly' model with the magazine set horizontally on the rear of the camera. In the US there have been some new Vistavision-type cameras built, most notably by ILM.

The size of the Vistavision frame is 1.485 × 0.991in. (37.72 × 25.17mm), an area of 1.471 sq. in. (949.4 sq. mm.) and an aspect ratio of 1.5 : 1. Each frame is 8 perforations long. If combined with anamorphic originals, image area at the top and bottom of the frame will be wasted; if used with the Academy format, image area at the sides will be wasted.

65mm

Like Vistavision, 65mm is most used today for multi-generation process photography; most of the cameras are leftovers from periods when entire pictures were shot on 65mm cameras, from which 70mm contact prints were made for projection. Notable exceptions to this are Disney, who use 65mm cameras for many of the special films made for Disneyland and Disney World, etc., and the Showscan process which uses 65/70mm at 60 fps.

A restriction to using 65mm negative anywhere else in the world but in the US is that only one laboratory in the western world, MGM in Culver City, Los Angeles, has facilities to process it.

The size of a 65mm frame is 1.912 × 0.87in. (48.56 × 22.1mm), 1.663 sq. in. (1073.1 sq. mm.), and the aspect ratio 2.2 : 1. Each frame is 5 perforations high. If used in combination with anamorphic original cinematography the advantage in image area is enormous; if used with Academy, the advantage is less.

Imax and Omnimax

These are exhibition processes which use special 65mm cameras to produce horizontal images for projection onto giant screens in purpose-built theatres.

The Imax image size is 2.74 × 1.91in. (69.6 × 48.5mm), 5.23 sq. in. (3375.6 sq. mm.), and the aspect ratio 1.44 : 1. Each frame is 15 perforations long. For Omnimax the picture area is quasi-elliptical.

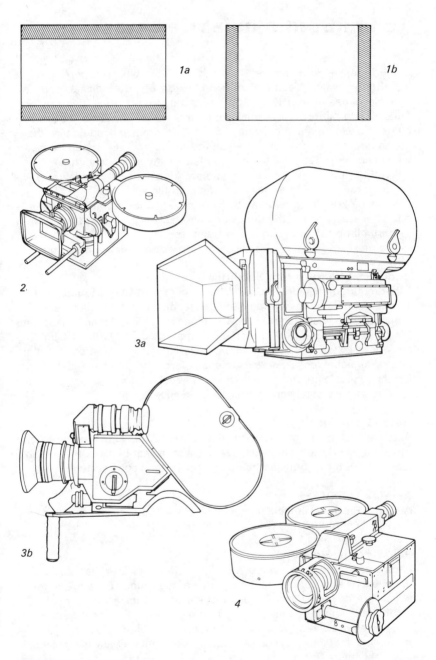

LARGE-FORMAT CAMERAS

1a. 35mm anamorphic-shape frame within a Vistavision frame; 1b. Academy-shape frame within a Vistavision frame; 2. 'Butterfly' type Vistavision camera; 3a. Super Panavision 70 studio; 3b. hand-holdable 65mm camera; 4. Imax camera.

16mm Studio-quiet Cameras

Camera noise is measured in decibels (db), which progress on a logarithmic scale. A camera noise reduction of 3 db indicates that the noise level has been halved; 6 db less is a quarter of what it was before. Thus a 22 db camera makes only a quarter the noise of a 28 db one and can be used closer to a microphone and in more confined conditions without the camera noise being obtrusive on the sound track, an important factor when choosing a camera to shoot a theatrical-type production.

Another important aspect of camera noise is its frequency, low-frequency noise being easier to muffle than high.

To use a 26+ db camera in studio or confined location conditions it is often necessary to swathe the camera in blankets or to use a lightweight camera blimp to achieve tolerable quietness.

The make and type of filmstock used may also affect camera noise.

Additional 'feature film' facilities
Other requirements for a 'studio' 16mm camera not always found on other 16mm cameras are exceptional image steadiness and flange focal depth registration to ensure the best possible image quality, Super 16 capability for blow-up to 35mm wide-screen format, usability with MH lighting anywhere in the world, a good video-assist system, time code option, interchangeable lenses, an exceptionally large, bright viewfinder image, interchangeable ground glasses, interchangeable short and long eyepiece configuration, crystal control and variable speeds, etc.

Aaton XTR and 7 LTR
Aaton claim the XTR model has a noise level of 23 db 'after running-in' and that their 7 LTR model may achieve this after a year of use. Other notable features are the Aaton clear number/SMPTE time code system.

Arriflex 16SRII
Arnold & Richter claim that later models of the 16SRII can be supplied with a noise level of 25.5 db.

Panaflex-16 'Elaine'
Panavision claim this camera has a noise level of less than 22 db. The Panaflex-16 incorporates all the features of the Golden Panaflex, many of which are new to 16mm. These include an in-shot adjustable 40–200° focal-plane shutter, dual-pin registration, optional spinning-mirror or pellicle reflex system, viewfinder contrast filters, illuminated ground glass frame-line markings, eyepiece leveller, alternative magazine positions, internal camera heaters, etc.

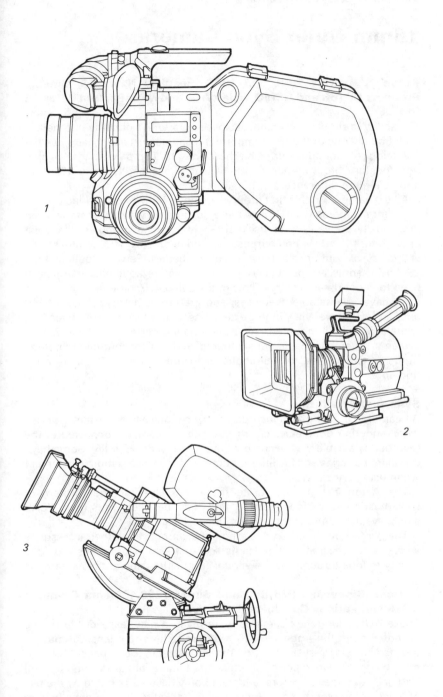

STUDIO-QUIET 16mm CAMERAS

1. Aaton XTR; 2. Arriflex 16SRII in studio mode; 3. Panavision 16 'Elaine'.

16mm Quiet Sync Cameras

Aaton 7, Arriflex 16BL and 16SR, Beaulieu News 16, Cinema Products CP16R and GSMO, Eclair ACL and NPR, Paillard Bolex 16 Pro

The ability to shoot sync sound, at close range, with a hand-held camera is undoubtedly one of the most important technological advances since the invention of sound itself. One has only to compare the television documentary programmes of today with those of the early 1960s to appreciate the difference.

All the cameras in this first group were designed when the principal use for 16mm cameras was TV news and documentary filming, and as such are equally convenient to use hand-held or on a tripod. While quiet enough for their designed purpose they do not measure up to film studio standards of camera quietness (24 db or better). Few are quieter than 28–30 db; some are positively noisy, and require additional blimping if used to shoot theatrical-type films in a studio environment.

All have orientatable eyepieces, and the newer models (Aaton, 16SR and GSMO) have viewfinder extensions available for use when the camera is tripod mounted. All have rotating-mirror reflex viewfinder systems, interchangeable lens mounts and crystal-controlled motors. Some offer facilities for automatic exposure control and video view-finding.

Sync-sound facilities

All cameras in this group incorporate sync-marker light systems for use when shooting double-system sound with the camera connected to the recorder by a cable via the camera battery (see page 80 & 86). Some have on-board batteries and facilities for time coding, which is more convenient when using crystal sync.

The Aaton 7 can incorporate the Aaton clear number system of sync-marking/scene-identification and may be used with their VCAR single system sound recording film magazines.

The Arriflex 16SR has a wide range of electronic and other accessories available which greatly increase its scope. It also incorporates a unique facility to look through the viewfinder from either side of the camera.

Auricon Cinevoice, Pro 600 and Super 1200, Cinema Products CP16 and various Cinevoice derivatives

These older, non-reflex cameras were given a new lease of life by the introduction of the Angenieux 10 × 12mm reflex zoom lens. All may be adapted for single-system sound-on-film recording (see page 112), and may be fitted with special shutters for filming off a TV monitor. All originally had mains motors, and could only become portable by the use of a power inverter, but may have been modified to incorporate a battery motor.

110

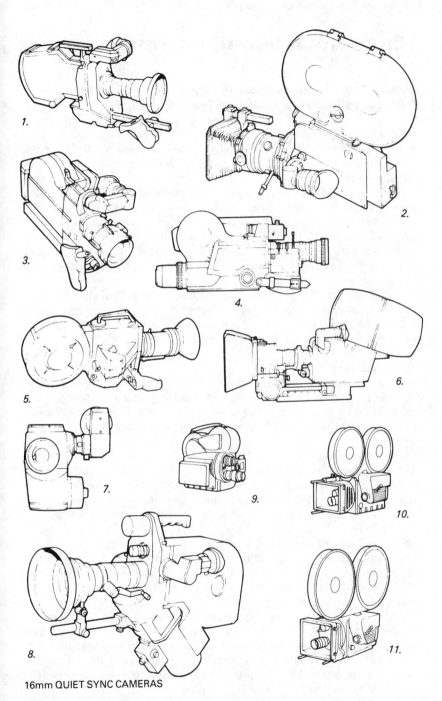

16mm QUIET SYNC CAMERAS

1. Aaton 7; 2. Arriflex 16BL; 3. Arriflex 16SR; 4. Beaulieu News 16; 5. Bolex 16 Pro;
6. Cinema Products CP16R; 7. Eclair ACL; 8. Eclair NPR; 9. Auricon Cinevoice;
10. Auricon Pro-600; 11. Auricon Super-1200.

16mm Sound-on-film Cameras

Arriflex 16BL, Beaulieu News 16, Canon Scoopic 200SE, Cinema Products 16RA, Paillard Bolex 16 Pro

Although much TV news coverage is done using video cameras there are many assignments when film is preferred for various reasons, ranging from lightness in weight and reliability through to the fact that they make less demands on battery charging facilities, which is often a problem in remote areas.

The urgency of TV news presentation demands the fastest possible means of getting the pictures on the screen. When film is used this invariably means the use of single-system recording whereby the sound is recorded on a magnetic stripe along the edge of the film, simultaneously with the picture. This method eliminates the need to transfer sound from ¼in. tape to 16mm magnetic coated filmstock and to synchronise picture and sound scene-by-scene.

All the cameras listed above may be adapted to record single-system sound. In addition, the manufacturers of some later cameras, most notably Aaton and Eclair, have produced magazines for their cameras which incorporate sound-recording heads.

Reflex viewing

Older sound-on-film cameras, principally those derived from Auricon Cinevoice cameras by the addition of a battery-powered motor and a 400ft. film magazine, are not true reflex cameras and depend upon the use of a non-interchangeable Angenieux reflex zoom lens for viewfinding purposes.

Later cameras, most notably the Arriflex 16BL and the Cinema Products CP16RA, have rotating-mirror reflex viewfinding systems and interchangeable lens mounts and so may be fitted with wide angle, wide aperture and telephoto lenses when necessary. This greatly increases the scope of the newsreel cameraman to film under difficult circumstances.

Noise and sound recording quality

These cameras are very good for what they are designed to do. They are not quiet enough for theatrical-type filming, and the quality of the recorded sound is not usually considered to be good enough even for serious TV documentary-type filming.

When portability is most important the Aaton, Arriflex and Cinema Products cameras may be used with on-board, totally automatic, recording amplifiers and directional microphones for one-man operation.

Any of the Aaton models (see preceding pages) may be used with their Velocity Controlled Audio Recording magazines, which give exceptionally high quality single-system sound recording.

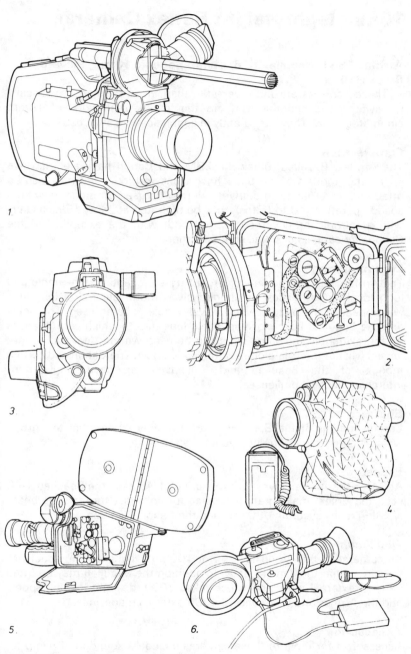

QUIET REFLEX SOUND-ON-FILM CAMERAS

1. Aaton VCAR camera with single-system recording facilities; 2. Arriflex 16BL showing film path for single-system sound recording; 3. Beaulieu News 16 camera; 4. Canon Scoopic 200SE fitted with a sound barney; 5. Cinema Products 16RA; 6. Paillard Bolex 16 Pro.

16mm Lightweight Reflex Cameras

Arriflex 16ST, Beaulieu R16, Canon Scoopic 16mm, Paillard Bolex H16

These cameras are more versatile than those designed specifically for sync sound shooting and are the 'maids-of-all-work' of 16mm cinematography. They vary greatly in sophistication, and cost.

Camera drive

The Arriflex, Beaulieu, Bolex H16EBM and Canon have electric drive only; other models of the Bolex have clockwork drive but may also be fitted with external electric drives. All may be used for moderately high speed operation (40 to 60fps), may be operated at 24 or 25fps usually with electronic or governed control and, with the exception of the Canon, are capable of single shot operation.

Lens mounting

The Arriflex has a three-lens divergent turret accepting wide angle and long focal length lenses simultaneously without fear that a long lens will appear in the picture when a wide angle is being used. The Bolex and the Beaulieu have close set triple-lens turrets which permit lenses of approximately the same length to be used without fear that longer lenses will cut into the picture of the wide angle. The Canon and certain models of the Beaulieu and Paillard Bolex have single non-interchangeable zoom lenses.

Shutters

Certain models of the Bolex H16 are the only cameras in this group which incorporate an 'in-shot' variable shutter.

Exposure

At 24fps the Arriflex gives an exposure of 1/48 sec., the Beaulieu 1/60 sec., the Bolex (making an allowance for light lost through the beam splitting reflex system) 1/80 sec. and the Canon 1/51 sec.

Film loadings

All cameras in this group take 50 or 100ft. daylight loading spools internally within the camera body. In addition the Beaulieu may be fitted with an external magazine which takes 200ft. daylight loading spools and the Arriflex and Bolex accept 400ft external magazines.

Accessories

Accessories for most of these cameras include a soundproof blimp for sync and sound shooting, sync pulse generator, watertight housing for underwater photography, microscope for cinemicrography, lens extension tubes for macrocinematography, endoscopes for internal medical cinematography and intervalometers for time lapse operation.

LIGHTWEIGHT REFLEX CAMERAS

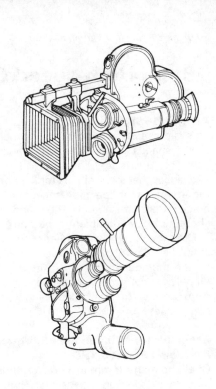

Arriflex 16ST

Beaulieu R16

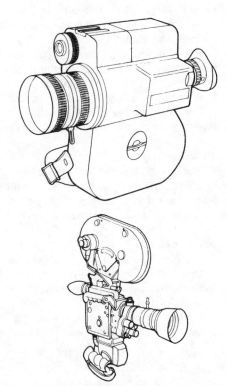

Canon Zoom D8-8

Paillard Bolex H16

16mm High-speed Cameras

Arriflex 16SR HS

This is a special version of the normal Arriflex 16SR camera designed to run at speeds up to 150 fps. Other than the film magazines, which are special to this model, the 16SR HS may be used with all the accessories and lenses that are available for the normal camera. Because of the special requirements of the high-speed movement this camera is somewhat noisier than the regular 16SR and so is not suitable for sync sound shooting in quiet ambient conditions.

The camera may be supplied with a servo-operated automatic exposure control accessory (this is a special modification that must be incorporated by the manufacturer), and if fitted with a lens which has an automatic diaphragm control it is possible to make changes in the camera's speed, from normal to high speed and vice-versa, with automatic exposure compensation.

Eclair GV16, Milliken DMB5, Mitchell Sportster and Photosonics/ Actionmaster 500 1PDL

Of all the many 16mm cameras originally designed and manufactured for industrial and scientific research, only the few listed above are used for general filming, and in the main this is sports analysis work.

All these cameras have intermittent film movements and various models are available up to 500 fps. Another Photosonics camera, the model 1W, is capable of 1000 fps. Cameras with continuous film transportation and incorporating rotating-prism optical compensation, and which are not often used for general filming, are capable of speeds of tens of thousands of frames per second.

The Photosonics has a facility to preset two camera speeds and to switch from one to another during a take.

Viewfinding

Of the above cameras, only the Photosonics 1PDL is a true reflex, and this is a fixed-prism type; all the rest require the use of an Angenieux reflex zoom lens for viewfinding. A boresight accessory is available for all cameras for accurate frame alignment.

Filmstock

Many high-speed cameras require film that is wound on spools, rather than in rolls, and double perforations. Older cameras originally supplied for industrial purposes may require film with a 0.3000in. perforation pitch instead of the usual 0.2994in. Before using any of these cameras it is important to check exactly what the filmstock requirements are and to allow sufficient time if it is not standard.

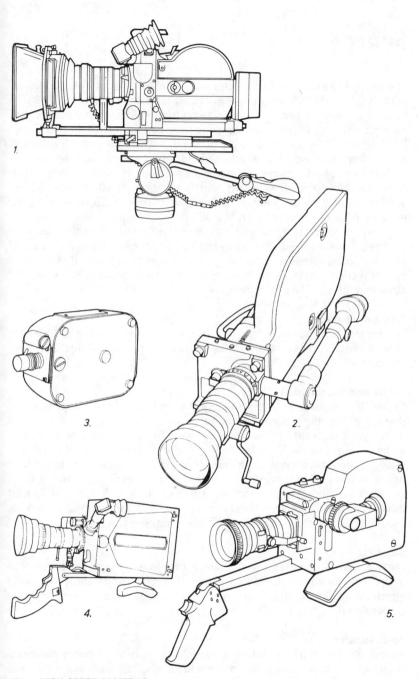

16mm HIGH-SPEED CAMERAS

1. Arriflex 16SR HS fitted with auto-iris lens and remote speed control; 2. Eclair
GV16; 3. Milliken DMB5; 4. Mitchell Sportster 164; 5. Photosonics/Actionmaster
500 1PDL.

Super 8

The projected area of a Super 8 frame is 33/1000 sq. in. This compares with 108/1000 for 16mm and 495/1000 for 35mm Academy. The size of each grain of emulsion is the same no matter what the format so that a single detail of information which is recorded on one grain of a Super 8 frame would be spread over $3\frac{1}{4}$ grains of a 16mm frame, 15 grains of an Academy frame and $17\frac{3}{4}$ grains of a 35mm anamorphic frame.

Furthermore, the same mechanical limitation in the accuracy which it is possible to achieve when film is perforated, about ± 0.0004in. applies equally to all gauges of film and therefore Super 8 must inevitably be more unsteady on the screen in comparison to the 16 and 35 mm formats by factors similar to the differences in their dimensions. On the other hand, Super 8 is invariably shown on comparatively small screens where these shortcomings are minimised. Super 8 is of most use to professionals as an inexpensive means of making experimental films and for sampling locations.

Camera speed
For amateur purposes, Super 8 cameras are run at 18 fps, 15ft. per minute. For professional use they should be run at 24 fps 20ft. per minute.

Films and magazines
Super 8 is at its best when the original camera film is projected and therefore the high contrast colour reversal film stocks are to be preferred. If duplicate prints must be made from a Super 8 original (and at best they are likely to be only marginally acceptable) the camera original should be shot on a low contrast high definition film stock which is intended for duplication. With rare exceptions, Super 8 films are packaged in daylight loading cartridges in 50ft. lengths. A special 200ft. cartridge, with either silent or magnetic edge striped stock, is available for single system Super 8 sound-on-film cameras.

Lenses
Most Super 8 cameras have a single non-interchangeable zoom lens and although some of these are very desirable, particularly the wide aperture varieties, this too is a restriction which must irk the professional.

Exposure control
Automatic exposure is almost an article of faith on Super 8 cameras. Although this is justifiable, adequate and often necessary for the amateur, unless the particular camera has a manual aperture override the professional is likely to find he has not the control he requires to cope with all conditions.

118

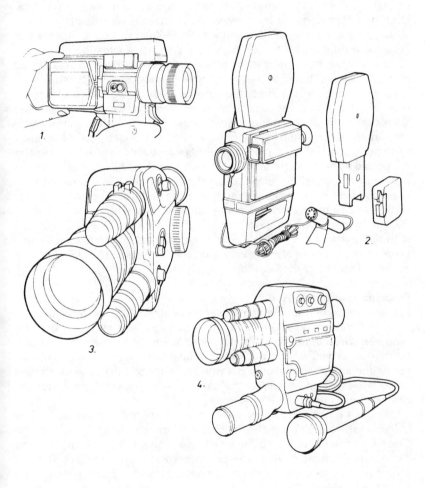

SUPER 8

1. The Super 8 cartridge system; 2. Kodak Supermatic 200 ft with 50 ft (15m) & 200 ft (60m) daylight loading cartridges; 3. Beaulieu 4008ZM. Sophisticated Super 8mm camera with 11:1 ratio zoom lens; 4. Beaulieu 5008-S. Professional Super-8 single/double system sound-on-film camera. Angenieux 6-80mm fl.2 zoom lens. Reflex viewfinding exposure control with automatic iris; both exposure meter and VU meter readings visible in the viewfinder.

Aids to Hand-holding a Camera

There are times when, for reasons of expediency and portability, a camera may have to be hand-held rather than firmly supported on a tripod, dolly or crane. There was a time when only newsreel cameramen regularly hand-held their cameras but now, with the advent of the floating camera system, hand-holding is frequently used in feature film production to enhance the interpretation of the script. When this situation occurs the camera operator usually endeavours to hold the camera so steadily, or move it so smoothly, that the audience is not aware of the technique.

To achieve such steadiness the camera must derive support from the most rigid parts of the operator's anatomy, the spinal cord and the shoulder. If a floating camera system is used it is worn like a vest, and if the camera is hand-held in the ordinary manner it must be rested squarely on the operator's shoulder, pressed firmly against the side of the head and supported by arms and elbows drawn well into hips and sides of the body.

Cameras of modern design, created with hand-holding steadiness in mind, are tailored to the human body and need little or no modification for static shots to make them eminently suitable for the purpose.

Older cameras, which have no more than a rubber eyepiece interface with the operator and with all their weight projecting forwards, can only be used inconspicuously with very wide angle lenses or require additional support if lenses of medium focal length are to be used.

Floating camera systems

For smooth camera movements over undulating surfaces, up and down stairs and into places where it would be impossible to lay tracks or use a mounted camera, floating camera systems are ideal. These consist of a reinforced jacket which the camera operator wears, an articulated, spring-loaded, shock-absorbing arm which supports the camera, a video reflex viewfinding system on the camera, and a small monitor for the cameraman to aim the camera by.

Using a floating camera is a skill which must be learned, and many camera operators promote themselves as specialist Panaglide or Steadicam operators. Like using a helicopter mount, the art is to touch the camera as little and as lightly as possible so as not to transmit to it any erratic human movements and to allow the camera support system to do its job unhindered.

For low-angle work either system may be used in an inverted mode. They may also be attached to moving vehicles, etc., to smooth out bumpy rides.

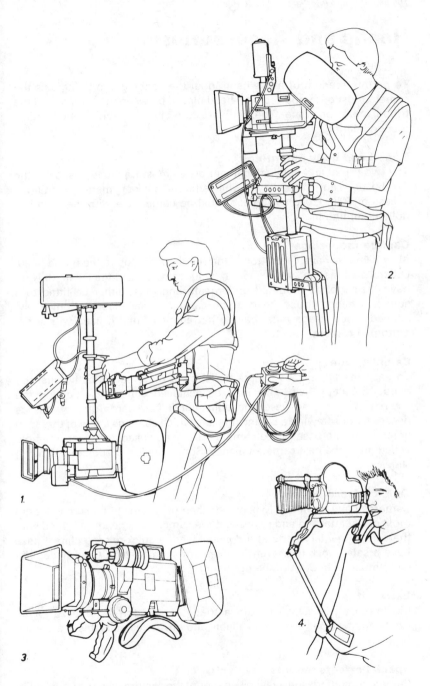

1. Panavision Panaglide floating camera system in inverted mode; 2. Cinema Products Steadicam floating camera system; 3. Panavision Panaflex in hand-holding mode, with short eyepiece, shoulder rest and left and right handgrips; 4. Arriflex 16 ST on a shoulder bracket.

Heads and Accessories

To permit freedom of movement about the panning and tilting axis the
camera must be supported on a head placed between the camera and the
tripod, dolly or crane. The simplest form has horizontal and vertical
friction bearings.

Tripod and dolly mountings

The two tripod and dolly attachment plates most frequently used are the
Arriflex bowl and Mitchell types, the latter mainly for cameras weighing in
excess of 50lb. (20kg). The head must be compatible with the tripod or
dolly mounting plate.

Camera mountings

Most cameras have flat bottoms and require a flat top to the tripod head.
Others, such as the Arriflex 35mm 'wild' cameras and the Eclair 16 NPR,
have their motors mounted underneath and must either be fitted to a
suitably shaped tripod head or be carried in an adapter. Conversely,
shaped tripod heads must have a flat adapter fitted if used with a flat
bottomed camera.

Balance slide

To ease the tilting movements the camera must be perfectly balanced
about the tilting axis. This may be achieved either by mounting the
camera on a sliding base and adjusting it backwards or forwards as
necessary or screwing a balancing plate which contains a row of threaded
holes on to the base of the camera. The head is secured using the hole
which gives the best camera balance. Some heads incorporate balancing
slides.

Quick release dovetail

Cameras have traditionally been attached by a ⅜in. 16 tpi screw but are
most easily attached and released if the camera and heads are fitted with
the complementary parts of a dovetail wedge quick-release plate. These
have a safety lock to prevent the camera slipping off a tilted head. The
locks must be in position before tilting.

Extra tilt

Maximum tilt is achieved with a triangular 'wedge' or 'cheese' plate.
Adjustable wedges are also available and on some heads this is a built-in
facility.

Special-effects mounts

Camera mountings are available to mount the camera with the nodal point
of the lens in the precise centre of both the pan and tilt axes of a head and
to rotate the camera about its longitudinal axis.

122

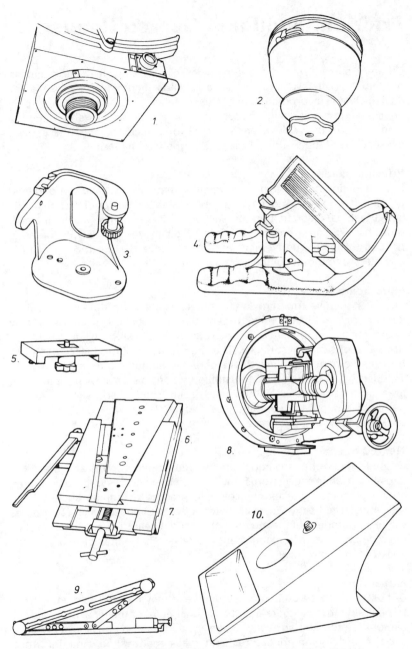

1. Mitchell-type fitting on underside of a geared head; 2. Arri bowl-type fitting; 3. Adaptor to attach Arri 'wild' camera with an underneath motor to a flat-top head; 4. Adaptor to fit an Eclair NPR camera to a flat-top head; 5. Adaptor to fit a flat-bottomed camera to a head made to take an Arri 'wild' camera; 6. Large dovetail quick-release plate; 7. Adjustable balance slide; 8. Turn-over camera mount; 9. Adjustable tilt wedge; 10. Fixed tilt wedge.

Friction, Fluid and Geared Heads

Different shots demand different types of pan and tilt control, and an operator will often wish to have several heads of different types available.

Many heads incorporate quick-release plates to enable the camera to be attached and detached in a simple manner, a built-in adjustable wedge to give extra tilt up or down, and a slide to correctly balance the camera irrespective of the weight of the lens or the film magazine.

Friction heads
Simple friction heads are particularly useful for very fast and comparatively insensitive camera movements. The inherent drawback of friction heads is in the initial static friction (or 'stiction' as it is sometimes called) which must be overcome before each pan or tilt movement. Greater force is needed to begin a movement than to continue it, so a friction head is unsuited to fine movements.

Fluid heads
The most popular tripod head for general usage is the 'fluid head'. This is similar to the friction head except that the stiction is almost totally overcome by interposing layers of a high-viscosity silicone liquid between the pairs of moving surfaces. The 'fluid flow' so introduced, dampens head movement and gives the cameraman something to 'push against'. The degree of damping is adjustable by controls which vary either the area or the thickness of the liquid layer. Fluid heads should have a perfectly smooth movement; no perceptible stiction or break-away, backlash, play, or fluid leak.

Geared heads
Geared heads offer the most precise movement control and are often chosen for shooting features and TV commercials or when using large studio cameras. It takes considerable practice to handle such a head efficiently. The heavy wheels provide a flywheel effect which contributes to the smoothness of the movements. Geared heads usually incorporate a gearchange system for both pan and tilt so that either of two or three speed ratios may be selected.

Nodal heads
Almost any geared or 'L' bracket-type head may be used as a nodal head to pan and tilt the camera about the nodal point of the lens, provided the camera is mounted correctly. Nodal panning and tilting are particularly used when filming miniatures and glass matte shots and for front-projection shooting to minimise image displacement when the camera is moved.

Motion-control special-effects rigs usually use an inverted 'trojan helmet' camera mounting for nodal-point panning and tilting.

124

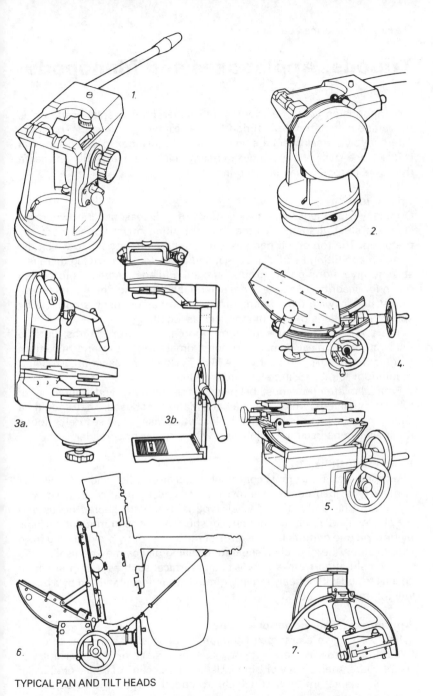

TYPICAL PAN AND TILT HEADS

1. Arriflex '35' friction head; 2. Ronford fluid head for Arriflex 35; 3. Ronford 'L-bracket'-type fluid head, used to raise tilt axis. May be used as a nodal head or, inverted, for low-angle work; 4. Worrall geared head; 5. Samcine-Moy geared head, incorporating quick release balancing slide and adjustable wedge; 6. Panaflex camera on a Panahead with adjustable wedge fully extended; 7. Trojan helmet nodal head.

Tripods, Appleboxes and Monopods

The tripod is an item of equipment older than photography itself, and is the standard method of supporting a camera in a static position. Alternatively a stack of square boxes, topped with a box to which a top-hat is fitted, or a stack of metal tubes or risers which clamp together and serve the same purpose, may be used instead.

Tripod legs

Originally tripod legs were always made of well-seasoned hardwood but stainless steel, titanium or other non-corroding metal is now normally preferred. The top of a tripod has a mounting plate or bowl to which the panning and tilting head is attached, and at the foot of each leg there is a spike to give a grip on the ground and a lug to enable the legs to be tied down for security. Tripod legs are extendable from their minimum length to just under twice that length. Further height adjustment is possible by spreading the legs or setting them closer together.

There are no standardised tripod nomenclatures or lengths, but the following are typical names and approximate minimum and maximum heights: Short, 20–32in.; baby, 22–36in; TV, 29–50in.; sawn-off, 31–54in.; medium or tall, 37–66in.; standard, 44–80in.

Particular attention must be paid to the handling and tightening of tubular metal legs, which may be badly dented if abused. They should be kept in cases when not required. Unless otherwise safely secured, tripods must always be used in conjunction with a spider or spreader.

Head mountings

The tripod mountings most commonly used are Arriflex and Mitchell. The Arriflex type incorporates a bowl leveller and is most often used with lightweight cameras. The Mitchell type is used with geared heads and may be levelled either by extending or shortening one or more of the legs, by moving one or more legs inwards or outwards, or by moving a leg from side to side. Alternatively a separate levelling device may be used.

When shooting from a slowly tilting surface, such as a ship at sea, a special tripod with a freely moving gimbal mounting, stabilised by a heavy weight, may be used.

Appleboxes and monopods/risers

When working in a cramped situation it is sometimes quicker to use a fixed and narrow camera support, such as a stack of boxes or a set of risers, rather than a dolly or tripod. Usually a selection of boxes or tubes of various heights are to hand which are added or removed to adjust the camera height, and some tubular systems have one section which may be wound up or down for fine adjustment.

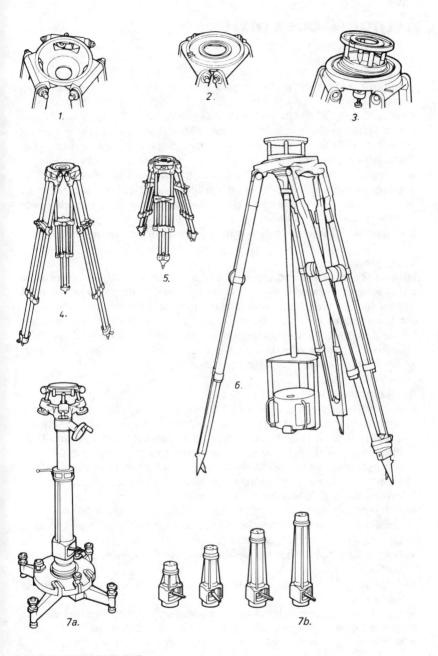

TRIPODS AND MONOPODS

1. Arriflex bowl-type tripod fitting; 2. Mitchell tripod fitting; 3. Gimbal tripod head;
4 & 5. Tall and short metal tripod legs; 6. Gimbal-head tripod; 7a. Elemack riser
column set with base, adjustable riser column and Mitchell-type head,
b. fixed-height risers.

Tripod Accessories

To prevent tripod legs from slipping or damaging a polished floor, a triangle, spreader or spider is usually used. These are three-pronged devices with slots or fixings for the foot of each tripod leg. They come in various forms. The flat metal type slides in and out and may be used as an aid to levelling the camera; the type with wheels on each arm (rolling spider) may be used to move the camera around between set-ups; the most simple type of all, the banjo spider, may also be used as an aid to levelling by allowing the tripod legs to be slid from side to side.

When working in conditions where the ground surface is uneven or unstable, making the use of a rigid spreader impossible, a triangle made of strong canvas or webbing is very effective. On sand or snow a groundsheet of canvas or plastic may be used to spread the load.

Tying down

For reasons of safety and security, a tripod must sometimes be securely attached to the ground or floor. The simplest way to do this is to nail three 'crows' feet' to the ground to locate the legs, screw a large hook into the ground immediately below the head, and secure a chain or rope between the tie-down eyes of the tripod and the hook eye. The chain or rope is then tightened by means of a turn-buckle or by twisting the ropes with a bar, which is then wedged between the tripod legs.

Accessories

- A *hi-hat* is principally used when a very low or screwed-down camera position is required. It may be Arriflex bowl or Mitchell type. Some are supplied with a spigot which may be attached underneath and then fitted into a lamp stand when a very high 'tripod' is required.
- A *levelling hi-hat* is a Mitchell-fitting type hi-hat which has a facility to level the camera. It may also be used between the tripod and the camera head as a leveller.
- A *hi-hat adaptor* is an Arriflex-bowl type hi-hat with a Mitchell-type underside which may also be used to convert a Mitchell-type tripod to take an Arriflex-bowl type head.
- A *scaffold clamp hi-hat* has an underside which may attach directly to scaffolding tube.
- A *paddle mount* is an Arriflex bowl attached directly to a length of scaffold tube.
- A *riser* is a spacing column that fits between the top of a Mitchell-type tripod top and the underside of a head to give additional height.
- A *low-boy* is a very low hi-hat.

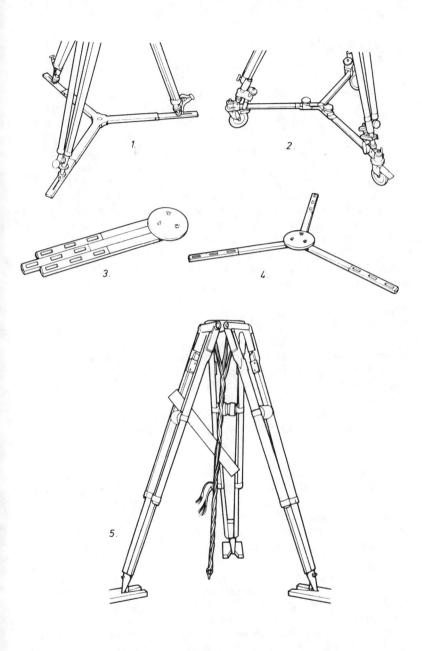

TRIPOD ACCESSORIES

1. Metal spreader; 2. Rolling spider; 3. Banjo spider (closed); 4. Banjo spider (open); 5. Tripod tied down by rope and tourniquet. 'Crows' feet' prevent the legs slipping.

Crab Dolly

The crab dolly can provide in-shot camera movements in all directions, up and down, forward and backwards, side to side, or a combination of any or all. To achieve this the camera and head are mounted on an arm or column which may be moved up and down by means of stored hydraulic or electric power. This, in turn, is mounted on a dolly which may be pushed in any direction, steered by the rear wheels or crabbed sideways.

Ideally, the rise and fall of a dolly mounting should be fast enough to keep pace with a person as he moves from a sitting to a standing position, i.e. if the camera is on a level with the artist's eyes at the beginning of the movement it should be possible to maintain that relative position throughout the action without the need to tilt upwards and risk including the top of the set or even the lighting gantry (grid) in the shot. A dolly should also be able to rise high enough to afford an over-the-shoulder shot of a 6ft. (1.80m) actor.

Running surfaces

Crab dollies fitted with pneumatic tyres are most suitable for use in situations where the floor surface is smooth, flat and level, permitting movement in any direction. If the surface is uneven it may be necessary to temporarily lay down a suitable surface, such as 8 × 4ft. (2.6 × 1.3m) sheets of ¾in. (20mm) thick plywood or blockboard or, if the movement is in one direction, tracks or deals.

Crab dollies with interchangeable wheels may be fitted with track wheels and used on tubular tracking in the same manner as a spyder dolly.

Accessories

Dollies may be given a little extra height with a riser and a little more reach by the use of a tongue. Seats and front and side platforms are provided to support the crew while tracking. All heavy-duty crab dollies take Mitchell-fitting heads and incorporate a leveller. If an Arri-bowl type head is used, an adapter is necessary.

Transportation

Before a dolly is taken on location, the width of any doors, stairways or lifts through which it must pass should be measured and compared with the width of the chosen dolly to make sure that passage is possible or to see if a narrower model is needed. It is bad practice to turn a dolly on to its side as this can upset the hydraulic system. In the last resort, if a dolly must be tipped in any direction, the boom should be tied down and the reservoir breather hole plugged. Tyre pressure should be maintained at 90 psi. It is always advisable to have a spare wheel and a tyre pump readily available in case of a puncture.

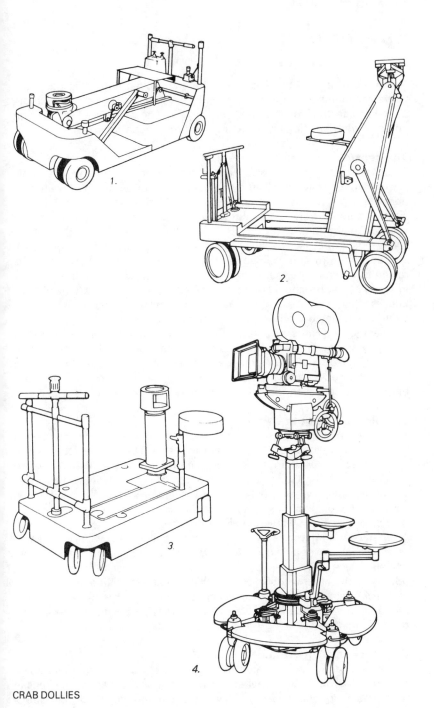

CRAB DOLLIES

1. Moviola crab dolly; 2. Fisher crab dolly; 3. Colortran crab dolly; 4. Elemack Cricket dolly.

Spyder Dolly

A compromise between a tripod and a crab dolly, the spyder dolly is a universal means of supporting a camera in a studio or on location, indoors or out. It can track over smooth or rough surfaces, or offer low or high angle camera positions, yet is compact and transportable.

The central column
A spyder dolly consists of a central hydraulically operated telescopic column which may be raised by the use of a foot pump and lowered by opening a valve. This up and down action is not suitable for in-shot rise and fall camera movements but these may be achieved by the use of a counterweight jib arm.

It is most important to release the locking clamps around the top of each section before raising or lowering the column. The column may then be raised by operating a foot pump situated on the side of the base unit or lowered by depressing a pressure relief valve. When a suitable height has been set the column clamp rings should then be tightened securely to avoid unsatisfactory operation or damage to the unit.

A seat for the camera operator may be attached to the centre section of the dolly and positioned where required. When this facility is used one or two 50lb (20kg) counterweights are provided which must be placed on an arm on the opposite side to the seat to ensure stability and freedom from tipping, and to lessen the twisting movement on the unit.

Wheels on a smooth surface
The wheels of a spyder dolly are mounted on individual arms and may be pivoted to many positions relative to each other. The normal settings are: 'full spread' for maximum stability, 'corridor' for use within narrow confined spaces and 'fully folded', when the dolly has 'to stand on a dime' or, more usually, when it is being transported or stored. No matter what combination of positions is selected the dolly may be steered by two wheels or crabbed by steering all four, as required.

When changing from a two-wheel steer mode to four-wheel crab, small reference arrows marked on each wheel casting ensure that the two wheels which have been used for steering are the correct way round relative to the other wheels before locking into the crabbing mode. Failure to check these results in unsatisfactory wheel alignment and crabbing movements. The steering/pushing handle may be positioned above any of the four wheels.

Rough or sloping ground
The spyder dolly can operate on tubular metal tracks quickly laid down over rough ground. Bogey wheels smooth out unevenness at the joins in the tracks. Floor and track running wheels are interchanged by releasing a securing bolt above each wheel.

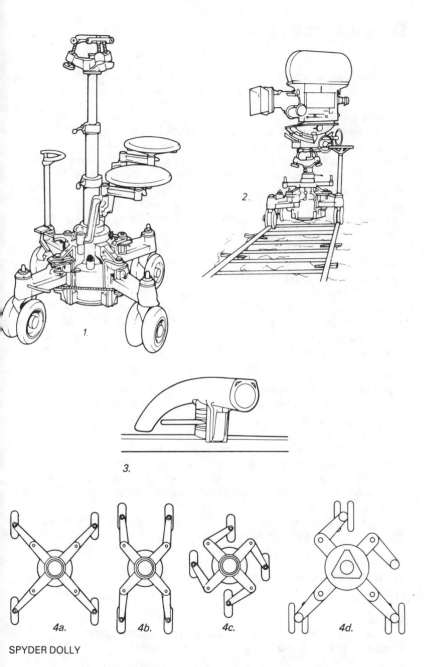

SPYDER DOLLY

1. Elemack Spyder dolly set at maximum height and with pneumatic wheels for smooth surface operation; 2. Spyder dolly set at minimum height and with bogey wheels on tubular tracking; 3. Flat-top track run-up section; 4. Alternative wheel positions: a. maximum stability, b. minimum width, c. minimum spread, d. three wheel for use on uneven surfaces.

Dolly Accessories

The shot possibilities when using crab and spyder dollies may be considerably extended by the use of a wide range of accessories.

Mini jib-arms

Jib-arms are short, usually counterbalanced, arms which fit on to the normal camera mounting position of a dolly and carry the camera and head at one end and sufficient weights to balance, at the opposite end. A jib-arm gives additional in-shot up-and-down and side-to-side camera movements and makes it possible to position the camera over a solid object, such as a table or a bed. It may be used in conjunction with the normal dolly up-and-down and tracking and dollying movements. As it does not carry the camera operator, the range of camera movements may be limited by the difficulty of the camera operator looking through the viewfinder all the time, unless a remote-control camera head is used.

Instead of, or in addition to, counterweights a link arm or cable may be fitted between the rear of the jib-arm and the base of the dolly so that as the centre column of the dolly is raised or lowered the jib-arm will be tilted up or down by leverage. By this means the possible amount of in-shot up-and-down movement of a dolly may be considerably extended.

Mini-jibs may often be folded into a compact form for transportation.

Crane-arms

Crane arms which carry the camera operator, and very often also the focus assistant, may be attached to the chassis of a dolly. If a crane-arm is attached to the centre column the column must be in its lowest, most stable, position.

Like jib-arms they are counterweighted, making it absolutely imperative that the camera crew must wear safety belts at all times and must stay on board the crane until sufficient weights have been removed from the rear, or added to the front, to prevent the crane shooting up, out of control, and causing an injury.

Very long crane-arms which use a remotely controlled camera (see page 138) may also use the chassis of a dolly as their means of support.

Snake arms

These are 'S'-shaped brackets used to give a low camera-head mounting position.

Tongues

Flat extension arms or tongues are used to offset the camera forwards or sideways, or to make it possible to use two cameras.

Seats and counterweights

Seats are available for the camera operator (and sometimes the assistant) which go up and down with the camera. If used on a dolly with a central column, a counterweight should be used on the opposite side.

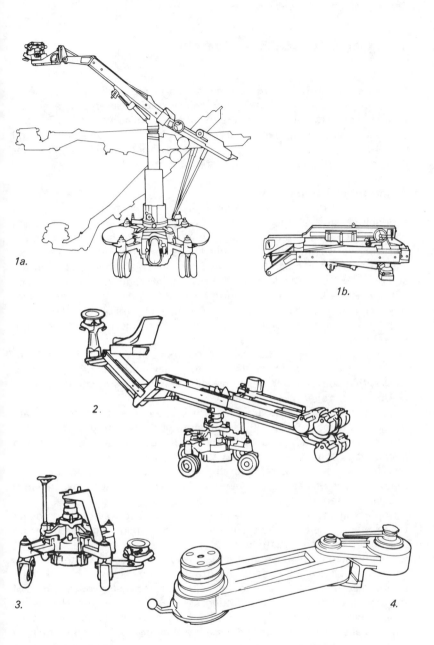

1a.

1b.

2.

3.

4.

DOLLY ACCESSORIES

1. Elemack Tipula jib, a. a link fitted between the rear of the jib and the dolly causes the arm to rise and fall as the dolly is raised and lowered, b. folded for transportation; 2. Elemack Jonathan jib (crane-arm accessory for three-dimensional camera movements, with the added possibility of carrying the camera operator); 3. Elemack snake arm, used for low-angle camera positioning; 4. Elemack rotating arm, used to extend and offset the camera position.

135

Large Camera Cranes

For three-dimensional camera movements in the traditional manner – with the possibility of carrying not only a studio camera but a geared head, the camera operator and the focus assistant, as well as the Director and a couple of large lamps as well, if required – a vehicle-mounted camera crane is necessary. Such cranes have petrol-driven engines for use on the road and silent electric drives for use in the studio.

Counterweight operation

The boom arms of large camera cranes used for motion picture production always operate on the counterweight principle and are controlled by an operator, a grip or a boom man, who stands either at the front or rear of the arm, from which position he can smooth out the transitions from and to rest, in a manner which is imperceptible on the screen. The standards of smoothness in acceleration and deceleration, without any jerkiness or bounce for the heights and speeds of movement of which a large camera crane is capable, cannot possibly be achieved by any known form of electric, hydraulic or other mechanically powered movement.

Large industrial-type 'cherry picker' hydraulic platforms are suitable for static camera shots or for mounting large, heavy lamps in high positions.

As with a dolly, a crane must operate either from a smooth, flat surface or from tracks specially laid down.

Counterweighted camera cranes which carry crew members are very dangerous without the strict discipline of not dismounting until after the grip in charge has adjusted the balance to compensate and said it is OK to dismount. A large crane may carry three or even four people at the front, and if one person steps off before his weight has been compensated for, the others will be catapulted upwards. Safety belts must always be worn in case this should happen.

Counterbalancing may be effected either with lead weights, by moving a heavy weight electrically along the arm, or by pumping mercury from one end of the boom to the other.

An advantage of lead weights is that the exact disposition of the weights can be seen. It is usual to have an extra weight box at the front end of the boom to accommodate sufficient weights to compensate for members of the crew mounting and dismounting. As the front end is usually on the ground when people get on and off, it is much easier to add or remove weights at this end than from the main weight box, which would then be high up and possibly out of reach.

Pumping mercury is a favourite method of adjusting the balance of very large cranes but, being toxic, it should be treated with respect. Should a leak occur, both the crane and the set would have to be decontaminated.

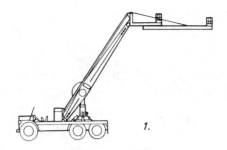

1.

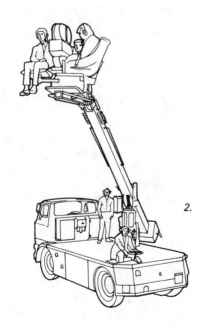

2.

LARGE CAMERA CRANES

1. Chapman 'Titan' camera crane; 2. Samcine 'Sam-Master' camera crane.

Remotely Controlled Camera Systems

Remotely controlled cameras fitted to long crane-arms, or suspended from cables, give camera positions that would not otherwise be possible, or safe, for a normal crane-mounted camera and crew to reach.

Louma camera crane

This is a very long camera crane-arm which carries a remotely controlled camera fitted with a video viewfinder. It is totally demountable and made up of the following elements, which may be carried anywhere and set up in positions that would be totally inaccessible to a vehicle-mounted camera crane of similar reach:

- *Crab dolly.* This may be steered by two wheels or crabbed in any direction, and may be used on a flat surface or on track. It has a sufficiently wide wheelbase to make it safe to carry a long arm.
- *Central column and fulcrum section.* This is tall enough to allow the boom arm to tilt up and down by the maximum amount without being obstructed by the dolly.
- *Boom arm.* Made up of a number of sections for portability and to make it possible to set the length to suit the shot. When very long arms are required it is usual to include additional bracing cables.
- *Camera mounting.* Consists of a system of mounting the camera about its centre of gravity, a remotely controlled camera platform, and the means to operate the camera and the lens from a distance.
- *Camera requirements.* The camera must be fitted with a video viewfinder, remote controls to focus and zoom the lens and adjust the lens aperture, and a small video camera to enable the focus assistant to look at the lens settings.
- *Counterweights* which are easy to handle.
- *Remote-control camera pan and tilt system.* Consists of a console with a video monitor with which the camera operators can view the scene as seen by the camera, control handles to pan and tilt the camera, similar to those of a normal geared head, and the necessary electronics.
- *Lens control package.* Servo controls for the lens functions, and small video monitors to view the scene and to see the lens settings.
- *Communications.* Earphones with boom microphones for all the crew to communicate with one another.

Skycam 'flying' camera system

This is a remotely controlled camera supported by four steel cables, each of which is attached to a computer-controlled cable drum.

By winding-in or paying-out the cables the camera may be made to move from side-to-side and up-and-down and to hover above an object at any height, in the manner of a helicopter.

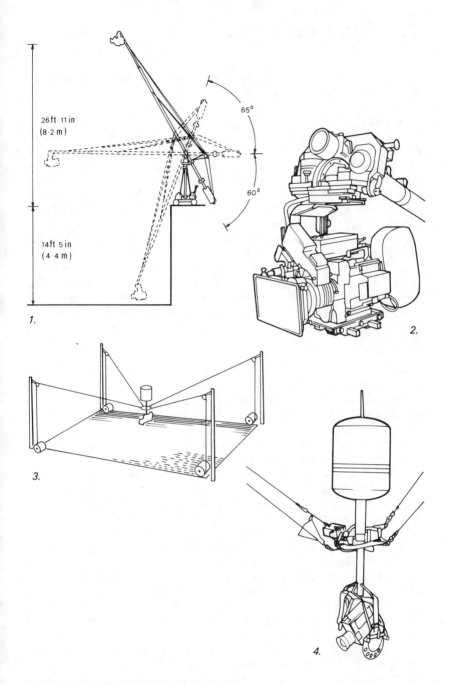

26 ft 11 in
(8·2 m)

65°

60°

14 ft 5 in
(4·4 m)

1.

2.

3.

4.

REMOTELY CONTROLLED CAMERA SYSTEMS

1. Louma camera crane in fully extended mode; 2. Louma camera crane camera
mounting; 3. Skycam cable-suspended camera system; 4. Skycam camera unit.

Tracking Vehicles

When a camera must travel faster than a man can push it along on a dolly, a motorised camera mounting is used.

Insert cars

The ideal system is the Hollywood-style insert car. The most sophisticated of these vehicles have 6 or 7 litre engine capacity, four wheel drive, automatic transmission, a steering wheel on either side, camera positions anywhere at the front, the rear, or on the roof, towing hitches for a target vehicle at the rear or to either side by means of outriggers, and a generator or alternator sufficiently powerful to run any amount of lighting that is required for daylight fill.

With a vehicle such as this almost any high speed and accurate tracking shot can be achieved.

Where the target vehicle has to be 'driven' by a non-driver, or must remain at a set distance from the camera, it may either be towed by an outrigger or mounted on a trailer which is towed. The same systems are used when a horse-drawn carriage is filmed without the horses in picture.

Bumps in the road may be smoothed out, to a certain extent, by partially deflating the tyres.

Tracking platforms

Platforms are often fitted to the roof or to the front or rear of the vehicle which is used to transport the camera equipment. Such arrangements do not have the potential of a proper insert car but are often good enough for an uncomplicated shot.

When setting a camera up on a tripod which is on a vehicle, care must be taken to ensure that it is very safely secured, especially if no safety rail is fitted, and the crew must hang on to the camera for their own safety.

When travelling on the roof of a car, the crew should always bear in mind that the driver might have to do an emergency stop at any moment. The driver must remember, when passing under low bridges or overhead wires, that he has people on the roof.

The ideal set-up is a tubular frame to which the camera is attached. This serves two purposes; it provides a camera mounting independent of the car roof so that movements of the camera crew will not affect the camera, and the crew are safely protected in case of a sudden stop.

Most important is a system of conversation or intercom between the driver and the camera operator. Only the man looking through the camera knows if the vehicle is being driven too fast or too slowly and he must be able to instruct the driver accordingly as the shot proceeds. One kick to go faster, two to go more slowly may be a good enough method for simple shots, but a microphone and speaker system is preferable.

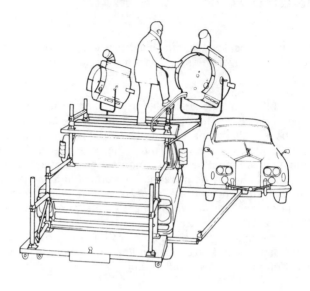

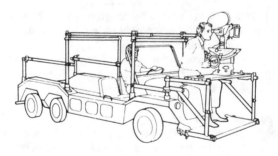

TRACKING VEHICLES

1. Insert car and towing vehicle
Casper insert car towing a target vehicle containing an actor who cannot drive.
The Casper also carries a generator and sufficient lights to fill daylight shadows
and illuminate the subject. Scaffold rails permit cameras to be fixed rigidly to film
from any angle.

2. Tracking vehicle
Sam Mini-Mook insert car and tracking vehicle.

141

Camera-to-vehicle Fixing

Very often it is necessary to attach a camera to the front or side of a car to shoot either a conversation or a 'point of view' scene.

Car rigs

A number of devices are available for attaching a camera to a car without the need for drilling holes or damaging the vehicle bodywork in any way.

The most simple means is a 'limpet' mount which has powerful suction cups to provide a secure hold. To use these devices the surface to which they are attached must be clean, smooth, non-porous, dust free, dry and reasonably flat. It may be horizontal or vertical or anywhere in between.

Other car rigs incorporate a beam which is supported across or alongside the car, and to which one or more cameras as well as lamps may be attached.

Yet another means is to build up a scaffold system by cross-bracing to various points of possible attachment in the vehicle and support the camera with the aid of a paddle mount.

Safety

Whenever a camera is attached to a vertical surface or to a moving vehicle it must have safety lines attached to support it should the principal fixing come adrift. If the ride is likely to be rough every movable and detachable part of the camera should be securely taped up. For some cameras there are special bracing systems available.

Failure to observe these elementary safety precautions and supply both 'belt and braces' means of attachment may easily lead to the destruction of an expensive camera.

Filming from a racing car

Occasionally a cameraman is called upon to film from a car being driven very fast. Under these circumstances he will find himself severely buffeted and subject to 'g' stresses.

The only possible way to control a camera under these circumstances is by using a tripod head which can be locked off fixed to the vehicle. Under severe circumstances fine control is really only possible with a geared head and a 'side finder' viewfinder for the operator to look through.

An image stabiliser will help smooth out the pictures if this is required. However, very often it is desirable to show just how rough the ride is, in which case it may even be necessary to add a little flexibility to the camera mounting.

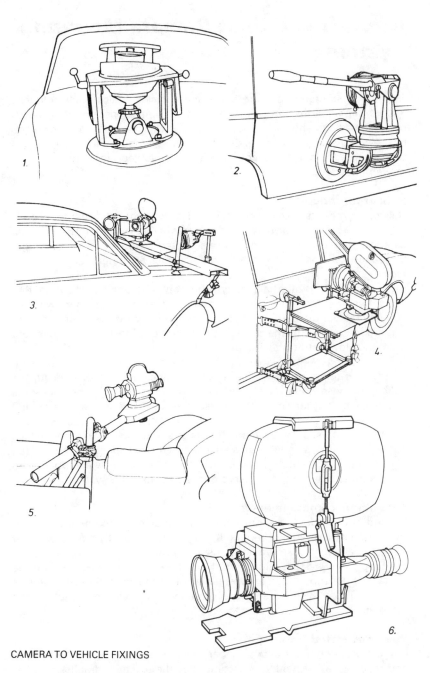

CAMERA TO VEHICLE FIXINGS

1. and 2. Limpet camera mounts attached to horizontal and vertical surfaces; 3. Cross-beam camera mount; 4. Car-door camera mount; 5. Camera attached to a racing car by a paddle mount, scaffold clamps and hose clips; 6. Special bracing system for a Panaflex camera.

Aircraft and Boat Camera Mounting Systems

Mounting cameras in aircraft, boats and vehicles, which pitch, roll, yaw and vibrate all at the same time, presents a camera operator with special problems if he or she wishes to take pictures which appear smooth and do not reveal the unsteady nature of the camera support. Perhaps the most difficult of all is the helicopter, which is subject to high-frequency movements.

Helicopter mounts

Helicopter mounts take several forms. The type most frequently used is the counterbalanced-arm type, which has a heavy counterweight that balances the camera in space. This system overcomes all the high-frequency roll, pitch and yaw movements which are inherent in helicopter flight.

When using a counterbalance-type helicopter mount it is important that it is set up with the camera in perfect balance so that the camera will stay put in whatever direction it is pointed, up, down or sideways, and that the camera operator aims the camera with only the lightest touch. The mount must be allowed to do its job unhindered.

For shooting 'point of view' shots with the helicopter flying in a forward direction, mounts are available to attach the camera on or beneath the helicopter nose cone, facing forward. In effect the pilot becomes the camera operator and the cameraperson just switches the camera on and off.

A more sophisticated system consists of a large spherical dome, which houses the camera and which is attached to the outside of the helicopter. The camera is remotely operated, using a video viewfinder, and incorporates a gyro-sensed, servo-operated stabilising system.

Jet aircraft camera mounts

Filming out of a fast jet aircraft presents problems if the degradation in image quality caused by shooting through a non-optically-perfect window is to be avoided. Camera systems are available to shoot through a periscopic lens system with the front of the lens protruding beneath the aircraft. Other mountings are available which replace the nose cone of a Lear Jet. These systems are mostly used when filming other jet aircraft air-to-air.

Power-operated levelling heads

Camera mountings are available which incorporate a gyro sensing device and maintain a constantly level camera by the use of hydraulics or other power system. They are particularly useful on boats.

144

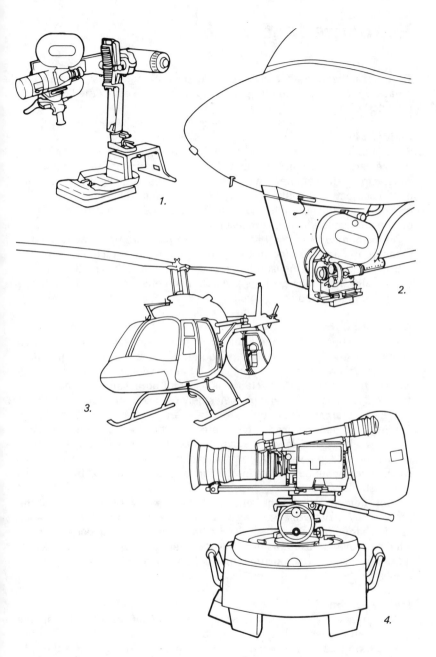

AIRCRAFT AND BOAT CAMERA MOUNTING SYSTEMS

1. Tyler counterweighted helicopter mount; 2. Fixed-position helicopter camera mounts for point-of-view filming; 3. All-axis gyro-stabilised, remotely controlled camera mounted in a sphere mounted on the outside of a helicopter; 4. Tyler gyro-controlled electro/hydraulic-stabilised camera platform for boats.

Exposure Meters

To assess the correct exposure an exposure meter may be used to measure either the incident light falling on the subject or the light being reflected off it.

Incident light
For a subject of average brightness, and particularly for scenes where people are important, incident light measurements are the most satisfactory. The cameraman should stand in the same light environment as the subject, and with a dome type attachment on his meter, point the meter in the direction of the camera. In this way all the useful light falling on the subject is effectively measured.

An incident light meter with a flat disc in place of the dome is used to measure the light coming from a particular lamp or direction.

Such readings are measured in foot candles or lux. This method is used to measure the intensity of the key light and control the fill light until the desired lighting ratio is achieved.

Reflected light
Take care when reading the light coming off a subject to ensure that an average brightness is measured. Theoretically, the measurement should be taken off an object or surface which has a reflectance of 18%. A grey card of this degree of reflectance is a useful accessory to refer to as a standard. Failing this, readings may safely be taken off a face or the back of the cameraman's hand if they are of average flesh tone. When taking readings off general scenes take care not to include too much subject matter of above or below average brilliance. To avoid including bright sky tilt the meter downwards. Automatic exposure meters built into cameras cause incorrect exposure settings when they are influenced by too much sky or shadow in a scene.

Spot meters measure the reflected light from a very small area of the scene. They may be used to measure either the most important area, such as a flesh tone of the leading artist, *or* the brightest and darkest areas from which a mean exposure setting may be determined. Spot meters are also good for measuring exposures from a distance, as when using telephoto lenses or shooting documentaries.

Light and shade
Sometimes there is as much as a three-stop difference between the incident and reflected light readings because the subject is over light or over dark. In such circumstances the general practice is to set the lens aperture to the mean of the two readings. When the latitude of the film cannot cope with the degree of light and shade within a scene the cameraman must decide which is the more important part of the picture and expose for that.

146

EXPOSURE READING AND METER TYPES

1. Incident light reading
The incident is directed towards the camera from the subject position.

2. Reflected light reading
The meter is directed at the subject from the camera angle.

Photo Research 'Spectra' meter
3. With Photosphere, for incident light readings.
4. With Photogrid, for reflected light readings.
5. With Photodisc, for determining contrast ratios.

Gossen 'Lunasix' meter
6. Set for 30° acceptance angle for reflected light readings.
7. With diffusing sphere in position for 180° incident light readings. and
8. With tele attachment in position for 15° or 7.5° incident light readings of particular portions of the subject.

Minolta Spot meter
9. Spot meters have an optical system through which the cinematographer views the scene.
10. Seen through the meter, a small circle indicates the area where the light is being measured.

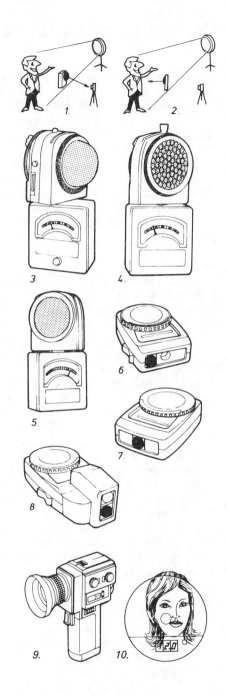

Colour Temperature

Sources of illumination differ in their colour balance according to their colour 'temperature'. A light of low colour temperature is quite red whereas light of high colour temperature becomes bluish.

Kelvins

Colour temperature is measured in kelvins (K) which represent the colour emitted by a theoretically perfect radiator as it is heated to a certain temperature.

'Mean Noon Sunlight in Washington DC' (5,500 K) is taken to be the average sunlight colour temperature. Tungsten filament lamps, normally used for motion picture lighting are 3,200 K. Photoflood lamps are 3,400 K.

Mireds

'Micro reciprocal degrees' (mireds) are kelvins divided into 1,000,000. They are a more workable measure of colour temperature. Unlike kelvins, they provide approximately proportional differences between colour temperature ratings in widely differing light sources. This makes it much easier to calculate the effect of any colour correction filter. Alternatively, decamired units, which are kelvin units divided into 100,000, may be used.

Typical mired and decamired values are:

Kelvin		Mired	Decamired
3,200	=	313	31·3 (tungsten artificial light)
3,400	=	294	29·4 (photoflood artificial light)
5,500	=	182	18·2 (average sunlight)
6,100	=	164	16·4 (typical daylight)

It will be noticed that mired numbers reduce as kelvins rise.

In the examples above there is a 200 K difference between the two artificial lights and 600 K difference between the two daylights and yet the difference in mired values, 18 mireds, is the same in both instances.

To change or correct colour temperature, it is necessary to introduce a colour filter to which a mired number may also be applied. Thus a +131 mired (Wratten 85B) correction filter is required when film which is balanced for tungsten light is used in average light.

Typical mired and decamired values for the most frequently used filters:

Wratten 85B camera filter	=	+131	+13
Wratten 85 camera filter	=	+112	+11
Wratten 85C camera filter	=	+ 81	+ 8
Full blue lamp filter	=	−132	−13
Half blue lamp filter	=	− 66	− 6·6
Quarter blue lamp filter	=	− 33	− 3·3

148

Approximate colour temperature values

Source	Kelvins	Mireds
Artificial light		
Domestic electric light bulb	2900	345
Photographic incandescent bulb	3200	312
Tungsten Halogen bulb	3200	312
Photoflood	3400	294
3200° bulb with $\frac{1}{8}$ blue filter	3400	294
,, ,, $\frac{1}{4}$,, ,,	3600	278
,, ,, $\frac{1}{2}$,, ,,	4100	244
,, ,, full blue filter	5550	182
1 volt drop in power supply to lamp, each	—10	
Carbon arc, LCT carbons, Y1 filter	3200	312
Carbon arc, WF carbons, full CTO filter	3200	312
,, ,, ,, $\frac{1}{2}$,, ,,	4032	248
,, ,, ,, $\frac{1}{4}$,, ,,	4651	215
,, ,, ,, WFG filter	5550	182
Daylight		
Dawn or dusk	2000	500
One hour after sunrise	3500	286
Early morning and late afternoon sunlight	4300	233
Summer sunlight	5500	182
Overcast Sky	6000	167
Sunlight blue-white sky	6500	154
Light summer shade	7100	141
Average summer shade	8000	125
Summer sky	< 30,000	> 33

Kelvin to Mired Conversion Table

Kelvins		100	200	300	400	500	600	700	800	900
2000	500	476	455	435	417	400	385	370	357	345
3000	333	323	312	303	294	286	278	270	263	256
4000	250	244	238	233	227	222	217	213	208	204
5000	200	196	192	189	185	182	179	175	172	169
6000	167	164	161	159	156	154	152	149	147	145

Mired to Kelvin Conversion Table

Mireds		10	20	30	40	50	60	70	80	90
100	10,000	9090	8333	7692	7143	6667	6250	5882	5556	5263
200	5,000	4762	4546	4347	4167	4000	3846	3703	3571	3448
300	3,333	3226	3125	3030	2941	2857	2778	2703	2631	2564

(Decamireds are Mireds divided by 10)

Colour Temperature Meters

It is not generally necessary to measure colour temperature unless for the purpose of balancing various sources of light. Provided that the colour balance of the scene is consistent overall, a modern laboratory can correct or introduce any colour cast to a scene, within wide limits. No laboratory, however, can compensate if the colour balance within a scene is patchy.

Cameramen sometimes measure the colour temperature of the light at a particular location only at the beginning of a day's shooting. Unless there is a drastic change in the ambient light conditions, they put the colour temperature meter away until late in the afternoon when the light begins to deteriorate noticeably. They then measure the colour temperature of the light again in order to make an overall change in the camera filtering, or to adjust the filtering of complementary lighting or filters controlling the daylight shining through windows etc.

With this knowledge they may change the lighting filters from a dull blue to a ½ + ¼ or even a ½ blue or, in the case of window filters, from a full to a ½ orange. At the same time the camera filter might be changed from an 85B to an 85C, or even an 81EF.

For this type of colour temperature measurement a two-colour meter is adequate.

Non-black-body light sources

Fluorescent and some types of metal-halide lighting present cameramen with special problems: although to the human eye they may look like normally balanced lighting, they are deficient in certain parts of the spectrum and have high peaks in others. To measure this type of lighting a three-colour meter is essential.

With early three-colour meters it was necessary to take separate readings of the red/green and the blue/green elements of the light and calculate which filter, or combination of filters, was necessary to adjust the light to suit either artificial-light or daylight balanced film stocks.

Later electronic three-colour meters automatically take separate measurements of the red, green and blue elements of the light, and may be switched to indicate which light balancing filter or which combination of colour correction filters is necessary for either type of filmstock.

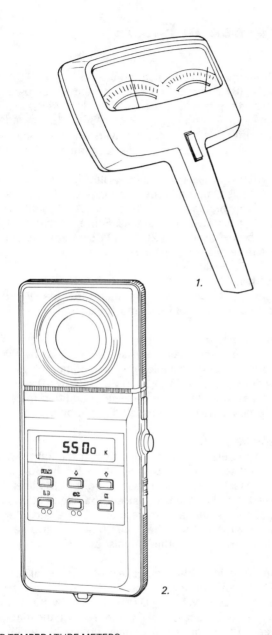

COLOUR TEMPERATURE METERS

1. Spectra three-colour colour temperature meter. Measures the blue/red and green/red light levels as well as the overall light level in foot candles or lux;
2. Minolta electronic colour temperature meter. Takes individual measurements of the red, green and blue light levels and calculates which light balancing or colour correcting filters are required to balance the light to artificial-light or daylight type film.

Colour Correction Filters

A frequent requirement is for a filter to convert 5,500 K (182 mireds) daylight to 3,200 K (312 mireds) for use with film stock balanced for exposure by tungsten light. A Wratten 85B (+131 mireds) will do this exactly. If a cooler result is required, a Wratten 85 (+112 mireds) filter may be used. The effect of any colour conversion filter may easily be calculated by converting the kelvin values to mireds and selecting an appropriate filter.

In conditions where an excess of ultra-violet light may give a blue cast to a scene, as in sea, high altitude and foggy conditions the 85B is the most effective conversion filter. A Wratten 1A (skylight) filter may be used with daylight balanced film stocks. Film balanced for 5,500 K (182 mireds) may be exposed to 3,200 K (312 mireds) tungsten light with the aid of a Wratten 80A (−130 mireds) filter.

Light balancing filters

For smaller adjustments in colour temperature the Wratten 81 (brownish) or 82 (bluish) range of filters may be used.

Colour compensating filters

Overall changes in the colour balance may be obtained by the use of colour compensating filters available in cyan, magenta, yellow, red, green and blue in densities of 0·05, 0·10, 0·20, 0·30, 0·40, and 0·50.

Magenta and green CC filters may be used in addition to colour correcting filters to compensate for fluorescent light imbalances.

Colour correcting filters

All colour correcting filters absorb a proportion of the light. Typical exposure increases are $\frac{2}{3}$ stop for the 85 and 2 stops for the 80A.

Filters made of glass or plastic are used in front of the lens. It is important that these filters be optically flat and parallel. Filters cut from sheets of thin gelatine sheet are sometimes set behind the lens or immediately in front of the film plane. Such filters must be absolutely free from dust, finger marks or other blemishes which would mar the picture.

Behind-the-lens gelatine filters increase the back focal length of a lens by about $\frac{1}{3}$ of their thickness. Thus a 0·0045in. thick gelatine moves the plane of focus forward by 0·0015in., i.e. by three times the distance considered to be acceptable when setting the flange focal depth of a camera. The error is not usually noticeable when normal focal length lenses are used, especially if they are well stopped down, but at full aperture it may well make it impossible to focus a wide angle lens to infinity or hold a zoom lens at the same plane of focus throughout the zoom range.

152

COLOUR CORRECTION FILTERS

Wratten Colour Conversion and Light Balancing Filters

Amber filter	Mired shift	Exposure increase	Blue filter	Mired shift	Exposure increase
85 B	+131	⅔ Stop	80 A	−131	2 Stops
85	+112	,, ,,	80 B	−112	1⅔ ,,
86 A	+111	,, ,,	78 A	−111	1⅓ ,,
85 C	+ 81	,, ,,	80 C	− 81	1 ,,
86 B	+ 67	,, ,,	78 B	− 67	⅔ ,,
81 EF	+ 53	,, ,,	80 D	− 56	⅔ ,,
81 D	+ 42	,, ,,	82 C	− 45	⅔ ,,
81 C	+ 35	⅓ Stop	82 B	− 32	⅔ ,,
81 B	+ 27	,, ,,			
86 C	+ 24	,, ,,	78 C	− 24	⅔ ,,
81 A	+ 18	,, ,,	82 A	− 18	⅓ ,,
81	+ 10	,, ,,	82	− 10	⅓ ,,

Colour Compensating Filters

Peak density	0·05	0·10	0·20	0·30	0·40	0·50
Cyan	CC05C	CC10C	CC20C	CC30C	CC40C	CC50C
Exposure increase in stops	⅓	⅓	⅓	⅔	⅔	1
Magenta	CC05M	CC10M	vCC20M	CC30M	CC40M	CC50M
Exposure increase in stops	⅓	⅓	⅓	⅔	⅔	⅔
Yellow	CC05Y	CC10Y	CC20Y	CC30Y	CC40Y	CC50Y
Exposure increase in stops	—	⅓	⅓	⅓	⅓	⅔
Red	CC05R	CC10R	CC20R	CC30R	CC40R	CC50R
Exposure increase in stops	⅓	⅓	⅓	⅔	⅔	1
Green	CC05G	CC10G	CC20G	CC30G	CC40G	CC50G
Exposure increase in stops	⅓	⅓	⅓	⅔	⅔	1
Blue	CC05B	CC10B	CC20B	CC30B	CC40B	CC50B
Exposure increase in stops	⅓	⅓	⅔	⅔	1	1⅓

To lighten a colour use a filter of similar colour.
To darken a colour use a filter of the
complementary (opposite) colour.

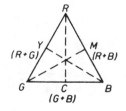

Neutral Density Filters

Neutral density filters are plain grey in colour and absorb light of all colours by an equal amount. They control the quantity of light transmitted, not the quality. They are referred to in terms of density which may be related to transmission. An 'ND 0·3' for instance, has a density of 0·3, transmits 50% of the light and reduces exposure by 1 stop. An ND 0·6 is 2 stops and ND 0·9, 3 stops.

Uses
Neutral density filters reduce the exposure at a given lens aperture without affecting colour, contrast or definition. They are used when a lens cannot be stopped down sufficiently in bright light conditions, allow the lens to be set at the stop which will give optimum definition or to be set at wider aperture in order to reduce the depth of field. Control of exposure by filtering is preferable to closing down the shutter for shots which involve fast movement of either the camera or the subject and which might otherwise 'strobe'.

Graduated neutral density
Filters which are partially clear and partially neutral density are used to reduce the exposure over part of a scene, to darken say, the sky or a bright wall in relation to the remainder of the picture. These 'grads' or 'wedges' must be used in a mattebox which has a sliding and rotating facility making it possible to position the filter exactly according to the scene, irrespective of height or angle. Unless the scene lends itself to the effect, it is not usually possible to pan and tilt the camera during a scene which has been set up with a grad, without the method of filtering showing.

When shooting 'day for night' i.e. simulating a night effect, sometimes two grads are used simultaneously, one for the top to control the sky area and the other from the bottom of the picture to control the foreground.

To alter exposure during a scene, as when panning from a dark to a light area or changing camera speed, and using a camera without a shutter which is adjustable in shot, a graduated ND filter may be slid across the front of the lens.

This method is preferable to that of adjusting the stop, which also affects the depth of field.

Cut gelatine
Occasionally it is desirable to darken part of a scene, as with a graduated ND, when the dividing line between the two areas is too uneven to use a straight line grad. Sometimes, a piece of gelatine neutral density filter may be cut to the desired shape. (See Selective filtering, page 160.)

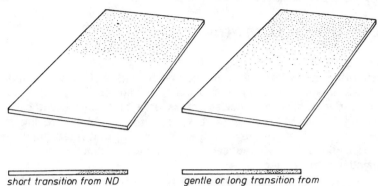

short transition from ND to clear

gentle or long transition from ND to clear

NEUTRAL DENSITY FILTERS

Name	Percentage transmission	Filter factor	Increase in exposure (stops)
ND 0.1	80	$1\frac{1}{4}$	$\frac{1}{3}$
ND 0.2	63	$1\frac{1}{2}$	$\frac{2}{3}$
ND 0.3	50	2	1
ND 0.4	40	$2\frac{1}{2}$	$1\frac{1}{3}$
ND 0.5	32	3	$1\frac{2}{3}$
ND 0.6	25	4	2
ND 0.7	20	5	$2\frac{1}{3}$
ND 0.8	16	6	$2\frac{2}{3}$
ND 0.9	13	8	3
ND 10	10	10	$3\frac{1}{3}$
ND 20	1	100	$6\frac{2}{3}$
ND 30	0.1	1,000	10
ND 40	0.01	10,000	$13\frac{1}{3}$
Combined colour correction and neutral density filters			
85N3 85BN3 etc.	32	3	$1\frac{2}{3}$
85N6 85BN6 etc.	16	6	$2\frac{2}{3}$
85N9 85BN9 etc.	9	12	$3\frac{2}{3}$

Graduated Neutral Density Filters:

Combination filters

Neutral density filters are obtainable in combination with coloured filters. An 85N3, for instance, is a Wratten 85 colour correction filter combined with an ND 0·3 (1 stop) neutral density. The use of a combination filter reduces the number of glass to air surfaces introduced, each one of which must slightly degrade the image.

Polarizing Screens

A polarizing screen is a neutral coloured filter that passes only those light waves which vibrate in one plane. Some light reflected from non-metal surfaces and from certain areas of a blue sky, is sufficiently polarized for such a screen to act as a method of controlling the selected light vibrations. By rotating the screen, unwanted highlights and reflections can be reduced or eliminated without effecting the remainder of the subject.

If two polarizing screens are mounted in combination and rotated until their planes of polarization are crossed then no light will pass.

Darkening blue skies
Light from a clear blue sky at right angles to the sun is strongly polarized and may be darkened by the use of a polarizing screen.

The effect varies according to the angle of the sun in relation to area of sky selected. If the sun is at 90° to the camera axis the skylight in the picture is partially polarized. If the sun is high in the sky polarization increases in the sky area near the horizon. If the sun is low, polarization is strongest higher up and in horizon areas at right angles to the sun.

Polarizing screens cannot be used for shots which involve long pans, (e.g. following an aircraft taking-off) because the depth of colour in the sky will vary so much during the shot that it would look unnatural.

Used to eliminate reflections
Many reflections from glass, glossy paint, polished wood and water are also strongly polarized and may be controlled to an extent which depends upon the angle of the surface in relation to the light falling on it. Reflections are most strongly polarized at 35° to the reflecting surface. Near 0° or at 90° there is no polarizing effect at all.

Polarizing screens are often used when filming through the windscreen of a car, especially if the camera is set at the optimum angle. They are also sometimes used when a road surface in the foreground of a scene is 'too hot'. This control is especially useful when shooting 'day for night'. Metal and other surfaces, which do not polarize light, may often be wetted to provide a polarizing effect.

Eliminating haze
Polarizing screens are useful when shooting distant landscapes and other occasions where it is desirable to cut through haze and absorb unwanted ultra violet light.

Polarizing the light
When shooting by artificial light complete control over all reflections, including those from metallic surfaces may be accomplished by polarizing the light source in addition to using a polarizing filter on the

POLARIZING SCREEN

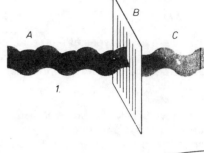

1. Polarized light passing screen
A. Vertically and horizontally aligned
light waves;   B. Polarizing screen
set to pass vertically aligned light
waves only;   C. Only the vertically
aligned light waves pass through.

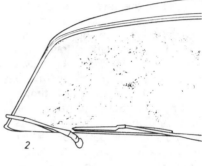

2. Shot taken from the front of a
car, without pola screen, shows only
reflections of the sky, clouds, trees
and buildings.

3. Shot taken from the front of a
car, using a pola screen, shows
details of the interior of the car and
its occupants. Reflections in the
windscreen are almost entirely
eliminated.

camera. Troublesome pack shots, paintings and backgrounds etc.,
which are difficult to photograph due to unwanted reflections may be
cleared of all reflections in this manner.

Using polarizing screens
Polarizing screens must be used in filter holders which may be rotated
to give optimum polarization. Exposure must be increased by $1\frac{1}{3}$ stops
when a polarizing screen is used.

157

Effect Filters

There are many types of filter and net which, in different ways, degrade the definition, contrast and colour saturation of the image, and create an 'atmosphere' over the whole picture.

Diffusers
Diffusers break up the overall definition of a scene, eliminating fine detail without affecting contrast or colour. They are often used when shooting close-ups of artists, particularly ageing actresses, and for degrading the best lenses to match the poorest.

Close-ups can take more diffusion than wide views, high contrast scenes more than those lit with flat lighting, dark haired artists more than blondes, dark colours more than high-key, to gain equivalent effects. A variable diffuser may be slid across a lens during a scene in such situations as an artist moving in to a close-up and requiring more diffusion than when at a distance.

Until a cameraman has gained experience he should treat diffusers with care and remember that it is one thing to create the required effect in one scene, another to produce an undetectable and balanced effect over an entire sequence of scenes. Typical, is the situation which arises when shooting an ageing actress, who requires a great deal of diffusion, talking to a young actor, who would normally be shot clear. In these circumstances it may be necessary to diffuse the actor somewhat to prevent the diffusion over the actress showing up.

Fog filters
Fog filters give an overall grey cast to a scene, reducing contrast, desaturating strong colours and simulating natural mist or fog. Scenes which are inherently low in contrast or contain fine detail take less fog effect than scenes which are inherently hard and bold. 'Double fog' filters degrade definition less than regular filters.

Low contrast filters
The effectiveness of low contrast filters falls somewhere between diffusers and fogs. They give slight fog, slight desaturation and slight diffusion.

Star filters
Star filters break up highlights, but have little or no effect on colour or on definition in the shadow areas. Pinpoints of light are seen to break up into characteristic light streaks in the directions of the lines engraved on the filter. The closer the lines on the filter, the longer and stronger the streaking. A star filter engraved with lines in the form of a square grid produce four-pointed stars and those engraved with two grids, one set at 45° to the other, produce eight-pointed stars.

158

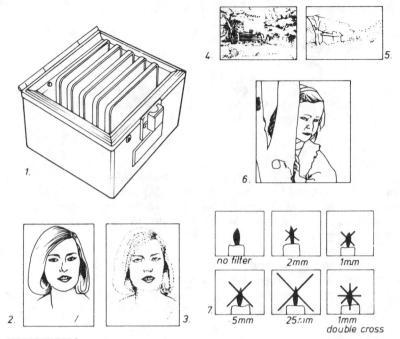

EFFECT FILTERS

1. Set of five effect filters
These may be diffusers, fogs, low contrast, stars, or black or white nets.

2 & 3. Diffusion
2. No filter;   3. Diffusion.

4 & 5. Fog filter
4. No film;   5. Fog effect.

6. Low contrast
Screen gives slight fog, desaturation and diffusion.

7. Star filters
A point light source photographed without any filter, with star filters having lines engraved at various distances apart, and with two sets of lines set 45° to each other.

Nets
Silk nets woven with a square weave have an even stronger effect than star filters. Nets woven with rounded corners give a slight overall softening to a scene. Black nets break up the image, give diffusion and slight desaturation. White nets give stronger desaturation than black. Brown nets impart an 'earthy' cast to a scene.

Nets may reduce the amount of light transmitted and should be held in front of an exposure meter to check the 'filter factor' before use.

Star filters and nets should be placed as close as possible to the front element of the camera lens but equidistant from all lenses to ensure a constant effect. They should be used with lenses set at wide apertures.

The Optical Flat

Occasionally a piece of plain glass must be placed in front of the taking lens of a camera. It must be optically flat, parallel and colourless, to avoid degrading the picture.

Noise containment
On certain cameras the lens must be blimped to ensure a minimum of noise emission. A special soundproof housing with an optical flat at the front is built around the lens. A Wratten 85B or 85 filter of the same size and thickness as the optical flat, can be substituted with this when shooting tungsten balanced film in daylight, to save an unnecessary extra glass-to-air surface.

Lens and filter protection
An optical flat can protect the lens from particles of grit or corrosive liquid when travelling fast and shooting in a forward direction, in close proximity to an explosion or in a sand storm or a storm at sea.

Selective diffusion
If petroleum jelly is smeared over part of the optical flat, selected areas of a scene may be diffused, the remainder clear.

Selective filtering
When a gelatine filter is used in front of a lens it may be mounted behind an optical flat to give it some protection from the elements. To filter only a part of a scene, a gelatine filter may be cut out to cover the area to be filtered and held in position by an optical flat. If such a filter is placed close to the lens the demarcation line between the two areas is sufficiently out of focus to be unnoticeable provided that the lens is not extreme wide angle or well stopped down.

A variation of this technique can make a white sky blue. A gelatine daylight correction filter is cut out to conform to the skyline and only the lower part of the scene is filtered. The unfiltered sky then photographs blue. It may also be necessary to cut out a suitable neutral density filter to darken the sky. Alternatively a blue filter may be cut out to conform to the upper part of the scene.

Gelatine filters can be cut without marking, while still wrapped between two pieces of protective paper:
1. Line up the camera and lock off securely;
2. Stop down to the shooting aperture;
3. Attach a piece of waste gelatine to an optical flat with a piece of adhesive tape;
4. Looking through the viewfinder, draw a line on the waste gelatine where the filter must be cut.
5. Place a piece of typists' carbon paper over the packet containing the

160

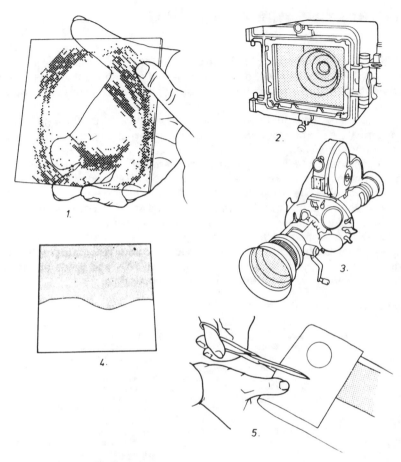

OPTICAL FLAT APPLICATIONS

1. Selective diffusion with a suitably treated glass screen.
2. Noise containment with the sound proofing effect of glass.
3. Lens protection by placing a flat over the camera lens.
4. Selective filtering which filters parts of a scene and not others.
5. Cutting a gelatine filter, held in a fold of paper.

gelatine to be used and place the marked gelatine over the top. Pencil over the line already drawn to trace the line through.

6. Cut round this line.

If a colour correcting filter is to be cut out for the lower half of the scene and a neutral density for the top, the two should be cut simultaneously so that they fit together accurately.

Filters for Black and White

Filters of many different colours may be used for daylight photography with B & W filmstock without the problem of putting a colour cast over the entire scene as would happen if such filters were used with colour film.

Filters are used in B & W cinematography to cut through haze, accentuate sky and cloud formations and to vary the contrast and tonal renderings of a scene.

A coloured filter will lighten those parts of a scene which are of similar colour and darken those which are opposite or complementary.

The stronger the colour of the filter, the greater the effect.

A yellow, orange or red filter lightens faces and darkens blue skies.

A very light yellow may be used to absorb ultra violet haze without noticeably affecting the tonal renderings of other colours.

All other types of filter normally used for colour cinematography i.e. diffusers, stars, nets, fogs, polarizing screens, NDs and grads etc. may be used equally well with monochrome film materials.

Filters: Factors and Effects

Wratten No.	Factor	Exposure increase	Colour	Degree	Daylight effect and use
3	1·5	½	Light yellow	Slight	Penetrates aerial haze
8	2	1	Medium yellow	Moderate	Corrects panchomatic colour balance
12	2	1	Yellow	Strong	Increases contrast
15	2·5	1¼	Deep yellow	Heavy	Lightens faces
21	3	1½	Light orange	Slight	Over correction
23A	5	2¼	Deep orange	Moderate	Heavy haze penetration
25	8	3	Red	Heavy	Whitens faces
29	16	4	Deep red	Extreme	Strong contrasts Dark blue skies Exaggerated clouds

MONOCHROME FILTERING

1. To lighten a colour use a filter of a similar colour.
To darken a colour use a filter of complementary (opposite) colour.

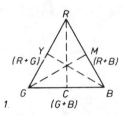

1.

2. Panchromatic film, no filter.

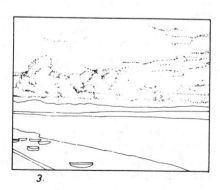

2.

3. The same scene using an orange filter.

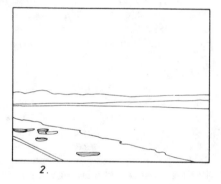

3.

Mattebox Accessories

In addition to filters and the Samcine Inclining Prism, a number of other useful accessories can be placed in front of a camera lens.

Cameraprompter

The Cinema Products Cameraprompter is a portable version of the prompting devices used on television cameras to superimpose a written script in front of the camera lens to enable the person on screen to read a text and look directly at the audience at the same time.

The text is written or typed onto a roll of clear plastic strip which is wound between rollers and mounted on the side of a special mattebox. It is illuminated by a battery-powered lamp from the rear of the lettering, and the reader sees it by reflection via an optical flat set at 45° to the optical axis. It is advanced by means of a variable-speed motor which may be remotely controlled by the reader or another person.

Panafade

The Panavision Panafade device is a pair of contrarotating polar screens which may be used to attenuate the light reaching the lens for the purpose of exposure control. Used with a Panastar camera it will automatically maintain a constant exposure as the camera speed is varied between, say, 24 and 120 fps, a difference of more than two stops.

Using two polar screens causes a loss of 2½ stops of light, requiring the basic exposure to be increased by this amount.

Lightflex

The purpose of the Lightflex system is to reflect a controlled amount of overall light back through the lens and onto the film as it passes through the camera for the purpose of 'flashing' the film.

The principal advantage of flashing the film in the camera, instead of having it flashed by the laboratory, is that any variation in the overall exposure setting affects the flashing to the same extent that the general exposure is affected, and therefore the degree of flashing is not affected by subsequent grading (timing) changes. Another advantage is that what you see through the reflex viewfinder is what you get on film, so the intensity of the effect may be set to suit the scene.

The Lightflex system (and flashing) is used to give additional exposure to the shadow areas, to increase the sensitivity of the film (particularly in the shadow areas), to reduce the contrast of a filmstock (particularly to modify reversal colour film to intercut with colour negative film), and to put an overall colour bias onto the shadow areas of an image, leaving the highlights virtually unaffected.

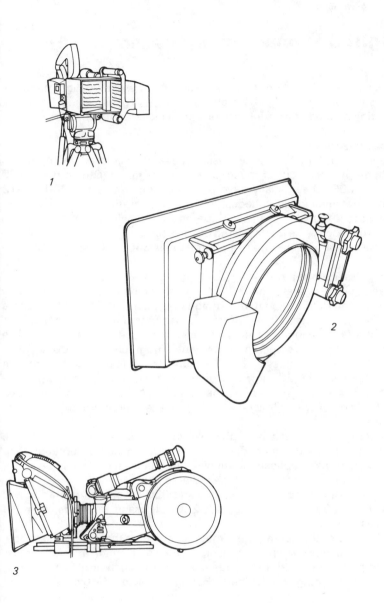

MATTEBOX ACCESSORIES

1. Cinema Products Cameraprompter portable prompter unit mounted on a
CP16-R/A 16mm camera; 2. Panavision Panafade variable neutral density filter;
3. Arnold & Richter Lightflex in-camera film flashing device.

Light Sources: Incandescent

Beyond the point where there is sufficient for exposure, light provides a means of enhancing the picture by imposing modelling, or detail, creating a mood or an atmosphere and 'filling' areas of shadow.

Incandescent bulbs

These lamps are the same basic type as those used for domestic lighting purposes but of much greater wattage, ranging between 200 and 10,000. They usually have a colour temperature of 3200 K (312 mireds) at their rated voltages. Initially comparatively inexpensive, incandescent bulbs blacken with age and lose their efficiency and as a consequence are now considered obsolescent.

The colour temperature of a photoflood is 3400 K (294 mireds).

Tungsten halogen bulbs

These bulbs use the same coiled tungsten filament as an incandescent bulb but operate at a very much higher temperature in an atmosphere of halogen gases. This effectively prevents almost all fall-off of brightness and loss of colour temperature due to blackening. The preferred colour temperature for cinematography is 3200 K (312 mireds). Like incandescent bulbs, tungsten halogen bulbs produce approximately 27–28 lumens of light per watt of electric energy consumed and although more expensive initially they last longer and, due to their compact size, may be used in smaller and more efficient lamp housings.

A tungsten halogen bulb gives exactly the same light output as a new incandescent light of equivalent wattage. Those incorporating their own reflector and optical system give out relatively more, as they make use of a greater percentage of the radiated light.

Wattages available are 150, 250 and 350 for battery operation and 200 to 10,000 for 120 or 220 and 240 volt usage, in a wide variety of shapes and forms.

Because of the nature of the material of which the envelope is made, tungsten-halogen lamps not incorporating a reflector and lens, must never be touched with bare fingers. A piece of cloth or gloves must be used when fitting a new bulb. Handling will cause blackening and premature failure. Should an expensive bulb be accidentally handled the finger marks should immediately be washed off with alcohol (white spirit is better than whisky).

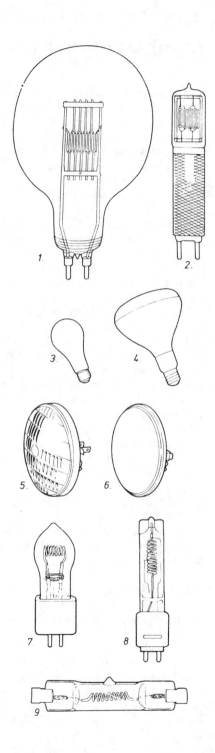

1. 10,000 w incandescent bulb;
2. Tungsten halogen bulb. Note
comparative sizes; 3. Normal
photoflood; 4. Reflector type
photoflood; 5. 650 w PAR-64 bulbs
with optical front glass; 6. 650 w
PAR-36 with clear front glass;
7. 600 w single-ended tungsten
halogen bulb; 8. 1000 w single-
ended tungsten halogen bulb;
9. Double-ended tungsten halogen
bulb (500-2000 w).

Light Sources: Non Incandescent

The most readily available light source, and the cheapest, is the sun. Bright and beautiful or miserable and dull it turns up for work exactly on time every morning and remains until it is scheduled to depart. Its quality, however, is completely inconsistent, except in rare locations like the middle of the desert. It can take every ounce of a cameraman's skill to control in such a manner that the results on the screen look as he wishes them to look, modelled as he wishes, and consistent for a whole series of scenes shot over a long period.

Carbon arc lamps

When a large quantity of controllable light from a single source is required, a 225 amp high-intensity carbon arc lamp, usually called a 'brute', is often used. Carbon arcs may be made to give light which approximates to either daylight or tungsten light by a suitable choice of carbons and filters.

Brutes require a specially generated high amperage low voltage DC supply and require heavy cabling between generator and lamp which must always be specially laid out. They are large, heavy and difficult to manoeuvre, require a heavy resistance unit, consume a pair of carbons at a fairly rapid rate (in a little over half an hour) and must be switched off periodically while the carbons are trimmed (renewed). Sometimes they splutter or make a noise or give off smoke and heat. They usually require one electrician to man each unit unless the producer is prepared to hold up the entire production while one man trims several lamps in turn. They require a special heavy duty stand with power operated lifting and are a significant item on any budget. Having said all that, when the light output of the type and power of which a brute is capable is required, there is no substitute other than the most powerful metal halide lamps.

A carbon arc lamp produces about 20 lumens of light for every watt of electric energy consumed.

Carbon arcs should never by operated without a glass in front of them, usually a fresnel lens, to absorb the excessive and dangerous UV light which they produce.

Metal halide lamps

These are highly efficient enclosed mercury arc discharge lamps which produce between 85 and 102 lumens of light per watt of electric energy. Metal halide lamps require an AC supply and must be used in conjunction with a ballast unit.

The light that they emit normally pulses at twice the rate of the AC supply frequency. In consequence, unless a special ballast unit is used specifically designed for filming purposes and which overcomes the pulsing problem, special precautions must be taken to ensure that the frequency of the supply, the camera speed and the shutter opening are compatible.

1. **Carbon arc**
A pair of carbons are consumed in
little more than half an hour.

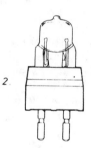

1.

2. **Metal halide (CID, CSI etc.)**
A 1000 w compact source iodide
metal halide bulb which is an
enclosed mercury arc discharge
lamp.

2.

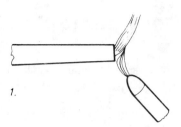

3. **Metal halide (HMI etc.)**
A 1200 w HMI mercury metal iodide
metal halide bulb.

3.

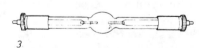

169

Controlling Sunlight

The great advantage of sunlight over artificial light is that it is cheap and covers a large area. Unfortunately its suitability is not always assured. It can be too bright (casting dark shadows), too high (blackening artist's eyes), from the wrong direction and inconsistent, making continuity of lighting difficult.

Weather forecasts

Weather forecasts in temperate parts of the world are not always correct. If sunshine is essential for a particular scene, it is always a wise plan to schedule an alternative 'bad weather cover' just in case.

Many a successful film has been made ignoring the weather, with scenes shot in sunshine put next to scenes photographed in dull conditions. Skill and co-operation on the part of the director, the cameraman and the laboratory can make differences unnoticeable by an audience.

High luminosity lamps

Metal halide lamps, carbon arc lamps (brutes) and the most powerful incandescent lamps are of sufficient brilliance, depending upon the strength of the sunlight and the size of area to be illuminated, to fill the hard shadows caused by sunlight or to substitute for sunlight.

Reflectors

The poor man's brute, these may be used singly or *en masse.* The ideal material for covering reflectors is silver coloured plastic-coated sheeting. This is available in various degrees of reflectivity ranging from the almost mirror-like to the type which disperses light over a wide area. Plastic reflector material will withstand rough handling, will not scratch or tear easily and may be cleaned as required. Reflectors which may be bowed can spread the light and reduce its intensity.

If the sun is in the wrong direction to be reflected satisfactorily, two reflectors may be used, a hard type to direct the sun on to the more normal soft type which redirects it to the subject.

Nets, butterflies, scrims, silks and blackouts

In hard sunlight it is sometimes necessary to place a large piece of semi-transparent or even opaque material between the sun and the principal artists and use artificial or reflected light to illuminate them independently. In this way, it is possible to light with all the modelling required for the highest standards of feature film production, while at the same time using daylight to illuminate the background. Care must be taken to ensure that the artificial light is the same colour temperature as the background lighting.

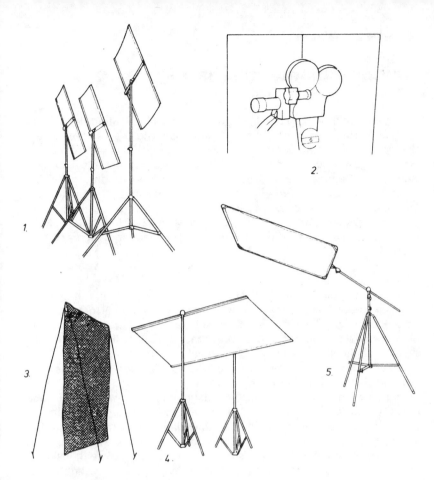

CONTROL OF DIRECT SUNLIGHT

1. **Mounted reflectors**
Reflectors may be used to redirect sunlight and if bowable may also spread the light and reduce the intensity.

2. **Polystyrene sheet**
Camera set-up in front of large sheets of white polystyrene which reflect just sufficient light back into the subject to fill shadows, reduce contrast and yet not produce any directional lighting of their own.

3. **Blackout**
Blackout which blocks out all direct sunlight from a particular area.

4. **Net**
A large 12 or 15 ft (3 or 4m) square of silk or net attached to a frame which may be rigged over a portion of a scene. Used especially where principal artists or action is set and should have individual lighting for modelling purposes.

5. **Silk**
5 ft (1.5m) square silk may be used to reduce harsh light falling on an individual actor.

Colour-Balancing Lighting

When shooting with colour film stock all light illuminating the subject, or photographed as background, should appear to the camera to be of the same colour temperature. This may be 3200K (313 Mireds), in which case any daylight illumination within the scene must be controlled with orange filters. Or it can be daylight, when an orange filter must be used on the camera, reducing the exposure by $\frac{1}{2}$ stop, and any incandescent lamps covered with blue filters, halving their effectiveness. Arc lights (brutes) may burn with daylight or artificial light (LCT) carbons and with a little filtering may be made to match any other form of lighting.

Balancing daylight

When lighting with incandescent light (3200K) any daylight may either be blacked-out completely or else orange coloured filter material must be placed over all windows and openings. Non-photographic orange filter material similar in colour to the Wratten 85 is available in 8ft.×4ft. sheets of rigid acrylic or in long rolls of gelatine or plastic film.

Acrylic sheets are to be preferred when an 'in shot' window is to be covered because it remains absolutely flat, giving only a single reflection from each lamp. Flexible plastic material, on the other hand, tends to buckle and show a multiplicity of reflections which are difficult to eliminate unless it is adhering to the window or stretched flat on a frame. If acrylic sheet is tilted, even a single reflection may be lost.

Acrylic sheets may be cut to size with an ordinary saw to fit inside an opening of specific size or simply hung up over the window on the outside.

These filters may be used repeatedly but, like any other materials containing red dyes they are subject to fading and should be stored away from strong daylight when not in use.

Additionally, sheets of neutral density acrylic may be used to balance the brightness of the exterior to that of the interior lighting. Sheets of ND 0·3, 0·6 and 0·9 may be piled one on top of the other, as necessary, and changed as the intensity of the daylight varies to make it appear constant from the inside.

Balancing artificial lighting

Artificial lights, being predominantly red in their colour balance, must be covered with blue filters to make them match daylight.

Heat resistant blue gelatine (plastic film) or glass filters often reduce the intensity of usable light by about 50% (1 stop).

Dichroic filters (partial mirrors which reflect only the red part of the light, leaving the remainder predominantly blue) are inconsistent in the colour of the light which they pass and should be checked before use.

Gelatine filters are available as full (—132 mireds), half (—66

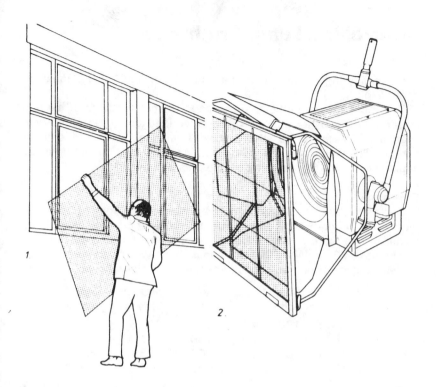

COLOUR BALANCE FILTERS

Window filter
1. Placing an '85' rigid acrylic window filter in position. Light entering a room will then be balanced to tungsten lighting

Lamp filter
2. Tungsten type lamp filtered with either a blue gelatine (plastic) filter or a dichroic filter to balance the light to daylight.

mireds) and quarter blue (—33 mireds) and so are the most controllable. If it is necessary to make the light more blue or red to suit the circumstances it is only a matter of choosing the correct degree of blue filter.

Gelatine filters are usually held in frames placed a short distance in front of the light. Unfiltered spill light must not be allowed to affect the scene, giving it a red cast. Some directors of photography insist that a gelatine filter must completely cover the front of the lamp to filter the spill light as well as the main beam.

Too much light may be as undesirable as too little.

Controlling Lamp Brightness

Creative lighting requires that the intensity of any lighting must be controllable.

The most simple methods are to flood or spot the lamp or move it closer or further away. If more control is required it may be necessary to change the lamp from a smaller to a larger one. Some lamps incorporate bulbs which have two filaments, in which case the light may be doubled or halved by switching on one or both filaments.

Dimmers

Variable resistances (dimmers) may be placed in a lighting circuit to reduce the brightness of a lamp. Unfortunately these also reduce the colour temperature of the lamps and so are only suitable for use with colour film up to the point that the colour change becomes noticeable.

Reducing the supply voltage affects the lighting as follows:

Bulb voltage	Supply voltage	Colour temperature K	Mireds	Light output
120 (240)	120 (240)	3,200	312·5	100%
120 (240)	110 (220)	3,100	322	75%
120 (240)	100 (200)	3,000	333	55%
120 (240)	90 (180)	2,900	345	38%

The voltage at the lamp head should always be correct. A volt meter is a useful accessory for checking purposes.

If the colour temperature of all the lighting is affected, the problem is less serious as an overall correction may be made at the printing stage. It is when just one or two lights are dimmed, particularly if they are illuminating an artist's face, that variations are noticeable.

Dimmers are normally used when an artist is seen to switch a practical light on or off or light a candle during the course of a scene. It gives a softer effect and reduces the jump from dark to bright, or vice-versa. Dimmers for lights of more than 5,000W are large and heavy items of equipment.

Shutters and reflectors

An overall means of reducing the intensity of a light without affecting the colour temperature is a venetian-blind-like shutter or reflector. These work very well, particularly from a distance. But the light should not be broken up into strips and the intensity at the top of the picture should remain the same as that at the bottom.

Wire mesh (scrim)

Fine stainless steel wire mesh, windowlite or scrim may be placed immediately in front of a light to reduce its brilliance. This method is particularly useful when partial control of the light beam is required to

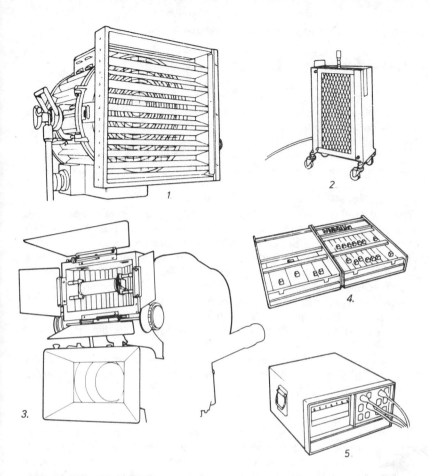

LAMP BRIGHTNESS CONTROL

1. **Adjustable shutter**
Controls lamp brightness without affecting colour temperature.

2. **Resistance dimmer**
5,000 w resistance type dimmer which may be used on AC or DC.

3. **Panavision 'Panalite' camera lamp**
This unit uses a variable reflector to dim the light and is particularly suitable for mounting on a studio camera.

4. **Berkey Colortran dimmer console unit**
Used in conjunction with dimmer pack 5.

5. **Berkey Colortran dimmer pack**
Consists of 12 × 3.6 kw and 6 × 6.6 kw dimmers, it operates from AC only.

even out the brightness falling at different distances from the source. For instance, if one lamp is illuminating two people, one of whom is five feet away and the other ten feet away, the light on the nearer person may be held back by using layers of wire mesh placed over part of the lamp face.

Lighting is expensive; too much is a waste, too little a disaster.

How Much Light?

A cameraman is often called upon to estimate how much lighting should be installed to illuminate a certain area. This may be a closet, a room, a hall, a cathedral or a football field.

Most British and American cameramen use the 'foot candle' as a unit of measurement. Elsewhere the 'lux' is used. 1 fc=10·76 lux, 1 lux=0·09 fc.

Lighting levels

When shooting in ambient light conditions the cameraman sets his exposure according to the light level, but where a scene must be lit he sets the illumination to a pre-determined level according to the exposure at which he wishes to work. For instance, if wishing to work at an aperture of T5·6 and using a film stock rated at EI 100 (exposure being the normal 1/50th sec.) then a lighting level of 400 fc (4300 lux) is required.

When lighting very large areas, money may be saved by using a faster filmstock (EI 400 or faster), faster lenses (f1·3 or faster), a camera with a wider shutter opening (200°) and force-developing the film (EI 1000 or faster).

Very low levels of lighting have an additional advantage in that any practical lighting such as street, vehicle or natural window lighting tends to stand out more.

Lamp efficiency

The amount of illumination produced by different types of luminaires varies enormously. Sealed-beam lamps, incorporating deep reflectors and pre-focused lenses, give the most usable light for the power consumed but have the disadvantage that the beam angle cannot be controlled other than by pointing groups of bulbs in different directions. Fresnel lamps are the most controllable and give the hardest shadows, but are comparatively inefficient. Soft lights, which spread light over a wide area, are the least efficient and give the softest shadows.

If the Peak Beam Intensity (candles) of a particular type of light is known for a particular flood spot setting, or the level of illumination at one particular distance is known, then by using the accompanying tables the level of illumination at any other distance may be calculated.

Because the light of the various types of luminaires varies so greatly, cameramen are advised to measure the light produced by the luminaires they most frequently use and keep their own notes in regard to Peak Beam Intensity at minimum and maximum beam angles. Manufacturers' figures and specifications are not always reliable or accurate for new lamps, much less for used equipment which can vary even more.

Assessing light coverage

No lamp used for general cinematography gives an absolutely even illumination. The standard practice is to measure the light level in the central and brightest part of the beam and measure the coverage to the point where the intensity drops to 50% of that in the centre.

Using a pocket calculator the level of illumination may be calculated using the formula: illumination=Peak Beam Candles÷Distance÷Distance. If the calculations are done in feet the answer will be in foot candles; if in metres, in lux. Such calculations are not accurate at distances less than 20x the diameter of the front of the lamp.

If the angle of the beam and the distance from the subject are known, the beam width may be calculated using the formula: Beam Width=the tangent of half the beam angle multiplied by twice the distance.

'How much light' tables

If the Peak Beam Intensity (candelas) of a lamp at a particular flood/spot setting is known or the level of illumination at one particular distance is known, then from the tables below the level of illumination at other distances may be calculated. (Not valid at distances less than 20 times the diameter of the front of the lamp.)

DISTANCE (FT.)

Peak beam intensity (candelas)	10	12	15	17	20	25	30	40	50	60	75
				Illumination (ft candles)							
10000	100	70	44	35	25	16	11	6	4	3	2
15000	150	100	67	50	37	24	17	10	6	4	3
22500	225	155	100	75	55	36	25	14	9	6	4
22750	350	235	150	115	85	54	37	21	13	9	6
50000	500	350	220	175	125	80	55	30	20	14	9
75000	750	500	333	260	200	120	85	50	30	21	13
115000	1150	800	500	400	300	180	125	70	45	32	20
170000		1200	750	600	425	270	190	110	70	48	30
250000			1100	850	625	400	280	150	100	70	44
400000				1400	1000	650	450	250	160	110	70
600000					1500	1000	650	375	240	160	100
900000						1500	1000	560	360	250	160

DISTANCE (M)

	3·0	3·5	4·0	5·0	6·0	8·0	10	12	15	18	22
				Illumination (lux)							
10000	1100	800	625	400	275	160	100	70	45	30	21
15000	1700	1200	940	600	400	235	150	100	67	45	30
22500	2500	1850	1400	900	625	350	225	155	100	70	45
33750	3750	2750	2000	1350	1000	525	337	235	150	100	70
50000	5500	4000	3000	2000	1400	780	500	350	220	155	100
115000	8000	6000	4500	3000	2000	1200	750	520	333	230	150
170000	13000	10000	7000	4600	3200	1800	1150	800	500	350	240
250000		14000	10000	6800	5000	2600	1700	1200	750	525	350
400000			16000	10000	7000	4000	2500	1700	1100	770	500
600000				16000	11000	6250	4000	2750	1750	1200	800
900000					17000	9400	6000	4200	2700	1850	1200
						14000	9000	6250	4000	2800	2000

How Much Light Lamps Give

The design of a luminaire affects the amount of useful light produced, the width and evenness of its beam, its capability of forming a shadow and its controllability. Sealed beam bulbs (PAR 36 and 64) and floodlights in deep elliptical reflectors give most usable lights, fresnel lamps are the most controllable and soft lights, which scatter light over a wide area, the least efficient in terms of light concentration.

Measuring light output

A lamp shone on a plain flat surface shows the distribution of its light.

The usable spread of a light is taken to be from the point either side of centre where the intensity falls to half that of the centre. The beam angle is from the half peak intensity points back to the lamp. To calculate the capability of a particular luminaire it may be necessary to know the angle of the light beam, especially at full spot and full flood. If reliable manufacturers' figures are not available the simplest method of ascertaining the beam angle is to set the lamp up at right angles to a wall (at least 20 times the width of the front aperture away), switch on, plot the beam width with an exposure meter noting the centre brightness and the points each side of centre where the intensity falls by half, draw two lines on the floor from these limits back to the lamp and measure the angle with a protractor. A more accurate calculation may be made using the formula:

$$\frac{\text{Beam angle}°}{2} = \frac{\frac{1}{2}\text{Beam width}}{\text{distance}} \times 2$$

To calculate the beam angle° using an electronic calculator with trigonometrical functions use the following order:

Beam width; ÷; 2; ÷; distance; =; Tan^{-1}; ×; 2;=

If the distance and the beam angle are known, the width or spread of the beam may be calculated using the formula:

$$\text{Beam width} = \text{Distance} \times \text{Tan} \left(\frac{\text{Beam angle}°}{2} \right) \times 2$$

or, by programming a trig function calculator as follows:

Beam angle°; ÷; 2, Tan; ×; distance; ×; 2; =

If the beam angle is known, the distance at which a lamp must be set to cover a certain area may be calculated using the formula:

$$\text{Distance} = \frac{\text{Beam width}}{2} \div \text{Tan} \frac{\text{Beam angle}°}{2}$$

which may be programmed on a trig function calculator viz:

Beam angle°; ÷; 2; Tan; M+; C; Beam width; ÷; 2; ÷; RM;=

178

BEAM ANGLE/LAMP COVERAGE

If the beam angle of a lamp is known, the coverage at a particular distance can be calculated from the Table below.

Beam coverage – distance (ft. and in.)

Beam angle°	10	12	15	17	20	25	30	40	50	60	75
				Beam width (50% peak illumination)							
10	1-9	2-1	2-7	3-0	3-6	4-4	5-3	7-0	8-9	10-6	13-1
15	2-8	3-2	3-11	4-6	5-3	6-7	7-11	10-6	13-2	15-9	19-9
22	3-11	4-8	5-10	6-7	7-9	9-8	11-7	15-6	19-5	23-4	29-0
30	5-4	6-6	8-0	9-1	10-9	13-5	16-0	21-6	26-9	32-0	40-0
40	7-3	8-9	11-0	12-4	14-6	18-2	21-9	29-0	36-0	44-0	55-0
60	11-6	13-9	17-6	19-6	23-0	29-0	35-0	46-0	58-0	69-0	87-0

Distance (m)

	3.0	3.5	4.0	4.5	5.0	6.0	8.0	10	12	15	18	22
10	0.52	0.61	0.70	0.78	0.87	1.05	1.40	1.75	2.01	2.62	3.15	3.85
15	0.79	0.92	1.05	1.18	1.32	1.58	2.11	2.65	3.16	3.95	4.74	5.80
22	1.17	1.36	1.55	1.75	1.94	2.33	3.11	3.90	4.67	5.80	7.00	8.55
30	1.61	1.88	2.14	2.41	2.68	3.22	4.29	5.35	6.43	8.00	9.65	11.80
40	2.18	2.55	2.91	3.28	3.64	4.37	5.82	7.30	8.74	11.00	13.10	16.00
60	3.50	4.04	4.62	5.20	5.77	6.93	9.24	11.50	13.86	17.50	21.00	25.00

Fresnel Luminaires

Placing a reflector behind a bulb to concentrate the light makes a lamp more efficient; placing a condenser lens in front of it to focus the light, makes it more controllable.

A fresnel lens is a whole plano-convex lens thinned down in a stepped form.

A fresnel lens makes it possible to flood and spot the light, a facility used either as a means of controlling the area covered or the intensity of the illumination at a particular point.

For maximum light output it is necessary to occasionally check that the reflector and lamp are correctly positioned on an optical axis with the fresnel lens.

Tungsten halogen bulbs

As already stated, tungsten halogen bulbs are more efficient than incandescent lamps in terms of light output over a long period and are therefore preferable. Special bulbs are available which may be used in any fresnel fitting as a replacement for the original incandescent bulbs.

When a tungsten halogen bulb is used in a fresnel fitting a wider angle of flood is possible due to the fact that these bulbs are more compact and are thus able to go closer to the lens.

Dual filament

A very useful type of bulb is one containing two filaments which, when used in a suitable lamp housing, may be switched individually. By this means it is possible to halve or double the light output of a lamp without affecting the colour temperature.

Cleanliness

Fresnel lenses and lamp reflectors attract dirt which becomes baked on to the surface. For maximum light output, bulbs, lenses and reflectors should be cleaned thoroughly and often.

Safety

When lamps are to be fixed above people, safety lines should be attached to all detachable parts, i.e. barn doors and filters, so that in the event of a support failing there will be no personal injury.

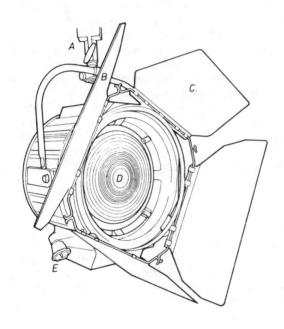

FRESNEL LUMINAIRE

This particular model may be hung from a rail or placed on a stand, fitted with either a single or double filament bulb, be operated manually or remotely by a long pole.
Various models take 100, 200, 750, 1000, 1250/2500, 2000, 2500/5000, 5000 or 10000 W bulbs.

Fresnel Luminaire Control

Because of their carefully designed optical system, i.e. reflector and fresnel lens behind and in front of the bulb, fresnel luminaires offer greater possibilities for control than any other type of lamp, even if they are not the most efficient in terms of light output compared with light produced, a most important consideration when lighting creatively and paying attention to modelling and the nuances of light and shade.

Doors, archways or windows which are never seen can be implied by throwing suitable shadows on the wall. As the bulb is moved towards the fresnel lens the lamp is flooded, as it is moved back towards the reflector it is spotted. When a fresnel lens lamp is first positioned it can be set to full spot for centering purposes and flooded out as required from there. If a cameraman or gaffer wishes to check the setting of a fresnel lamp he should stand in the artist's position and, with the lamp switched on, look at it through a dark glass or contrast-viewing filter. The filament will be seen as a bright spot relative to the centre of the lens.

Barn doors
Fitted to the front of the lamp housing immediately in front of the fresnel lens, barn doors are large flaps which may be hinged open or closed individually or rotated as a unit. They control the spread of light, create shadows and prevent spill light shining into the camera lens or elsewhere that it is not required. Most effective when the lamp is at full flood they have little effect apart from softening off the edge of the light when the lamp is at full spot.

Barn doors set to produce a vertical beam of light are said to be set 'English', and 'Chinese' when horizontal.

Snoots are wide tubes which fit onto the front of a lamp. They restrict the light to a circular pattern.

Pole operation
Lamps which are hung from overhead fixtures and are out of reach for normal control purposes may be fitted with special control knobs in the form of a cone with a bar across it. A long pole with a hook on the end of it may be inserted into these cones to actuate the various lamp controls. Pole operation may be used for switching on or off, for panning and tilting the lamp and for adjusting the flood and spot setting. The opening of the barn doors and their rotational position may also be set by pole operation (knobs are individually coloured for easy recognition).

Local lighting
When a cameraman wishes to illuminate just a very small area, smaller or more irregular than he might be able to control with barn doors and to save cluttering up the set with flags, etc., aluminium foil, as used in kitchens for baking, can be placed across the front of a lamp and a hole made as required to pass just the right amount of light.

182

FRESNEL LUMINAIRE CONTROL

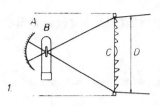

Reflector lamp
1. Fresnel set in spot position;
2. Fresnel set in flood position.
When the bulb and reflector are far
from the fresnel lens the light beam
is narrow. When the bulb and the
reflector are close to the fresnel the
beam is full flood.
A. Reflector; B. Bulb;
C. Fresnel; D. Light beam.

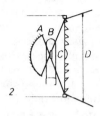

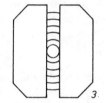

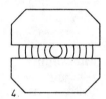

Barn doors
3. Barn door set 'English'.
4. Barn door set 'Chinese'.

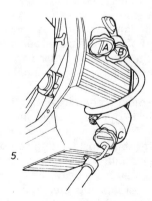

Pole operation
Pole operated controls.
A. Tilt control; B. Pan control;
C. Flood/spot control.

General Purpose Lighting

'A great deal of light with little control' is a fair description of many tungsten halogen luminaires which do not have a front fresnel lens.

Open bulb lamps
A bare tungsten halogen lamp with an open front and an efficient reflector behind the bulb will give more light than the equivalent fresnel lamp. It is possible to vary the beam diameter and intensity of these lamps by moving the bulbs backwards in relation to the reflector, but the barn doors are completely ineffective other than as a means of gently shading off the light. If a sharply defined shadow is required a flag or gobo must be placed some distance in front of the lamp.

These luminaires, being compact and efficient, are very suitable for use as small lightweight units that may be easily and cheaply transported. News and documentary cameramen, especially, make great use of them. They are available in 250, 650, 800, 1000 and 2000 W sizes.

Multi-lights
A number of compact 650 or 1000 watt sealed-beam tungsten halogen bulbs, each of which incorporates a parabolic aluminised reflector (called PAR bulbs) and a collecting lens in front, are often mounted together in groups of 4, 6, 9, 12 or more. Groups of nine 650 watt PAR 36 bulbs are often called a 'nine light' or a 'mini-brute'.

Groups of twelve or more 1000 watt PAR 64 bulbs are often called 'maxi-brutes', and groups of 24 are sometimes called a 'Dino-light'. These lamps are often suspended very high up to give a hard over-all light.

Multi-light luminaires usually incorporate the means of switching bulbs on and off to increase or decrease the light output without changing the colour temperature. When very few bulbs only are lit, say two or four and the unit is placed close to a person or object, there is a danger of multiple shadows.

The most economical PAR bulbs to use are the plain white 120 v types. It is usual to run them paired and in series, where the mains supply is 220 or 240 v. They are available with either 'spot', 'medium' or 'flood' optical systems, but most lighting companies standardise on the medium type.

A nine light 'FAY' lamp draws over 50 amps of power at 120 v and so requires suitably heavy cabling. It is sometimes advantageous to wire smaller groups together so that lighter cables may be used. For instance, four 120 v bulbs wired in pairs and placed in series, draw less than 11 amps from a 240 v supply and so may be operated off a normal wall plug. Two such 'four light' groups may be placed side by side to form an 'eight light' and powered off individual wall plugs.

Multiple lights are often used in conjunction with white reflectors to give 'bounce' soft-lighting.

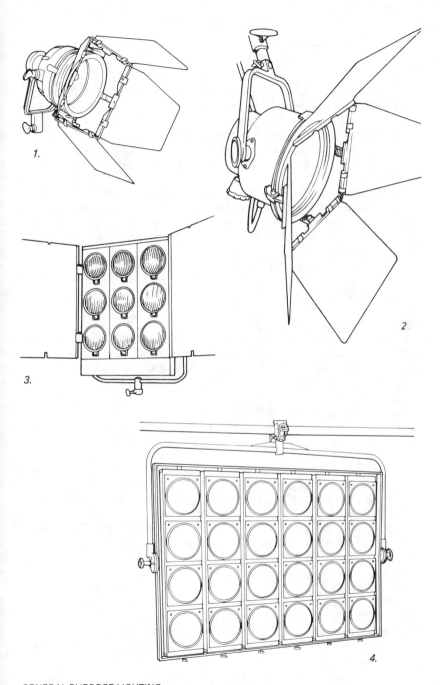

GENERAL PURPOSE LIGHTING

1. 650 watt 'Red head' quartz light; 2. 2K 'Blond' quartz light; 3. 9 × 650 watt 'Mini brute'; 4. 24 × 1000 watt Maxi-brute.

Soft Lights

Modern colour film stocks have greatly reduced the need for much of the hard lighting of the days of black and white which would separate a foreground subject from its background.

Soft lights, which illuminate a wide area from a large area source give a shadowless light akin to that of a northern sky, which is kind and flattering to both the artist and to the apparent skill of the cinematographer.

Shadowless lighting requires that the source of the light be broadly based. Hence some soft light fittings are 4ft. (1·2m) across. Smaller units are available which only give a shadowless light if they are placed close to the subject or if several such lamps are placed side by side to form a broad source.

Soft lights are often used in conjunction with hard lights to provide a fill light with which to reduce the contrast of the lighting without creating double shadows.

Bashers, broads and scoops

Luminaires with one or two open bulbs surrounded by a matte white reflector, are often placed close to the camera as fill lights. They soften the shadows around the artists' eyes and under their noses and chins and give lively looking pin-point reflections in the pupils.

Blimp basher and obie lights

Lamps fixed to the camera immediately above the lens are also used to fill in the shadows of artists' faces, particularly when shooting close-ups.

If the artist and the camera move closer together or further apart, it is necessarily to control the intensity of the light to maintain a constant illumination. This must not affect the colour temperature or the even spread of the light. It may be done by passing successively thicker layers of fine mesh in front of the lamp to reduce the light output without recourse to reducing the voltage to the lamp which would, of course, redden the light (see page 160).

Studio fittings

Clusters of large bulbs, surrounded by wire frames from which white netting is draped are sometimes hung high up in a studio. These give a very soft overall basic light, rather like that from a white sky and are particularly useful when very large open sets, such as street scenes are to be illuminated.

In the US, these units are known as Chicken coops.

Sky pans, large white dishes 2 or 3ft. in diameter with a single 5000 or 10,000 W bulb mounted in front are still used in film studios to illuminate cycloramas and backgrounds. Compared with modern

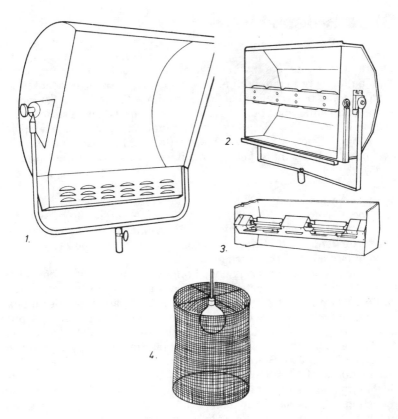

SOFT LIGHTS

1. 4000 W softlight;   2. 2000 W 'Zap' softlight;   3. Lampholder rotated for
bulb replacement;   4. Studio white netting overhead light.

cyclorama lighting, as used in TV studios, they are very inefficient and
make it difficult to obtain absolutely even illumination . . . but traditions
die hard.

Colour temperature
As all of these types of lamps rely upon the light being reflected, it
follows that the reflection surfaces should be kept a pure white and very
clean in the interests of efficiency.

Shadowless Lighting

Where soft lights are not available or where even broader based illumination is required, normal lamps such as fresnels, floodlights and even arcs and metal halide lights may be made to produce a flat form of illumination either by 'bouncing' the light off a broad white surface or by placing a very large sheet of translucent material between the lamp and the subject. Such a sheet might be 10ft. (3m) across. The shadows become softer as the reflector or diffuser is moved further from the lamp.

Bounced light

The most simple and readily available white surface from which to bounce light, especially on location, is a white ceiling. Lamps may be tipped upwards, and, if necessary, barndoored or flagged (goboed) to prevent direct light from reaching the subject.

Similarly a light may be bounced off a white wall or a white painted piece of plywood or hardboard fixed in a suitable position. Sheets of white polystyrene are often carried around on location for this purpose. They have the advantage of being extremely light in weight and slightly flexible and inexpensive. Lumps may be broken off to make the sheet fit into some restricted space. Silver space blankets used by campers are popular in the United States.

An additional advantage of using bounce light where space is limited is that the lamp may be sited high and out of the way while the reflecting surface takes up only a minimum of space, far less than would be taken by a similarly placed soft light.

Translucent materials

Various materials may be placed a short distance in front of a 'hard' luminaire to diffuse and broaden the area of a light. Most commonly used, because they are so inexpensive are tracing paper, greaseproof paper, spun glass, heatproof opalescent plastic, dacron, windolite or other such materials.

Ground or frosted glass may be used in an obie light or other similar. Such glass is often cut into thin strips to prevent cracking due to heat.

Areas of hard lighting may be created by making holes in the translucent materials. Holes may be patched with transparent tape to increase diffusion.

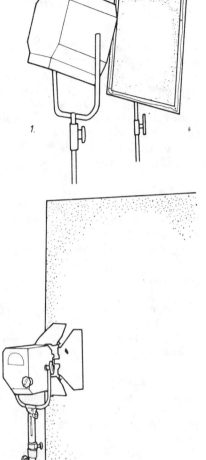

1.

1. **Transmission**
A large sheet of translucent material,
such as spun-glass tracing paper
placed between the lamp and the
subject.

2. **Reflection**
Incandescent lamp directed towards
a white painted board or polystyrene
sheet to provide 'bounce' softlight.

2.

Carbon Arc Lamps (Brutes)

When the need is there and time and money are also available, 225 amp arc lights (brutes) are often used to fill in hard sun shadows, simulate sunshine and/or to light a large area from a single source and direction. Brutes are heavyweight equipment, require a DC generator, heavy cables, heavy transportation; usually one electrician to operate each lamp, extra time to set up compared with other lights and time to trim and change carbons every forty minutes.

However, where a great deal of controllable light is required there is no real substitute for a brute.

Modern versions

Many who have not used the latest lightweight and compact arc lamp equipment may be reluctant to use brutes because of stories and experiences of the past but like all other equipment used in motion picture production, brutes have undergone much development in recent times and are now smaller, lighter and less of a drama to use than heretofore.

Two lightweight units are available, both of the same power (225 amps), one with the standard 24¾in. (630mm) fresnel and the other with a 14in. (355mm) lens.

The 'baby' model may be supplied with a choice of fresnel condenser lenses, the 'hot' lens giving a wider angle than the 'cold' lens.

Older models

Notwithstanding the foregoing remarks, the previous generation of equipment, where the mechanism may be detached from the body of the lamp for ease of handling and transportation purposes, is still much used.

Because the combined weight of the body and mechanism of a full size brute is considerable, such lamps can not be supported on normal lighting stands but use special heavy-duty units, usually called 'molevators', which incorporate electrically operated elevation, powered by the same supply as the lamp.

Technical considerations

The 225 amp carbon arc lamp requires a 73 volt DC electrical supply. A resistance must be placed in the supply line near the lamp head to reduce the voltage from the 115v usually available.

The supply is connected to a pair of carbons which are touched together to strike the arc and then drawn apart to create a flame of intense luminosity.

As the arc burns the carbons are consumed and an automatic feed mechanism moves the carbons continuously towards each other, keeping the gap constant.

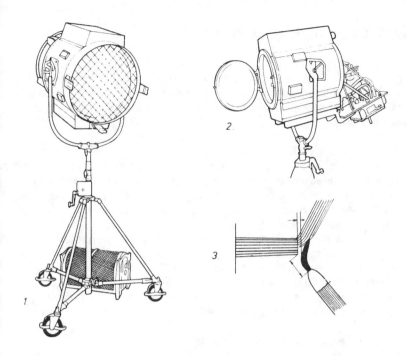

CARBON ARC LAMPS

1. **Brute**
225 amp lightweight Brute, mounted on lightweight wind-up stand and resistance.

2. **Baby Brute**
Baby Brute with 14in fresnel lens open and its mechanism tilted out.

3. **Carbons**
Normal appearance of burning arc and relative positions of carbons, which are adapted to maintain a consistent separation while the lamp is operating.

Colour temperature
The colour temperature of the light from a carbon arc may be selected by the type of carbons burned and the filter used viz:

Light	Carbon Type	Filter
'Daylight'	White Flame	WFG, Y1
3,200K (312 Mireds)	White Flame	MT2+Y1, MT/Y, Full CTO
3,200K (312 Mireds)	Yellow Flame	YF

Cyclorama Lighting

Special luminaires are available for illuminating cycloramas and backdrops, which have an asymmetric pattern of light distribution and ensure that a large surface may be illuminated evenly by lights placed overhead only.

Placing cyclorama lighting
In order to achieve an even distribution of light from varying distances a very sophisticated lamp reflector design must be employed. It follows that equal care must be taken in placing the lamps at the correct angle of incidence to the backing, at the correct distance away and with similar distances between lamps.

To cover a surface 26ft. (8m) high, for instance, a typical brand of cyclorama light must be set level with the top of the backing, be tilted down at an angle of 20°, be at a distance of 10ft. (3m) from the top and be spaced 8ft. (2·5m) apart.

Special luminaires are also available for placing on the floor when it is inconvenient to use the proper overhead lights.

Cabling systems for cyclorama lighting
Where cyclorama lights are made up into clusters of four lamps, each with a different coloured filter, in a permanent situation, it is most convenient to use a wiring loom made up of 9 core cable specially designed for the purpose.

Traditional backdrop lighting
Studios very often use large luminaires with open lamps and a simple matte white reflector, called skypans, to illuminate backdrops. Because they give a symmetrical light distribution they should be set at a greater distance away from the illuminated surface than the more modern luminaires.

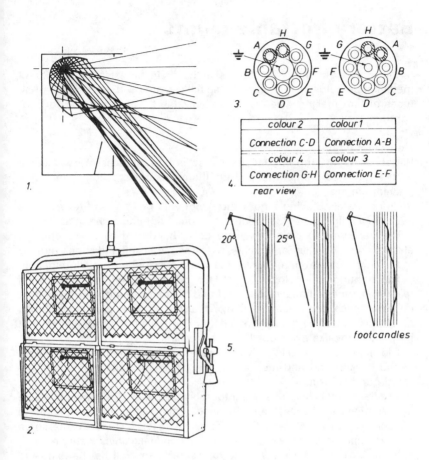

colour 2	colour 1
Connection C-D	Connection A-B
colour 4	colour 3
Connection G-H	Connection E-F

rear view

CYCLORAMA LIGHTING

1. **Top light**
Asymmetric pattern of light distribution of a cyclorama top light.

2. **Cyclorama lighting unit**
A group of four lights, red, green, blue and white, give full control of colour.

3. **Cyclorama cable**
Colour code for 9-core cyclorama cable.

4. **Cable connection**
Cyclorama units in permanent or semi-permanent installations are most
conveniently connected to the dimmers and power supply with a special 9-core
cable.

5. **Evenness of illumination**
With correct placing a cyclorama light gives overall even illumination from a
single direction.
Incorrect angle of setting results in uneven illumination.
Incorrect distance of lamp from backdrop results in uneven illumination.

Battery Portable Lights

Small lightweight units with 150, 250 or 350W 30v tungsten bulbs or 200W metal halide bulbs, using a flicker-free ballast, are used extensively for all types of film making when it is impracticable to use any other form of lighting.

Newsreel usage

Battery portable lights are one of the most important accessories available to the newsreel cameraman. With them, insufficient light can rarely prevent filming.

Unfortunately, having a hot centre spot with rapid fall-off towards the edges, such lights are not conducive to good lighting technique.

The very way in which they are used, hand-held by a non-creative electrician or assistant or attached to the camera itself and aimed directly at the centre of action, makes for the worst possible form of illumination.

The lighting effect looks even less pleasant when reproduced on television, where the faces burn out and the background, which the light does not reach, goes black. At its worst, a shot of, say, a person arriving at an airport, filmed by the light of a battery portable lamp shone directly at him, may look like a snowball in a coal cellar.

The situation may be improved by pointing the centre beam of the light at the background and just letting the edge light fall on the principal foreground subject.

Like flashlights used for still photography, exposure for battery portable light filming may be calculated by dividing the distance from the light to the subject into an exposure factor. To calculate this factor the cameraman should stand, say, 10ft. away from the light and take an exposure reading with an incident light meter. The exposure factor will be the exposure given, multiplied by the distance.

Documentary use

One of the most useful applications for battery portable lighting is in the TV documentary field, where interviews and other close-ups of people are frequently photographed in any and all types of daylight. Here, such a lamp can improve on the ambient light. Even on a sunny day, hard shadows about the interviewee's face may be filled by a spotted battery light held two or three feet away, just out of the picture. On a dull day a battery light may be used to give modelling and lift a face out from the background.

When used in daylight a blue filter must be fitted over the light to correct the colour temperature. It is advantageous to use the dichroic type of daylight correction filter which will pass more light than blue glass or gelatine.

194

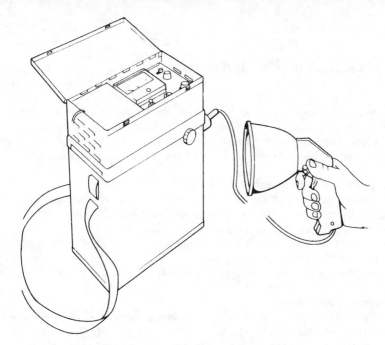

BATTERY PORTABLE LIGHT

Lightweight unit of the type used by newsreel or documentary cameraman or by feature film cameraman when other types of lighting are impracticable. The controls are incorporated with the battery pack.

Feature use
In the controlled conditions of feature film production, there are occasions when battery lights are more convenient than mains lighting and provided they are treated like any other light, there is no reason why they should not be as acceptable as any other lamp of the same (limited) output.

Fuses
If the battery unit has a fused circuit at least two spare fuses should always be readily at hand.

Battery/mains interchangeability
Certain lamp heads may be used either for 30v battery-powered operation or for a 120 or 220/240v mains operation, by the simple expedient of changing the bulb to suit the supply voltage. This system is fine as long as the user remembers which bulb is in the lamphead. Failure to do so makes the economy of interchangeability an expensive luxury.

Transportable Lighting

Not every cameraman, by a long way, thinks in terms of arc lights, 10Ks or nine-lights when he needs extra illumination. Perhaps, many rarely use lamps more powerful than 1,000 or 2,000 watts and limit themselves to the types which they are able to carry and fit personally.

Compact and lightweight
The folded size, weight and convenience of lamps, may determine whether or not any lights are to be used for a particular job. Luminaires of this type invariably use tungsten halogen lamps. Some may be spotted and flooded; others give a shadowless soft light. Others again are just very versatile general purpose fittings. Clip-on fittings may obviate the need to take a stand for every lamp carried.

Power requirements
Transportable lamps are likely to be used only with available mains supplies rather than with specially generated power. It is important therefore that the cameraman have some rudimentary knowledge of how much light may be run off what plugs, and with which cable.

The power drawn by different wattage bulbs is as follows:

	240v	220v	120v	110v
375 watt Photoflood	1·6	1·7	3·2	3·4
500 watt Photoflood	2·1	2·3	4·2	4·6
650 watt Tungsten halogen	2·75	3	5·5	6
800 watt Tungsten halogen	3·33	3·66	6·66	7·33
1000 watt Tungsten halogen	4·2	4·55	8·33	9·1

When arriving in a strange city, especially in one of those countries where voltages may differ even between one part of a city and another, the quick and simple method of checking the voltage is to look at the rating marked on an electric light bulb or an appliance in the room. It is reasonably safe to assume that this is also the voltage on the wall sockets. Cameramen from 120v countries may use their lamps in 220 or 240v countries by taking with them plugs and sockets which connect pairs of lamps in series.

Plugs and sockets
Different countries use different plugs and in the course of time a cameraman who travels widely will collect a varied selection. Sockets fitted with thermostats for controlling central heating appliances should not be used for lighting. They may switch off during a take.

In addition to all the lamps, featherweight stands and clip-on devices he needs the cameraman should also take a screwdriver, a supply of fuse wire and a light with which to find the fuse box when he has blown the fuses. An inexpensive volt meter may also be useful.

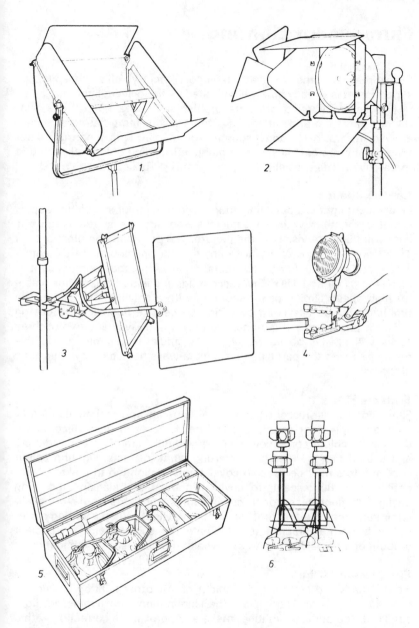

TRANSPORTABLE LIGHTING

1. Lowell foldable softlight;   2. Lowell 1000 W Quartz Light;   3. Lowell Porta-Kit. An outfit which folds down to a very compact size;   4. Ianiro 650 W Quartzcolor Jupiter 1 lamp;   5. 2 × 1000 W lanbeam lamps complete with stands, etc., packaged as a single outfit;   6. Colortran Porta-Kit. Enough light in a suitcase to illuminate an area 10 × 10 × 10 ft to 150 foot candles.

Fluorescent Lighting

Sometimes a scene such as an airport, factory, office, hospital, or supermarket is already amply illuminated by fluorescent lighting.

Fluorescent lighting presents problems. It does not have a continuous spectrum and cannot be given a colour temperature as a light derived from a 'black body' source. Any reading with a normal colour temperature meter is likely to be highly misleading unless taken with a three-colour type specially designed for this purpose.

Camera speeds

Fluorescent light is a pulsating source and if the frequency of the supply is not compatible with the camera speed and the shutter angle the light will fluctuate visibly in the picture. The optimum combinations for 50 Hz operation are 25fps, with any shutter opening or 24fps, with a 170–175° opening. For 60 Hz operation at 24fps, the optimum shutter angles are 144 and 180°. Fluorescent lighting is particularly unsuitable for high speed filming or for shooting with a small shutter angle. The problem may be alleviated by wiring successive fluorescent tubes on different phases of a three phase supply. In this way any two of three tubes will always be lit. Many sports stadia are illuminated in this manner so that the participants should always have a continuous view of the ball.

Suitable filters

Film shot by fluorescent lighting, without an appropriate filter, may have an unpleasant green cast and be deficient in reds. Recommendations for colour correction filters vary widely, are often contradictory and should only be used as a starting point for tests. Lighting colour control filters may be used to cover tungsten lighting to make it compatible with fluorescent, to cover windows for balancing incoming daylight to fluorescent, or to cover fluorescent lights to make their illumination match either artificial light or daylight. When shooting close-ups it is normal practice to illuminate the subject with a sufficient amount of artificial lighting to overwhelm the fluorescent illumination.

Fluorescent fill light

An alternative to matching the colour of any other lighting to fluorescent light *in situ* is to complete the illumination with fluorescent light similar to the principal lighting, make an approximate correction with a camera filter and leave it to the laboratory to make the final correction at the printing stage. Fluorescent luminaires, which may be used on normal lighting stands, may be placed at eye level as fill-lighting to eliminate eye shadows and other dark areas which would otherwise result from lighting which was totally overhead.

198

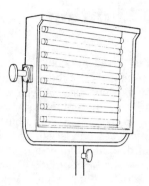

FLUORESCENT LIGHT

Recommended Wratten CC filters for use with various types of fluorescent tubes.
The following are intended as a guide and can form a basis on which the
cinematographer may proceed on a trial and error basis.

Tubes available in the the UK

Fluorescent Lamp type	Colour film types			
	3200K (313 Mireds)		Daylight (183 Mireds)	
	filter	factor	filter	factor
Northlight and artificial daylight	Wratten 85	$\frac{2}{3}$ stop		
Daylight	Wratten 85+10M	1 stop	20R	$\frac{1}{3}$ stop
White	20R+10M	$\frac{2}{3}$ stop	30B+10M	1 stop
Warm white	20R+10M	$\frac{2}{3}$ stop	20B	$\frac{2}{3}$ stop
Warm white deluxe			30C	$\frac{2}{3}$ stop
Cool white			10R+10M	$\frac{2}{3}$ stop
Cool white deluxe			10C	$\frac{1}{3}$ stop
Natural and colourite	10R	$\frac{1}{3}$ stop		

Tubes available in the USA

Cool white	50M+60Y	$1\frac{1}{3}$ stop	30M	$\frac{2}{3}$ stop
White	40M+40Y	1 stop	30M+20C	1 stop
Warm white	30M+20Y	1 stop	40M+40C	$1\frac{1}{3}$ stop
Daylight	40M+30Y	1 stop	85B+30M+10Y	1 stop
Deluxe warm white	10Y	$\frac{1}{3}$ stop	30M+60C	$1\frac{2}{3}$ stop
Deluxe cool white	10M+30Y	$\frac{2}{3}$ stop	20M+30C	1 stop

The above recommendations are made by the British Lighting Council and
Kodak.
The filters referred to are Wratten CC and 85 ranges.

Fluorescent fill light

Fluorescent tubes similar to those in the ceiling fittings may be fitted to this
luminaire and used at camera level to eliminate shadows without affecting
colour balance.

Metal Halide Lighting

Metal Halide lamps are enclosed mercury arc light sources with metal halide additives which produce an enormous amount of light for the amount of electric energy they consume. A typical MH lamp will produce between 80 and 100, and even more, lumens of daylight-balanced light per watt of electricity, while by comparison a blue-filtered conventional tungsten halogen lamp produces only about 14 lumens per watt.

For 3200K (312 mireds) operation either a daylight-balanced MH bulb may be used, in which case the MH output will remain very high, or the MH lamp must have a full CTO filter, which will reduce the MH lamp efficiency to approximately 60 lumens per watt and the equivalent colour tungsten bulb output will be 27 lumens per watt.

MH bulbs may be single or double ended, operate only off AC power supplies, require a ballast unit between the power supply and the luminaire, must incorporate a high-voltage igniter circuit (which is usually contained within the lamp head and must be fitted with safety switches), and for most types of bulbs the lamp head must be completely lightproof except for the glass front through which the light shines (to prevent the emission of dangerous UV light). For all these reasons MH and tungsten luminaires are not interchangeable.

Advantages
The principal advantage of MH lighting is that all but the most powerful lamps (4000W and above) may be operated off a single-phase AC power supply and cabled by comparatively lightweight cables. Enough light to fill the shadows caused by sunlight or to illuminate a large area can be carried around in a small vehicle and operated off available power. Even if a generator is required it can be much smaller than heretofore.

Disadvantages
An inherent problem with MH lighting (under normal circumstances) is that the light it emits is not of a constant brightness but decays by 60–85% twice every AC cycle. To ensure that scenes illuminated by MH lighting show no flicker on the screen, due to uneven exposure between successive frames, the supply frequency, the camera speed and the shutter angle must be constant and compatible. This problem may only be overcome by the use of a ballast unit especially designed for cinematography which will produce light which has no decay time and which makes filming possible at almost any camera speed and with almost any shutter angle.

Even if a cameraman does not deliberately set out to use MH lighting he is bound to encounter it when filming in floodlit sports stadia and other public places where this form of lighting is almost always used.

MH bulbs, except in sealed units, must not be touched with bare fingers as this will cause the quartz envelope to blacken.

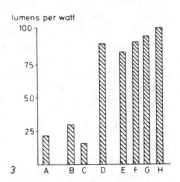

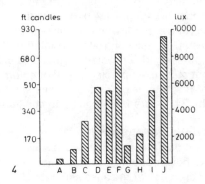

METAL HALIDE LIGHTING

CSI Cluster
1. Cluster of 4 × 1000 W Thorn CSI lamps (left) mounted in especially designed sealed beam units with a choice of lenses which give pre-set beam patterns and greatly improved light output.

HMI lamp
2. Typical luminaire using an Osram HMI bulb with fresnel lens beam focusing. This particular unit is an LTM Luxarc 2500.

Comparative efficiency
A. Carbon arc;   B. Tungsten halogen;   C. Tungsten halogen with blue filter;   D. 1000 W CSI;   E. 575;   F. 1200;   G. 2500;   H. 4000 W HMI.

Comparative lamp output
a. 1000;   B. 2000;   C. 5000;   D. 10000 W Tungsten Halogen fresnel luminaire;   E. 1000 W CSI with OMS beam spreader;   F. 1000 W CSI with OME beam spreader;   G. 575 W HMI in a fresnel luminaire;   H. 1200 W;   I. 2500;   J. 4000 W HMI in a fresnel luminaire.

An electronic 'shock absorber'.

Metal Halide Lighting Ballast Units

A ballast unit must be interposed between the AC power supply and an MH bulb to: 1, Provide an electrical resistance when the arc is struck, to prevent a short circuit across the supply and effectively extend the life of the electrode and of the bulbs; 2, To smooth out small variations in the mains supply; 3, To keep volts/amps relationship constant throughout the life of the bulb (as the bulb ages and the electrodes burn away, the gap increases causing an amperage drop and a rise in voltage) and 4, To reduce the voltage at the lamp head as required.

Choke ballast units
The standard ballast unit, as used for flood lighting, is the 'choke coil' type. It is the simplest, least expensive and probably the most reliable. It consists of heavy copper windings around a core of steel plates.

The problem with using a choke ballast is that the resultant light intensity is not of constant brightness but pulses twice every AC cycle and if the AC frequency (Hz) powering the lamps and the camera speed/shutter angle are not consistent and compatible, uneven exposure will result. Under controlled conditions the uneven exposure of successive frames is not a problem. With 50 Hz at 25 fps any shutter angle is possible but at 24 fps a precise 172.8° opening is necessary. With 60 Hz at 24 fps a 144° shutter is optimum but any shutter angle is possible if the 60 Hz and the 24 fps are both exact and constant.

Triplicated lighting
Groups of three lamps, each powered by a separate leg of a three-phase AC power supply, mounted close together and far enough away from the subject as not to cause separate shadows, or used for reflected soft light, will give flicker-free light at any camera speed and shutter angle.

Square-wave ballast units
Unlike sine-wave AC, with its rhythmic change from one direction to the other, square-wave is engineered to maintain a more or less constant level of current (like DC) until it is switched almost instantaneously to the other direction. With no peaks and troughs of current and therefore even lighting intensity, MH lighting using a square-wave ballast power supply may be used for filming under any circumstances.

High-frequency ballast units
MH lighting may be made flicker-free by the use of a high-frequency AC generator or by first converting 50 or 60 Hz AC to DC and re-converting it as high-frequency AC. 200–2000 Hz has been used for various applications. With high-frequency AC the peaks and troughs of light occur so rapidly they are smoothed out, each frame being exposed by many peaks of light.

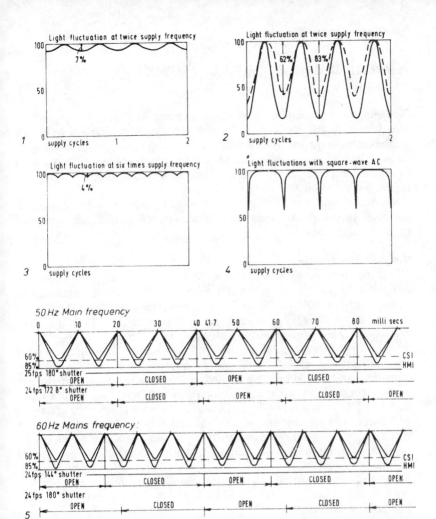

1. Normal tungsten lighting. Note light intensity falls by 7% between AC supply cycles.

2. Comparison between various types of MH lighting. CID, CSI and similar lighting (shown dotted) drops by 62% between cycles; HMI and similar (solid line) drops by 83%.

3. Triplicated lighting. Gaps between individual troughs of light are filled by light powered by another leg of a three-phase AC power supply.

4. Square-wave power supply. The troughs of light between AC power cycles are of very short duration.

5. MH lighting and exposure time compatibility.

50Hz (above): note that at 25 fps the shutter opens and closes in sync with the power supply and that by using a 172.8° shutter at 24 fps the exposure is exactly 1/50 sec, which also synchronises with the lighting.

60Hz (below): a 144° shutter is open during two pulses of light and closed during three, and a 180° shutter is open and closed during successive periods of 2½ pulses of light.

Metal Halide Lamp Types

Two shapes of MH bulbs are available to cinematographers: single- and double-ended. The single-ended is available on its own or enclosed in a sealed-beam lamp unit. All are available in a range of wattages and to give either daylight or 3200K colour temperatures. An older version of the single-ended bulb, CSI, is also available in a colour temperature which approximates to 4000K.

MH bulbs used in fresnel-type luminaires may have a wider spread or a narrower beam of light than their tungsten equivalents, owing to their smaller overall size.

Single-ended bulbs

The colour temperature of CID lamps approximates to 5500K (daylight), CSI bulbs to 4000K, and CIT bulbs to 3200K. They are all available in wattages of 400, 1000 and 2500. The 1000 watt size is available in standard or 'Hot Restrike' versions, the former requiring a cooling-down period of several minutes before switching on again.

Some single-ended bulbs do not produce harmful UV light associated with most other MH lighting and in consequence may be used in open-fronted luminaires. The 2500W bulb has the same dimensional configuration as a normal 2000W tungsten bulb and may be used in a standard 2K luminaire provided the necessary control circuitry is fitted.

The 1000W versions are available as bare bulbs for mounting in a luminaire or mounted in a pre-focus type sealed-beam unit with a choice of spreader lenses giving beams of various shapes and degrees of divergence.

All can be operated off 110–240v single-phase AC power supplies.

Double-ended bulbs

Double-ended MH bulbs are available in 5600 and 3200K versions and in wattages ranging from 200 to 12000W. They must be fitted in special fresnel or flood-type luminaires equipped with the necessary control circuitry, protection against emitting dangerous UV light, and safety switching in case the lamp is opened with the light switched on.

The 200W version is usually fitted in portable units powered by rechargeable batteries.

MH bulbs up to 2500W require a 110–240v single-phase AC power supply; the larger types, 4000W and above, require a 380v three-phase supply.

Double-ended bulbs require a warming-up period of about three minutes when first lit, after which they may be switched on and off at will.

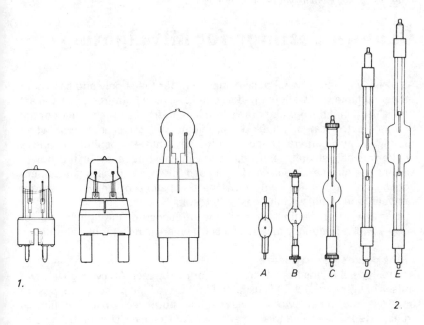

1.

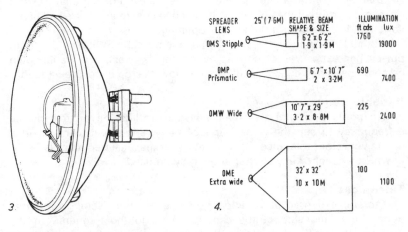

SPREADER LENS	25' (7 6M)	RELATIVE BEAM SHAPE & SIZE	ILLUMINATION ft cds	lux
OMS Stipple		6'2" x 6'2" 1·9 x 1·9 M	1760	19000
OMP Prismatic		6'7" x 10'7" 2 x 3·2M	690	7400
OMW Wide		10'7" x 29' 3·2 x 8·8M	225	2400
OME Extra wide		32' x 32' 10 x 10M	100	1100

3.

4.

METAL HALIDE LAMPS

1. 200, 1000 and 2500W single-ended CID type MH bulbs; 2. 200, 575, 1200, 2500 and 4000W double-ended HMI-type MH bulbs (6000, 8000 and 12000W types not shown); 3. 1000W single-ended CID bulb in a sealed-beam lamp unit. 4. Beam characteristics of various sealed-beam lamp units.

205

Camera Settings for MH Lighting

As already stated, several possibilities exist for the supply and control of power suitable for MH lighting. If a square-wave or high-frequency ballast unit is used or if the lighting draws from a high-frequency alternator or the lighting is triplicated, no flicker problems will be encountered when filming at any camera speed or with any shutter opening. Should a choke-coil ballast unit be used, however, the frequency of the power supply, the number of pulses of light used for each exposure, the camera speed and the shutter angle must be compatible or uneven exposure between one frame and the next will result.

It is a wise precaution to check the frequency of the lighting power supply with a frequency meter, especially when using a mobile alternator.

Light pulses per exposure
At the normal mains frequencies of 50 or 60 Hz, each AC cycle giving two pulses of light per cycle, it is usual to film by two light pulses per exposure and use the other two for viewfinding purposes while the film is transported. To achieve this, an exposure of exactly 1/50th or 1/60th sec. must be set. At 24 fps this means a shutter angle of 172.8% or 144° respectively.

If it is desirable to photograph at slower camera speeds or wider shutter angles, more than two pulses of light per exposure can be used, and if at higher camera speeds or smaller shutter angles, one light pulse per frame.

If the fps is exactly divisible into the frequency, e.g. 25 or 30 fps (50 or 60 Hz) then any shutter angle may be used as the camera will then pick out the same portion of the light cycle for each exposure and there will be no variation, irrespective of the shutter opening.

With 60 Hz power supplies, at 24 fps, it is possible to film by 2 ½ light pulses per exposure so long as everything is exact. Any variation in camera speed or frequency will cause a slow ⅓ stop exposure variation.

Variable frequency
With a mobile alternator it is usually possible to adjust the rpm to generate a frequency to suit the camera-speed/shutter-angle and to maintain it within very close tolerance. To shoot at 24 fps the ideal frequency is 48 Hz, at which frequency any shutter angle may be used.

Tolerances
The tolerable degree of variation from the optimum settings depends upon the relationship of the camera speed to the frequency. If the frequency is exactly divisible by the camera speed the tolerance is high, otherwise these settings, and the shutter angle, must be quite exact.

Single-ended bulbs have a greater tolerance than double-ended.

SETTINGS FOR FLICKER-FREE MH OPERATION

Flicker-free windows for 24 fps with 48 and 50Hz, and for 24 fps with 60Hz.

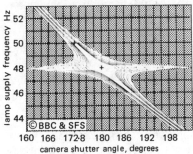

24 fps/48 & 50 Hz/180 & 172º SHUTTER

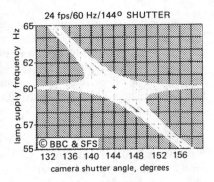

24 fps/60 Hz/144º SHUTTER

Optimum shutter angles (°)

Camera speed (fps)	Supply frequency	
	50Hz	60Hz
8	172.8 or 144	any, but 198 optimum
12	172.8 or 129.6	any, but 180 optimum
16	172.8 or 115.2	192 or 144
18	194.4 or 129.6	162
20	any, but 144 optimum	any, but 180 optimum
22	158.4	198 or 132
24	172.8	any, but 144 optimum
25	any, but 180 optimum	150
26	187.2 or 93.6	156
28	100.8	168
30	108	any, but 180 optimum
32	115.2	192 or 96
36	129.6	108
40	144	120
48	172.8	144
50	any, but 180 optimum	144
60	not possible	any, but 180 optimum
100	any, but 180 optimum	not possible
120	not possible	any, but 180 optimum

Optimum supply frequency (Hz)

Camera speed (fps)	Shutter angle			
	165°	170°	180°	200°
8		48	or 60	
12		48	or 60	
16	52.4	50.8	54	48.6
18	58.9	57.2	54	48.6
20		50	or 60	
22	48	46.6	66	59.4
24		48	or 60	
25			50	
26	56.7	55.1	52	46.8
28	61.1	59.3	56	50.4
30			60	
32	69.8	67.8	64	57.6
36	39.3	38.1	72	64.8
40			60	
48	52.4	50.8	48	43.2
50			50	
60			60	
100			50	
120			60	

24 fps/60Hz light intensity variation cycle (assuming the camera to be running at precisely 24 fps)

Power supply variation	Light intensity variation cycle
60Hz ± 0.0025	3 min. 20 sec.
60Hz ± 0.005	1 min. 40 sec.
60Hz ± 0.01	50 sec.
60Hz ± 0.02	25 sec.
60Hz ± 0.05	10 sec.

Formulae to calculate flicker-free MH settings

Two light pulses per exposure:
Shutter angle = camera speed × 360 ÷ supply frequency
Supply frequency = camera speed × 360 ÷ shutter angle
Camera speed = supply frequency × shutter angle ÷ 360

Any number of light pulses per exposure, 50Hz supply:
Shutter angle = camera speed × 3.6 × number of light pulses per exposure
Camera speed = shutter angle ÷ 3.6 ÷ number of light pulses per exposure

Any number of light pulses per exposure, 60Hz supply:
Shutter angle = camera speed × 3.0 × number of light pulses per exposure
Camera speed = shutter angle ÷ 3.0 ÷ number of light pulses per exposure.

Strobe Lighting

Sometimes called the lively light, strobe lighting, with a single ten millionth of a second exposure for each frame, gives a crispness to fast moving detail that makes each and every particle almost touchable.

Another advantage is that strobe lights are cold and very useful when filming biological or botanical specimens or ice-cream or anything else that will melt, wilt or otherwise deteriorate under the effect of hot incandescent lighting.

Use in commercials
Few things look less convincing at the end of a commercial than a frame hold of a cascade of crisp and crunchy cornflakes looking like a muddy blur which belies the commentary and mars the action. Photographed with a strobe light each flake will look so crisp it could almost be picked off the screen. A shower of water, too, is a most suitable subject for strobe lighting.

Synchronizing with the camera
Because the exposure period of a strobe flash is so brief, the equal of a shutter opening of less than a tenth of a degree at 24 fps, each flash must be synchronized with the camera. This may be done by means of a contact fitted to the inching knob of the camera, if there is one, or by an electronic synchronizing device.

To ensure that the camera and flash are correctly synchronized the camera should be run and the movement observed by the light of the strobe units to ensure that the flashes occur when the shutter is fully open. Either the lens or the camera door must be removed to check this.

Strobe consoles have a facility for plugging in 'viewfinder lights' which flash 180° out of synchronism with the principal lights to give illumination during the viewfinding period. These lights must be switched off when checking synchronism. An intermediate flash is advantageous when filming people, because 48 flashes per second is found far less disturbing than 24.

Power and frequency
Small strobe lighting outfits accommodate up to ten two-joule Xenon discharge heads, each producing about the same light output as a 750 W incandescent lamp. Although not very powerful compared with the discharge lights used for still photography they are, however, quite adequate for close-up and pack-shot work.

Strobe lighting designed for cinematography may be run either in synchronism or wild at speeds of up to 30 fps.

Care must be taken never to operate the strobe lights at around 17 flashes per second which may trigger an epileptic fit in someone susceptible to this.

The colour temperature of strobe lighting is 6000K (167 mireds).

208

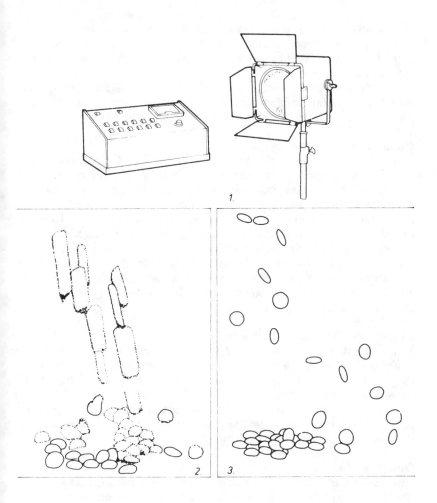

STROBE LIGHTING

1. Dawe strobe light console and lamp lead.
2. Falling beans photographed with normal lighting. Movement registers on the film as a blur. The same beans photographed by strobe lighting. Individual beans are clearly defined.

Lighting Stands

Lights need something on which to be supported or hung.

They may be placed on floor stands, suspended overhead or supported by a suitable fixture attached to another structure.

At the lamp-stand interface, the heaviest types of lamp are fitted with a $1\frac{1}{8}$ inch spigot. Lightweight lamps may have either a $\frac{5}{8}$ inch diameter spigot or socket.

Stands are available in a profusion of types, weights and shapes. Stands for use on location should be no heavier than is necessary but robust enough to carry a lamp without it waving about in the wind.

General purpose stands

Traditional type stands, designed many years ago for studio use and made of steel and bronze castings, are a time wasting nuisance on location when rapid set-ups and wrap-ups are an economic necessity. They are too heavy to transport and manhandle, bulky when folded, laborious to erect, and being so heavy are always on castors. They are therefore more easily knocked out of position when kicked accidentally.

Modern stands, developed in recent years especially for location usage, are light in weight, compact when folded and have a wide range of possible heights. Some have tops which accept any type of lamp attachment and have one leg which may be extended for use on sloping ground or stairs.

Stands for heavyweight lamps

The heaviest lamps of all, brutes, require suitably heavyweight stands equipped with electrically operated elevation and lowering. When used over soft or rough ground they are often mounted on a large three wheel dolly called a desert dolly.

Lightweight brutes and the heaviest incandescent lamps are most conveniently mounted on wind-up stands which make it possible for one man to raise a heavy lamp by hand.

Overhead fixtures

The most simple system of overhead lighting is that constructed from a grid of scaffold tubing onto which lamps may be clamped as required.

More sophisticated installations incorporate facilities for raising and lowering the lamps to any required working height as well as for manoeuvring them from side to side or forwards and backwards. Adjustment of the lamp functions may be carried out by means of a long pole or by remote control.

Such systems are much favoured in studios designed for TV production, leaving the floor clear for multi-camera operation.

In film studios, a series of lighting gantries or parallels (grid walks) are usually rigged around the perimeter of a set and elsewhere.

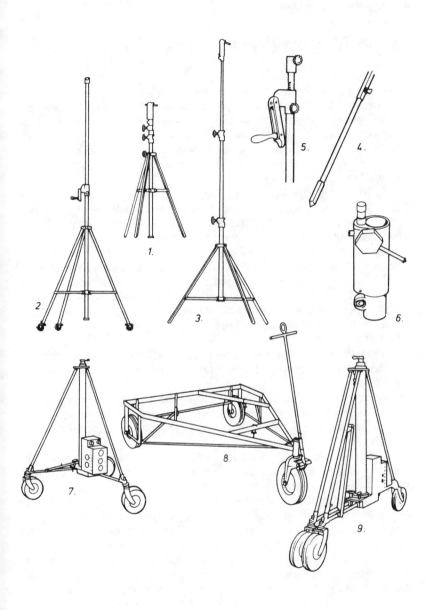

LIGHTING STANDS

1. Lightweight stand set low; 2. Wind-up stands set high; 3. Lightweight stand set high; 4. Extending leg used when setting a stand on a slope or on stairs; 5. Handle of wind-up stand; 6. Universal adaptor, takes lamps with $1\frac{1}{8}$in, or $\frac{5}{8}$in spiggots or sockets; 7. Heavy duty stand with electric elevating mechanism capable of taking a regular brute; 8. Desert dolly used to transport brutes on stands; 9. Brute stand in folding position.

Lamp Mounting Accessories

There seems to be no limit to the devices which have been designed and are available for placing lamps and other light control equipment in position exactly where they are required. The following are descriptions of some:

Overhead hanger, anti-G or pantograph; An overhead lamp carrier which may be moved up and down, the lamp remaining as set without any need to tighten locking screws.

C or G clamp, furniture clamp, Mole grip, Mole wrench, gaffergrip, Gator Grip, etc.; various clamping devices usually incorporating a lamp spigot which may be attached to any suitably-placed scaffold pole, piping, wood batten, door frame, railing, flat, etc.

Floor stand, turtle, spyder, T-bone, wall or floor plate or bracket; flat surfaced plate with lamp spigot attached at right angles or parallel which may be used to stand a lamp on the floor, or with the aid of nails or screws, to attach a lamp to any wall or other suitable flat surface.

Bazooka, trombone, extendible telescoping or adjustable hanger; various forms of tubes with means of clamping at one end and a lamp spigot at the other.

Extension arm; a means of clamping a lamp adaptor to the upright of a stand of vertical pole to place a lamp lower or a second lamp on a stand.

Two- or three-lamp cluster bars, hangers or heads; the means of putting two or three lamps on one stand from one central spiggot.

Trapeze, hanger or stirrup hanger; a means of suspending lamps from above.

Limpet, suction cup, sucker, vacuum cup; originally made for handling plate glass, used to attach equipment to any smooth non-porous surface, particularly of an automobile.

Polecat, jack tubes, Acrows; an extendible tube which may be securely locked between floor and ceiling or two walls either to support lamps directly or to support cross tubes from which lamps are suspended by means of C or G clamps, etc.

Century stand; special type of stand used for flags and other light control media which has three legs at right angles to the upright of the stand, each at a different height so that several stands may, if necessary, be grouped closely together without the legs of one interfering with another.

Knuckle, head, clamping disc; pairs of round discs with deep grooves to secure flags etc., in such a manner that they may be positioned exactly as required. Two, attached to extension arms may be used in combination to make the unit more adaptable.

Camera adaptor spigot or spud; a means of using a lamp stand as a camera tripod.

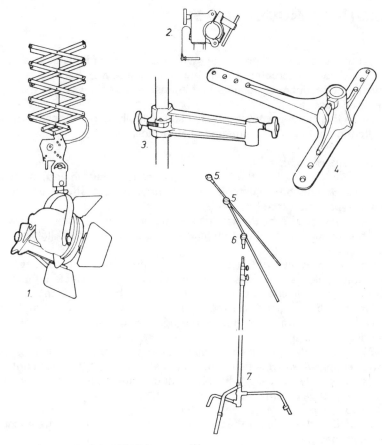

LAMP MOUNTING ACCESSORIES

1. Pantograph overhead fitting;   2. Scaffold clamp;   3. Extension
arm;   4. Floor stand;   5. Flag knuckle on extension arm;   6. Knuckle on top of
stand;   7. Base of century stand.

Boom, overhead arm; a means of placing a lamp overhead, some distance from its stand.

Flat plates; plates which may be taped to a wall using strong 'gaffer
tape'. Care must be taken in using this equipment on location not to
tape to expensive wallpaper or some other surface which may be
damaged when the tape is removed and cause the owner of the
property to demand an expensive redecoration job.

Lighting Accessories

Illumination becomes 'lighting' as, with the control of individual lamps, the cameraman creates highlights and shadows, harshness and diffusion, direction and balance and intensity and colour within the elements of a scene.

To do this there are tools which, used skillfully, can not only harness the lighting but also promote mood and atmosphere.

Light control accessories

Barn doors: Fitted on the front of a luminaire to cut off certain areas of light. Should be adjustable and rotatable. Most effective with a fresnel type lamp set at full flood.

Cucoloris, cookie or ulcer: Opaque material considerably cut away which, placed in front of a lamp, causes a broken pattern of lighting on a background.

Dichroic or Macbeth: Glass colour correcting filters. Dichroics reflect unwanted colours and pass a greater percentage or usable light than coloured glass (Macbeth) or gelatine but tend to be inconsistent.

Diffuser: Spun glass, tracing paper or other translucent material placed in front of a lamp makes the light source less directional and reduces its intensity.

Dimmer: A device which reduces lamp brilliance by reducing the power supply. A variable resistance reduces voltage; a thyristor control, which may only be used with AC, reduces the amplitude of the AC cycle. Both severely affect colour temperature.

French flag, dot or target: A small opaque flag, carried on an articulated or flexible arm that may be clamped almost anywhere; used for local shading.

Gel or filter holder or colour frame: Used to hold coloured gelatine or other flexible filter material in front of a lamp.

Flag or gobo: Opaque mask set on a separate stand independently of any lamp. Used to throw shadows or mask off unwanted light. Gives a sharper cut-off with all types of lamp than does a barn door. A *finger* or cutter is a long, narrow flag.

Net or lavender: Flag made of black or coloured netting to soften and reduce the intensity of a lamp.

Scrim: Stainless steel wire mesh used to control light intensity without affecting point source direction or colour temperature. A *double scrim* consists of two layers of mesh. *Half scrim* covers only half the lamp and is principally used to even out the light falling on a scene from a lamp set at an angle. Half scrims especially, are usually mounted in circular frames which may be rotated to set at the correct angle. All frames may be colour coded as an indication to the cameraman of what scrim is in position. Windowlite is used for the same purpose and may be folded or torn to achieve control.

LIGHTING ACCESSORIES

Barn doors; Cucoloris; Dichroic or Macbeth Filter; Diffuser; Dimmer; French Flag; Gelatine Filter Holder; Flag, Gobo, Net or Lavender; Scrim and Half Scrim; Shutter; Snoot; Cable Ramp; Safety Cable; Safety Wire Grille; Sand or Water Bag. (Left to right, top to bottom).

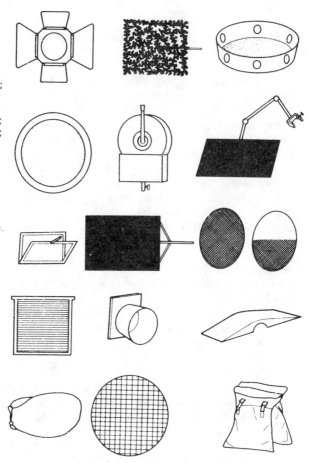

Shutter: A device to progressively control light intensity without affecting colour temperature or beam pattern.

Snoot: A cylindrical mask used to control spill light and reduce the circle of illumination.

Non-creative accessories

Cable ramps: Slopes placed either side of cables laid across a road to prevent damage from passing vehicles or accident to pedestrians.

Safety equipment: Fail-safe devices used to ensure that any lamp placed above people, especially the general public, is harmless in case of failure. Includes attachment wires, to secure barn doors, etc., to the lamp housing, safety pins to prevent spigots which are set upside-down from falling out and wire grills to prevent falling glass should a bulb shatter.

Sand or water bags: Used to keep stands etc., in position. May be filled locally.

215

Power Supplies for Lighting

No matter what the production, be it newsreel which requires little supplementary lighting or a major feature film to be shot on location, the power demand for lighting purposes is likely to be considerably more than is available on site for that purpose. Very often, if the demands are modest, it is possible to draw sufficient power from wall outlets, if necessary drawing from sockets in several rooms or even floors and spreading the load. Often more is obtainable by taking the supply at the mains at the point where it comes into a building, and if more than that is required then a temporary supply of one or more mobile generators is needed.

Whenever possible an examination of the location should be made beforehand and the entire lighting requirement considered in advance.

Planning

When planning a lighting installation the following should be born in mind:

1. The lighting requirement in terms of types, sizes and numbers of the various luminaires available.
2. The maximum amount of lighting that may be used at any one time.
3. The nature of the power required, AC or DC for normal tungsten lighting, DC for carbon arcs, AC for metal halide.
4. The nature of the power available, AC or DC, what voltage, single or three phase AC, how many amps to be drawn at maximum (amps=watts÷volts, watts=volts×amps).
5. That the supply is adequately fused, the location of all the fuse boxes, the rating and types of fuses and that spares are or will be available on site.
6. The point or place at which the entire supply may be switched off in an emergency.
7. That if AC is used, an adequate earth (ground) cable may be available.
8. The lengths of cable runs of various capacities required from the point of supply to the furthermost lamps.
9. That if working off a company supply the phone number of the local supply emergency maintenance depot is at hand, just in case a sealed fuse is blown, and, in the case of a major demand, that arrangements are made for a company engineer to be present during the shooting. In certain areas this is not only advisable but obligatory when more than a certain amperage is being drawn.
10. If the power is to be drawn from more than one leg of a three phase supply, the lighting should be so planned that cables, lamps and equipment on one phase are not sited within touching distance of equipment drawing power from the other phases. There

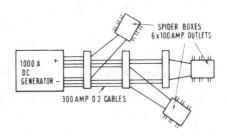

Cabling from 1000A DC Generator

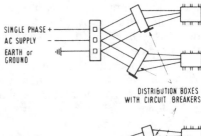

Cabling from single phase AC

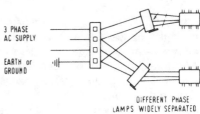

Cabling from three phase AC

must be no chance that anyone might touch two items of equipment that are 'live' across different phases and so get a double voltage electric shock.

WARNING

Electricity is dangerous, in some ways more dangerous than a gun, for at least it is possible to see if a gun is loaded or safe.

It behoves everyone working on a film location to ensure that all electrical equipment is in a safe condition, is treated with the respect that it deserves and that there is no chance of a stray child or visitor to the set being able to touch a live cable.

217

Cabling

Some knowledge of cables and their capacities is necessary when considering the lighting requirements for shooting a sequence and in understanding the gaffer's problems on location.

Voltage

The voltage available at the head of the lamps inevitably drops as the distance from the supply is extended or as the load factor on the cables is increased. As the voltage drops so does the intensity of the light and the colour temperature. A 5% drop in voltage at the lamphead will result in a drop of 60K (6 Mireds) in colour temperature, reduce light output by 17·5% and increase bulb life by 200%. Cable runs should therefore be as short as possible and the cables themselves must be of adequate gauge to minimise losses.

When working on location voltage may drop during the peak demand period when all the neighbours switch on electric cookers, air conditioners or electric heaters at the same time.

Within limits cables will carry increased loads for reduced periods of operation. Resistance increases as the temperature of a cable rises and, in consequence, cables carrying loads above the normal rating must be allowed sufficient time to cool down as necessary.

Cable should not be used partially wound on a cable drum or tightly coiled. This situation creates excessive heat by inductance, which will reduce the capacity of a cable by 50% or more and destroys the current carrying capacity of the cable forever by annealing the metal.

If necessary two or more cables may run side by side, in parallel, to increase the cable capacity; alternatively the voltage at the supply end may be increased to compensate for losses. Voltages should be measured at the lampheads to ensure that colour temperature is consistent.

Amperage

The maximum amperage that a cable carries and the voltage losses incurred depend upon the cross sectional area of the cable and the type of metal used.

Aluminium cables of *similar size* to copper have 84% of the load capacity, are 57% lighter and cost only half as much. To carry a *similar load* it is normal to use aluminium cables which are one gauge thicker than copper. There will still be a weight saving of almost 30% and less likelihood of the cable being stolen. Such cables are usually preferred for location usage. The very thick single core cables used to feed power from its source to the distribution boxes, known in the UK as 'Point two', in the US as 'Four zeros' and in metricated countries as 120mm², are capable of carrying a continuous load of 250 amps and an intermittent load of approximately 350 amps. Thus three or four such cables must be used, in parallel, for each pole from a 1000 amp generator if it is being used to its full capacity. With AC an earth

218

CABLING

Cable (250 amp) lugs

1. Technicolor lug brazed on to copper cable;
2. Lug crimped on to aluminium cable.

Where the power supply 'emerges' from the generator, or the distribution board of the local electricity supply company, wide flat strips of copper are usually provided onto which the cables which carry and distribute the highest currents must be attached by what are usually known in the industry as 'Technicolor Lugs'.

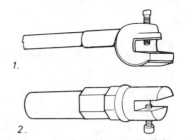

Lugs may be brazed or crimped on to copper cable but only crimped onto aluminium to prevent inter-reaction between dissimilar metals which eventually breaks down the joint.

Distribution cable sizes

Standard metric size mm²	Nearest imperial size inches²	AWG	Nearest US Circ Mils	Recommended maximum amp load – 100% usage
4	0.007	12	6530	25
6	0.01	10	10380	42
10	0.145	8	16510	57
16	0.0225	5	33100	76
25	0.04	3	52630	100
35	0.06	2	66370	120
50	0.06	0	105500	150
70	0.1	00	133100	180
95	0.15	000	167800	220
120	0.2	0000	211600	250

These are standards laid down for use with metric size cables. Other ratings may pertain in other situations. Increased capacity is possible when the load is intermittent.

Watts/amps table

Watts	Amps. 110/120 v	Amps. 220/240 v
1,000	9.1	4.6
2,000	18.2	9.1
5,000	45.5	23
5,850 (9 × 650 w.)	53.2	26.6
10,000	91	45.5
25,000	225	113
50,000	450	225
110,000	1000	500

Wattages may be aggregated to find the maximum load that may be drawn at any one time.

(ground) cable must be run in addition to the supply and return. This cable need only be half the capacity of the power cable and should be in good electrical contact with the earth, or a water pipe or object which is well planted in the ground. Single phase AC requires a three-core cable and three-phase a four-core cable.

Plugs and Connectors

Domestic plugs and sockets, at best, will not carry more than about 10–15 amps, enough only for 2000 or 3000 watts of lighting, and the cabling of houses and offices will rarely carry more than 30 amps, spread out over several outlets. For film work it is therefore necessary to provide a purpose power distribution system, including cables, plugs and sockets.

For low-voltage AC or DC (no more than 110 volts) Kleigl stage plugs are much used, but for higher-voltage AC plugs and sockets with a greater safety factor must be used.

High-voltage AC power distribution

For lighting large areas or using a great number of luminaires, 380 volt three-phase AC is likely to be drawn off the mains and split into three 220–240 volt legs. To handle such power there are many statutory safety requirements that must be observed. Special five-pin plugs and sockets, coloured red, are used for three-phase; three-pin, coloured blue, are used for single-phase. Lighting on different legs of a three-phase supply must never be placed within touching distance of one another.

The AC plugs and sockets most often used for film work come in 16, 32, 64 and 132 amp sizes, although different manufacturers may vary from this. Most of the types of plugs were used on building sites long before they were used by film makers and so are rugged and splashproof.

An AC distribution system must always be properly grounded and fused, and must have facilities to break the circuit at frequent intervals in case of an emergency; larger systems will incorporate an earth-leakage detection device to break the circuit automatically should there be a fault. For safety reasons it is usually preferred to distribute all AC power by a single multi-core cable as this eliminates the possibility of making incorrect connections; but if single core cables are used, plugs and sockets which carry up to 600A are available.

Domestic plugs and sockets

Care should be taken not to overload domestic plugs and sockets, the capacity of which varies from country to country. If the load which is plugged in is critically close to the maximum the connection should be made or broken with the luminaires switched off and the lamps switched on progressively to avoid a surge which may cause the fuse to go prematurely.

Kleigl plugs and sockets

For low-voltage power distribution, particularly DC, Kleigl plugs are used in earthed (grounded) and fused 1in. and ½in. wide versions. The 1in. type will carry up to 100 amps (12,000W of lighting from a 120v supply) and the ½in. type, 50 amps. Two ½in. types may be plugged into a 1in. socket, providing great versatility and economy of sockets.

PLUGS AND CONNECTORS

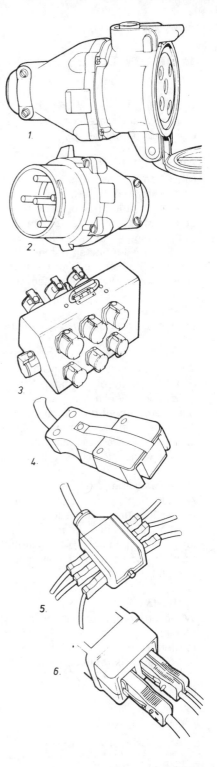

1. Mareshal decontactor type DS socket.

2. Mareshal decontactor type DS plug.

3. Mareshal decontactor type DS distribution system.

4. 1 in Kleigl stage plug. Fused and earther (grounded) type.

5. Six pocket Kleigl distribution box.

6. Two pocket distribution box showing 1×1 in plug and $2 \times \frac{1}{2}$ in plugs in similar sockets.

221

Generators

When film production requiring artificial lighting must be carried out in places where there is no suitable mains electricity supplied, a mobile generator is required.

AC or DC?

Most lighting, with the exception of MH, which requires AC, or carbon arcs, which require DC, may be run off either type of power. The choice of one or the other may be based on a number of considerations, and many generators incorporate both an AC alternator and a DC dynamo. Whether high-voltage AC or low-voltage DC power is chosen, it will be necessary to check that all tungsten halogen bulbs are of the correct voltage.

If an AC generator is to be used for MH lighting it will need to have a sensitive speed-control system to maintain an accurate AC frequency.

Silent generator

Perhaps not as quiet as a camera, but nevertheless inaudible from 20 yards, the modern 'silent' generator should not cause the sound department problems when shooting quiet dialogue scenes nearby.

The most usual size is about 1,000 amp output, sufficient to run 4 brutes or 80 kilowatts of incandescent light. Generators as powerful as 2,000 amps are not unknown, and at the other end of the scale the 250 amp size may be mounted on a small 'go anywhere' vehicle.

A silent generator independently mounted on its own prime mover chassis is far more practical than a generator mounted on a multi-purpose vehicle which also carries the camera and other equipment.

Portable generators

A small highly portable alternator which will generate up to 3,000w of AC power is a useful accessory to have available when away on a remote location. It may be used to provide a working light after dark (releasing the large silent generator), for charging batteries and for powering camera heaters and barneys. It may also be used to power an electric kettle or percolator.

Altitude

When ordering a generator for a particular assignment remember that efficiency will be reduced if the location is at high altitude or at high temperature.

Efficiency is reduced by $3\frac{1}{2}$% for every 1000ft. (300m) above 500ft. (150m) and by 2% for every 10°F (5°C) rise in temperature above 85°F (30°C).

222

MOBILE GENERATOR

Typical silent generator. It may generate 1000 amps of DC or 100 kW of AC power.

Effect Lighting

Sometimes certain lights must be made to look brighter than the normal light level in order to be meaningful in the scene. Usually such a light must be at least two stops (four times the foot candles or lux) more than the overall lighting level to show.

Practicals

Few things look more amateurish, in terms of lighting, than to see an artist carrying a torch or candle about a set with the lighting coming from another direction. To see a shadow of what is supposed to be the source of the lighting completely takes away all credibility.

To overcome these problems, more powerful bulbs, usually photofloods, may be fitted in place of the normal practical lamps.

The back of a lampshade may be cut out, provided it is out of sight of the camera to make a lamp look meaningful. Orange filter material can be fixed inside a lamp to give it a warmer tone to simulate gas or candle light compared with daylight.

Small bulbs may be replaced with tungsten halogen bulbs of the type normally used for battery portable lights, the 30v supply being provided by a battery belt worn by the artist.

Special 'candles' are available with the inside hollowed out to accommodate a bright bulb which illuminates the artist's face as though the light was coming from the candle flame.

The beams of car headlight bulbs are usually too directional for filming purposes and may have to be replaced by luminaires powered by a towed generator.

Effects spotlights

Where a 'spotlight effect' with a clear-cut beam is required, a special lamp must be used. Such lamps incorporate an optical system to focus the light, an iris to control the size of the beam, filter slides for colour effects, a mounting system to make it easy to follow and a sight to make it possible to aim the spot accurately before the beam is opened up. The most powerful effect spotlight available uses a 4000w HMI bulb and is capable of making a round spot effect even against sunshine. It is particularly handy for use in a large stadium.

Lightning

Off-screen lightning flashes, casting hard shadows, may be created by striking an arc. A pair of carbons, connected to a DC supply, are mounted on a scissor-like device in such a manner that they may be brought together and instantly separated.

Repeated flashes may be created by reversing the polarity of the current supply to the carbons in an arc lamp and holding them closely together. This will cause considerable spluttering.

EFFECT LIGHTING

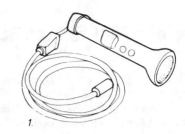

1. Light with 250 W tungsten halogen bulb.

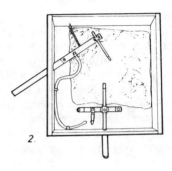

2. Lightning effect box.

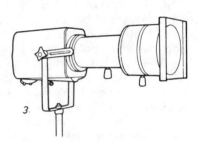

3. Follow spot light.

4. 30 v, 250 W 'candle'.

Electrical Effect Equipment

A little motion or atmosphere introduced into a scene will lift it out of the ordinary and give it an added quality of realism. This is part of the creative art of feature film making compared with that of, say, newsreel filming (which also has skills of its own).

Wind
Artificial wind is used to bring an exterior scene to life. For close work electrically powered fans may be used. These are specially designed for film making purposes and give the maximum effect for the amount of noise they make. Provided the only movement required is that of gently mussing the leading lady's hair, the fan should not interfere with the sound recording department. To stir up the atmosphere over a large area, much larger wind generators are available and for hurricane-force winds, engine driven aircraft propellers are used, when post sync dialogue will most certainly be necessary.

Fog
Small amounts of low hanging mist may be made by pouring hot water on to troughs of dry ice and directing the mist to where it is wanted by small battery operated fans or sheets of plywood or card. For larger fog and haze and smoke effects a fog-maker machine is required. This must be filled with a special juice and plugged into a power supply to heat the liquid. As this fog consists largely of tiny droplets of oil, it must not be allowed to contaminate equipment and other materials that may be spoiled. Other juices, to chase the fog away, to perfume the air, to eliminate obnoxious smells or to exterminate bugs may be put into the same type of fog-making machine.

Firelight
A flickering firelight effect on walls, ceilings or artists may be created by dangling strips of silk in front of two or more lamps. The silk strips should be moved around by a small fan and the lamps alternatively brightened and dimmed on dimmers.

Cobwebs
A special fan incorporating a nozzle which dispenses a thin stream of glue may be used to construct cobwebs.

ELECTRICAL EFFECT EQUIPMENT

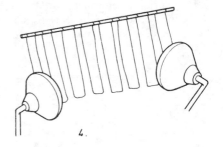

1. Wind machine;

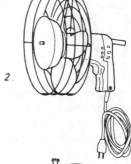

2. Cobweb spinner;

3. Fogmaker;

4. Firelight effect.

Special Effects Equipment

Certain items of equipment are necessary to create combined images, whether or not the images will be combined at the time of shooting the foreground image (by front or back projection) or later on an optical printer in the laboratory (travelling matte).

Front projection
A popular way to combine a live-action foreground with a pre-photographed background image is by front projection.

The background image is projected onto a retro-reflective screen which reflects all the light directly back to source. By projecting the image via a partial mirror set at 45° between the projector and the camera, and placing the entrance pupils of both lenses coincident in space, an object placed in front of the screen is exactly in front of its own shadow when viewed through the camera.

Because the amount of light required to produce a bright image on a retro-reflective screen is so little compared to that required to illuminate the foreground, light from the projector falling on the foreground is too little to be noticeable by the camera, even if it is plain white.

When a moving image is projected it is necessary to synchronise the projector and camera shutters so that both open and close simultaneously. This may be achieved by an electronic synchroniser which slaves one motor to another or by using stepper motors on both units.

A special rig is required that holds the projector, the partial mirror and the camera in exact relationships, one with another, and has facilities for making fine adjustments to eliminate fringe shadows.

Blue screen for travelling matte
Foreground images to be combined subsequently with background, and even other foreground images, on an optical printer are normally photographed in front of an intensely blue screen. While a brightly lit blue-painted solid backing may be used, the preferred method, especially for very large backings, is a backlit translucent screen illuminated from behind by fluorescent lighting run off a DC power source.

For certain scenes it is sometimes more desirable to use a white screen, in which case the blue backing can usually be interchanged for a white one, or a jet black backing, in which case black velvet curtains are used.

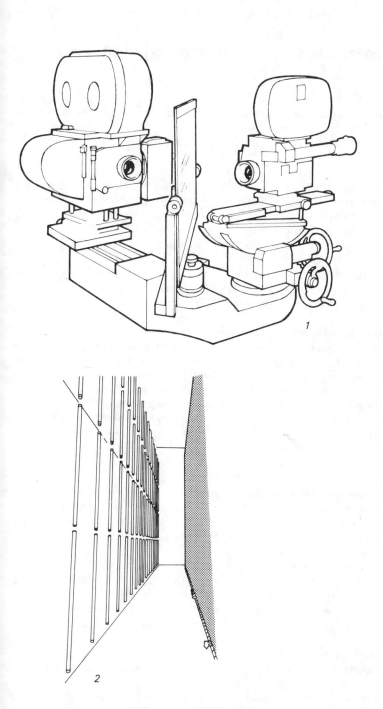

'ON FLOOR' EQUIPMENT FOR CREATING COMBINED IMAGES
1. Samcine front projection rig; 2 (right) with Stewart back-lit translucent blue travelling matte screen, (left) fluorescent strip lights.

Computers in Cinematography

Computers have many applications in film making. They may be used to plan and monitor a production, to control the operation of the camera, to produce images which may be transferred to film and in the laboratory for photometric control, and in all manner of situations in between.

'Wire frame' drawings of solid objects

The 'wire frame' image of a familiar object may be achieved by loading a computer with a modified Computer-Aided Design program, programming in the necessary elevation drawings of an object, setting up a plotting tablet opposite a stop-motion camera, in the dark, and filming a tiny point light source on the end of a plotting pen as it creates a line drawing. If the computer and a stop motion camera are programmed to repeat the plot over and over again and the camera to film a little more of the operation each time, the scene will appear on the screen as a travelling light source which progressively draws the object.

Motion-control cameras and objects

The ability of the computer to repeat movements over and over again, to within very fine dimensional tolerances, makes it much used to film miniatures of spacecraft and other inanimate objects. The computer can be programmed to coordinate and repeat the movements of the camera pan, tilt about the entrance pupil of the lens, rotate about the optical axis, move the camera up and down, side to side and forwards and backwards, similarly move the model, and control camera forward and reverse running at any selected exposure rate, shutter opening and lens capping, lens aperture, focus and zoom, lighting control, and so on.

Computer-generated information

Microcomputers are an ideal tool, when planning a production, to estimate the cost of making a film, to schedule the shooting period in the most economical manner and to keep tabs on production costs.

A small battery-operated computer may be used to do all the arithmetic of cinematography, including those involving optical calculations. Using a computer it is possible to predict depth-of-field limitations far more accurately than is possible with tables or calculators.

Computers are used in laboratories and cutting rooms to keep track of camera takes, edit cuts and the location of individual pieces of film.

Computer synchronisation

A computer-generated time code recorded onto both the picture and the sound track at the time of shooting may be used to identify what image goes with which piece of sound, and synchronisation may be done at any point in a take without the need for a clapper board.

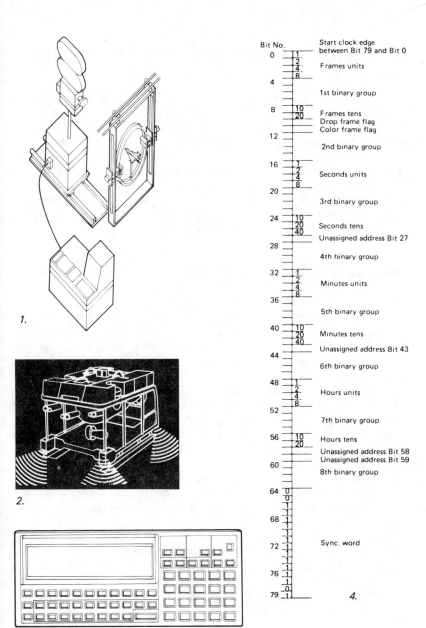

Bit No.		Start clock edge
0	1	between Bit 79 and Bit 0
	2	
	4	Frames units
	8	
4		
		1st binary group
8	10	Frames tens
	20	Drop frame flag
		Color frame flag
12		
		2nd binary group
16	1	
	2	
	4	Seconds units
	8	
20		
		3rd binary group
24	10	
	20	Seconds tens
	40	Unassigned address Bit 27
28		
		4th binary group
32	1	
	2	
	4	Minutes units
	8	
36		
		5th binary group
40	10	Minutes tens
	20	
	40	Unassigned address Bit 43
44		
		6th binary group
48	1	
	2	
	4	Hours units
	8	
52		
		7th binary group
56	10	Hours tens
	20	
		Unassigned address Bit 58
		Unassigned address Bit 59
60		
		8th binary group
64	0	
	0	
	1	
68	1	
	1	
	1	
72	1	Sync. word
	1	
	1	
76	1	
	0	
79	1	4.

COMPUTER-ASSISTED CINEMATOGRAPHY

1. Computer-controlled, motion-controlled camera rig; 2. 'Wire frame' computer graphic image which may be photographed step by step by a film camera;
3. Portable computer used to display production information; 4. SMPTE time code data structure.

Motion Picture Camera Techniques

To know and understand the equipment used in professional motion picture making is one thing, to understand its application and the techniques involved is another. In David Samuelson's complementary book, *Motion Picture Camera Techniques,* he not only takes the reader through all the processes of film making to which the equipment is applied but also describes many of the organisational aspects of film making which are not covered in any other book.

Planning the day to make the best use of sunlight, transporting equipment safely and shipping it through international borders using the 'ATA Carnet de Passages for Temporary Import', are some of the early topics.

Things every second assistant cameraperson should know

Loading magazines, keeping camera report sheets, looking after equipment in a dusty environment, shooting in the wet, in the cold and in the dark, shooting news and documentary interviews, shooting colour film for video transmission and shooting with metal halide lighting are all topics that the young junior on a camera crew will need to know about, and this book deals with each one separately and comprehensively.

For the more advanced reader

All the basic special-effect processes likely to be encountered on the studio floor are described. Front projection techniques, travelling matte cinematography, miniatures, glass mattes, high speed, stop motion and time lapse are all described in sufficient detail to enable the newcomer to understand what the long-established experts are talking about and require to be done.

For the would-be specialist there are pages describing animation rostrum cinematography, underwater filming techniques and shooting from a helicopter.

For those planning a career in cinematography

The final twelve topics of David Samuelson's book are devoted to graphic job descriptions of all the specialist opportunities open to anyone embarking on a career in cinematography. The work of all members of a feature film crew is described, as are the jobs of those working in the fields of special effects, news and documentary and TV commercial film making. Even the work of the camera grip, an indispensable member of the camera crew, is covered in *Motion Picture Camera Techniques,* published by Focal Press.

Index